THE DOCTRINE OF REGENERATION, AND OTHER SERMONS

by Thomas Halliday

COPYRIGHT INFORMATION

The Doctrine of Regeneration, and Other Sermons
by Thomas Halliday
Edited and updated by C. Matthew McMahon and Therese
B. McMahon
Copyright © 2011 by Puritan Publications

Published by Puritan Publications,
A ministry of A Puritan's Mind
4101 Coral Tree Circle #214
Coconut Creek, FL 33073
www.puritanpublications.com
www.apuritansmind.com

First Electronic Edition, 2011, USA
First Hardback Publication, 2011, USA

eISBN: 978-1-9374662-4-4
ISBN: 978-1-9374662-3-7

ORIGINAL TITLE PAGE

Sermons
by
the Late
Reverend Thomas Halliday,
with
A Memoir
by
Andrew Symington, A.M.

"...He, being dead, yet speaketh." Hebrews 11:4

Glasgow,
Printed By Andrew Young,
For David Halliday, Dumfries:
Sold by M. Ogle, and T. Nelson, Edinburgh
Alex Gardner, Paisley
1878

TABLE OF CONTENTS

MEMOIR

by Andrew Symington, A.M.

DEATH, in every instance of its occurrence, calls up solemn reflections in the thoughtful mind; but in some cases a person feels more impressed and astonished, and experiences a greater difficulty in giving an unhesitating acquiescence in the wisdom and equity of *Providence*. Never should the question, "Wherefore hast thou made all men in vain?" be put in the spirit of doubt or of challenge; for he who inquires into the ways of God should bear in mind the Divine greatness and rectitude, the narrowness of his own views, and the influence which his own interests have over them. But in some cases the question presses with peculiar urgency. The death of an infant, who has only lived an hour, and of a man who has lived eighty years —of the youth who has auspiciously entered upon public life, and of the man who has served God and his generation fifty years, are, in their relation to the immortal spirits concerned, and to the infinite duration into which they have entered, momentous beyond conception, but they affect the observant survivor differently. With all its mournful regrets, the mind acquiesces, while it beholds the servant, worn with toil and crowned with honor, released from his labors and dismissed into rest; but in the other case, besides the melancholy reflection excited by every occurrence of mortality, the heart experiences a feeling of pain, and suppresses with difficulty questions which it cannot solve. The emotions, in these cases, differ as do those of the observer of nature who beholds, on the one hand, the faded leaf falling from the tree which has yielded its fruit in its season, and, on the other, the tender bud nipped by the frost, or the blossom prematurely withered on the branch where it lately presented the fairest hope. How often do we observe young persons, distinguished by capacity of understanding and sensibility of heart, by genius, and acquirements, and education, adorned with every amiable disposition and accomplishment, and these too consecrated by unfeigned piety, sinking into an early tomb, and becoming in our estimation lost to the world, and to the church, to their generation and to posterity! When the eyes of sanguine expectation have begun to be fixed upon them, and their "names are much set by," death not infrequently marks them as its victims. Providence, with awful majesty and irresistible effect, thus carries into execution its irrevocable purposes; and, after reproving us for undervaluing or overvaluing its gifts, and for possessing them without a due sense of the supreme propriety of God in them, leaves us to cherish their memory, as the only improvement we can now make of them. The subject of the present *Memoir* affords an affecting instance of this appointment of Providence. He had just entered upon the labors of the sacred ministry, in circumstances the most hopeful and encouraging, when it pleased the Great Master to call him hence. When presenting to his friends and to his congregation, a few of his written Discourses, as a memorial of departed excellence, we shall submit the few particulars of his life of which we have been able to obtain the knowledge.

The Reverend THOMAS HALLIDAY was born at Farthingwell, in the parish of Dunscore, Dumfriesshire, on the 18th of November 1799. He was the second son of Mr. David Halliday and Mrs. Helen Stott, who, with three sons, survive to lament their first domestic breach. Mr. D. Halliday inherited by his mother the small property above named, being a division of the land of Farthingwell, which had been in the possession of that line of family from almost time immemorial. Mr. John Glen-dinning, his maternal uncle, had finished the usual course of education for the sacred ministry, and was just about to obtain license to preach, in the connection of the Reformed Presbytery, when an event occurred, similar to that which has occasioned our present mournful task. Mr. Glen-dinning died at Pentium! His nephew had secretly resolved that if ever Providence gave him a son and inclined his heart to the sacred office, he would make every sacrifice in his power to give him the requisite education. And after this desire of his heart was accomplished, and in circumstances peculiarly happy, it pleased Providence early to remove the dedicated youth. But the case was so hopeful for himself, and so honorable in relation to the church, that the parents can never for a moment regret any sacrifice they have made; nor are they to conclude, in the fullness of their grief, under a dispensation they feel as severe, that their pious dedication was rejected. It will be the first concern of religious parents to surrender their children to the Lord. And may they not, in submission to God, dedicate them to his special service, and by continued prayer, instruction and encouragement, foster the desire of a good work? Although we sometimes observe sovereignty in these things commanding our silent awe, who knows in how many instances the church of God may have received her ministers, in connection with the secret pious dedication of parents? Some parents may aspire to this office for their sons, from the respectability or emolument connected with it, and others may, in both of these views, look down upon it with contempt, as befitting only the mean and the poor; but the Christian, judging rightly, will magnify this office, as investing him who discharges it faithfully with the highest honors, and imparting to him the richest rewards. Hannah is not the only parent in Israel, whose man-child has been lent unto the Lord all the days of his life, and who has considered the special service of God on earth, in connection with the enjoyment of him in heaven, as the highest consummation for which children could be wished, or which could be wished for children.

The subject of our *Memoir* was early dedicated to God in baptism, and it was his privilege to receive what may be called a strictly religious education. Prayers were offered to God in his behalf; he was accustomed to attend at the family altar, when the morning and evening oblations were presented to the God of the families of Israel; the elements of religious knowledge were communicated, on his earliest susceptibility of receiving them; he was taken to the sanctuary on the Sabbath; the example of industry, order, and piety, was always before him; and the sequestered situation of his paternal residence happily secluded him from many of impositions which assail our youth in a dense population. Domestic prayer, example, and instruction, the ordinary, and, in connection with the preaching of the Gospel, the most frequently blessed means of grace, there is reason to hope were blessed to him; as it appears, that besides that constitutional sedateness of character by which he was distinguished, he manifested from early years serious impressions of mind. The importance attached to the domestic constitution in the erection of the church of God of old, and the continued obligation of its duties, ought never to be overlooked, by parents or others. "All the nations of the earth shall be blessed in him," says the Lord concerning Abraham; "For I know him, that he will command his children and his household after him, and they shall keep the way of the Lord, to do justice and judgment; that the Lord may bring upon Abraham that which he hath spoken of

him." The duty and advantage of domestic; instruction
should ever be strongly inculcated. Other plans for the
religious instruction of children, however necessary
from a degenerated state of society, and imposing from
the devotedness of laborers, the extent of operation,
and hopeful success, should not be permitted to
displace or supplant an institution which God has
expressly provided and authorized, and to which he
has promised his special benediction. Parents are the
most valuable auxiliaries to the ministers of the Gospel,
and their instructions form, perhaps, the most ordinary
means of beginning spiritual good in the rising
generation. Domestic instruction, let it be observed, is
not in the place of the preaching of the Gospel, but
cooperates with it, in preparing the soil, watering the
seed, driving away the devouring fowl, and watching
against the insidious enemy. Many who have had the
best opportunity of observation, have acceded to the
sentiment, that "in a regular state of the church, and a
tolerable measure of faithfulness and purity in its
officers, family instruction and government are the
usual means of conversion, and the public ordinances of
edification." To the former, many as well as the
deceased, have occasion to trace their first serious
impressions, and shall have reason to bless God for
domestic instruction, while they live and forever.

Mr. Halliday, when a child, was distinguished
by precocity of mental power. Before he had completed
his second year he could distinguish the letters of the
alphabet. So soon as he was taught to read he
manifested a taste for books, and an ardent thirst for
information. He diligently applied himself to the books
that were within his reach, and was known frequently
to leave his puerile sports and betake himself to
reading. When about ten years of age he had made
great proficiency in arithmetic, and was able to solve,

with readiness and accuracy, the most difficult questions in Hutton's system. About this time he began to learn the elements of the Latin language, and continued four years studying Latin and Greek, in the parochial school; laying a foundation for that respectable acquisition in language, and taste for classical literature, for which he was afterwards distinguished. From the parochial school he was sent to the Dumfries Academy, where he joined the highest class, and stood at the head of it, or contended for this honor with another competitor. Here he also attended a French Class, and acquired a knowledge of the elements of this language which was useful to him afterwards. When in Dumfries, he was distinguished for his close application. His landlady said of him, "Though the King were passing in his coach, it would not take him off till he had got his lesson." He was of a very reserved disposition, and said little respecting his future designs. He had expressed to his landlady a strong desire to go to College, which she communicated to his parents. After he had entered his second quarter at Dumfries, he was taken home, and immediate preparation made for sending him to Edinburgh.

The following is an outline of Mr. Halliday's academical curriculum. He was sent to the University of Edinburgh in November, 1815, when he had just entered his sixteenth year, and he joined the second Humanity and second Greek classes. In November 1816 he entered the senior Greek and the Logic classes. In the following session he attended the senior Greek, Moral Philosophy, and Mathematic classes. In 1818 he attended the Natural Philosophy class, and a private Hebrew class.

The writer has it not in his power from personal acquaintance, to say anything of this period of Mr.

Halliday's history. But his fellow-students attest that his application was unremitting, and that his appearance in the classes, was not only respectable but superior. He commanded the respect of those to whom he was known by his abilities, and by his intelligent conversation and propriety of conduct. Many of the students from Dumfriesshire consulted him respecting the classes they should enter, and applied to him occasionally for assistance in preparing their exercises. He was regarded with deference for his talents and the soundness of his counsels. He manifested an unquenchable thirst for knowledge, and an invincible perseverance in his application, difficulties rather stimulating than discouraging him. And when pursuing with the greatest ardor, the study of the different branches of Philosophy, he always discovered a partiality for sacred science. This was the ulterior point at which he aimed, and other things were viewed as preparatory. It is pleasant to observe, that at this time he appears to have lived under deep impressions of divine things. I shall give the testimony of a companion, who lived with him during the two last sessions he attended College. "I regarded him more like a father than a fellow-student, and from the most intimate acquaintance with him I had never cause to change my opinion. His advices to me were uniformly for my interest, and his example was worthy of universal imitation. His thirst for science and philosophy, though very great, was not equal to the desire which he had for a knowledge of divinity and an acquaintance with revelation. In the prosecution of his studies, no difficulty however great deterred him from the pursuit. His perseverance was almost beyond conception, as it was, at all events, beyond anything I ever knew. What was better than all these qualities, he had a most profound regard for sacred and divine things. The deep impressions which he had of religion were visibly manifested in the whole of his conduct and conversation. The graces of the Christian character, in fact, have seldom been more prominently manifested in a young man. In short he seemed to have been destined for another and a better world." Mr. Halliday was a youth of great reserve, and retired from public view. It is gratifying to find one to whom all his privacy was known, testifying thus not only to his diligence as a student, but to the excellence of his conduct, and to his piety.

The vacations between the sessions of College were spent under his father's roof, and he improved the opportunity afforded him of applying himself to study. He distributed his time methodically, as every student should do who is emulous of a profitable appropriation of it. The morning and forenoon he devoted to close study. After dinner he recreated himself, for half an hour or so, with some manual employment, and returned to his study, continuing in it till 8 o'clock in the evening. About this time he walked in the fields, with a book in his hand, sometimes reading aloud, and at other times reciting favorite passages which he had selected. He was in the habit of selecting pieces of poetry and recreating himself by recitations. He was a careful observer of nature, and marked minutely the progress of vegetation. And being enamored with astronomy, as young minds usually are, and as young and old ought to be, he often made remarks on the appearances of the heavens. At one time he remained without till after midnight, observing an eclipse of the moon, and marking carefully its different stages. Knowledge gives its possessor an unspeakable advantage. The traces of Divine wisdom are everywhere in the works of God, and when the eye and the mind have been trained by observation, and by sound philosophy, and the heart is under the influence of true piety, the works of nature become a temple irradiated with Divine glories. Mr. Halliday discovered a quick relish for the beauties of nature, and his taste was to him a source of enjoyment. Dark though the face of nature may be, on those revelations which the Christian essentially needs, it aids his views of the Divine power and wisdom and goodness; and philosophy, in this way sanctified to her proper use, becomes subservient to faith and devotion. Happy, peculiarly happy indeed! Is that observer of the works of the Almighty,

> "—who with filial confidence inspired, can lift to heaven an unpresumptuous eye, And smiling say, 'My Father made, them all.' Are they not his by a peculiar right, And by an emphasis of interest his, whose eyes they fill with tears of holy joy, whose; heart with praise, and whose; exalted mind with worthy thoughts of that unwearied love that planned and built, and still upholds a world so clothed with beauty for rebellious man?" "Happy who walk with Him! whom what he finds of flavor or of scent, in fruit or flower, or what he views of beautiful or grand In nature, from the broad majestic oak, to the green blade that twinkles in the sun, prompts with remembrance of a present God. His presence who made all so fair— perceived. Makes all still fairer. As with him no scene is dreary, so with him all seasons please."

I can well suppose these passages of his favorite poet, fully verified in the evening walks of young Halliday.[1]

---

[1] Besides being quickly alive to the beauties of nature, Mr. Halliday was not insensible to those of art, particularly when they were illustrative of science, and sub-served what is useful. As an

The history of a young man immured in his room, and devoting himself to reading, study, and writing, it would he uninteresting as tedious to give in detail. But the effect is told in his future eminence. And would the youthful reader know the true secret of attaining usefulness and eminence, he may safely behold it lies in persevering diligence, without which no man can reasonably hope to excel. Mr. Halliday's

---

evidence of the ingenuity of his mind, and of his mechanical activity, I may mention, that having seen, in the Natural Philosophy class, a model of Barker's centrifugal mill, he succeeded on his return to his father's, in constructing one for himself. This hydraulic machine is of simple construction, and capable of useful application. It consists of a vertical pipe, turning on a pivot at the lower extremity, and having an axis attached to a frame on the upper end, in which it is free to move. Toward the lower extremity of the pipe, and at right angles to its axis, are attached two arms or smaller pipes, with closed external ends, and an adjustable orifice near to each end, but plated on opposite sides that the water may flow in opposite directions. The water received into the vertical pipe and discharged by the orifices throws the whole into a rapid rotator motion; the power depending not altogether on the perpendicular height of the water, but on the centrifugal force that is generated in the arms. By attaching machinery to the axis to receive its motion, this engine may be applied to many useful purposes; and so correct were the views of our young mechanic, that by his direction, his friends succeeded in constructing a mill, which serves all the purposes of a threshing machine, and is thus employed by them. Several others have been formed from it in the vicinity, and in other places. Mr. Halliday's ingenuity appeared also in a simple contrivance for regulating the supply of water. When the reservoir, or dam, was full, the pressure caused too great a discharge of water for the pipe. By forming a cone-shaped plug adjusted to a proper orifice, and attaching it by a rod to a lever, whose other arm is connected with a block of wood which floated in the water, the evil was remedied; for in proportion as the surface of the water fell, the other end of the lever was elevated, and the plug thus gradually rising, opened the way for a larger discharge. This simple contrivance had the most perfect success. But Mr. Halliday soon abandoned mechanical recreations altogether, absorbed in studies of a higher character.

study of secular learning, was distinguished by constant diligence, and painful perseverance. His active inquiring mind was always at work, and without enjoying the facilities to which many have access, the result was happy. His history as a student is one of humble retirement. If he might be without some of the advantages to be derived from general company, and frequent intercourse with the world, he also happily escaped many snares. His time was not squandered, his mind was not dissipated with frivolity, his morals were untainted, his ambition had received no worldly excitement, and he advanced to higher studies, and came forward to public life, with a character which even an enemy could not reproach.

When Mr. Halliday had completed his academical career, his next care was to determine for future life. Notwithstanding an early and prevailing bias to the study of Theology, he did not proceed to it merely as the next in a system of education. His mind was affected with the peculiar importance and solemnity of this study, as connected with preaching the gospel. He viewed it as something quite different from a step to secular advancement, or an avenue to respectability and comfort in life. His mind seems to have been aware of the necessity, both of personal piety and of a call unto the work of the ministry. Indeed these things had impressed his mind from an early period of his studies; for sometime in the vacation, after his first session of College, he had said to one of his friends, that "he thought that perhaps he could learn to preach, but there was a Divine call to it of which he was not certain." Before entering formally on the study of divinity, he made it his care to form an ecclesiastical connection, and proceeded to it with much thoughtful inquiry. Two things seem to have engaged his attention—his own personal religion, and the profession he should adopt. The former of these is in danger of being neglected, or is too easily disposed of, by those who give accession to the church, and by candidates for the Christian ministry. From the nature of the subject, from natural modesty, and from the danger of being deceived in a matter of so great importance, or of incurring the charge of ostentation where humility is so becoming, the matter may sometimes be too little the subject of conversation. It cost Mr. Halliday much thought, and in this, as in other things, he acted much on his natural reserve. In a confidential conversation which the writer of this had with him, a few weeks before his death, the subject was introduced with a view to commence a regular correspondence, and to prepare the way for more particular conversation at a future time. Although the subject was introduced with much delicacy, it could not escape Mr. Halliday's penetration, that apprehensions were now entertained as to his recovery. With great modesty and diffidence, he said, "that when studying philosophy, his mind had been almost in danger of indifference or skepticism, but that about the time he joined the church, if he was not mistaken, his mind had been brought to some decision in this matter, that had never been shaken." he made no specification of times or circumstances; but the conversation was dropped in view of being resumed, at a future time— his dissolution, although feared, not being at this time contemplated as so immediate. It was the opinion of the writer at the time, and he has been confirmed in it from conversation with Mr. Halliday's friends, that he had been brought under religious impressions in early life, and that feeling himself laid under a necessity of self-examination, in the view of a first approach to the Lord's table, he had entered very seriously upon this work, subjecting himself to strict self-scrutiny, and had obtained some rest and comfort in views of the gospel; and that he perhaps looked back to this time as the beginning of his confidence. He read carefully Newton's *Letters*, and Scott's *Force of Truth*. The latter of these seems to have made a particular impression on him, as appears from the disposition accurately to distinguish between the Arminian and Calvinistic theology, which is prominent in his early compositions, of which the following are a specimen. I am mistaken if he did not refer to this period of his life, in the use of the scripture expression, "the beginning of confidence," in the last letter that he wrote, which we shall afterwards introduce in its place. But long before this time his mind appears to have been deeply affected with the sentiments of religion. When very young, on the morning of a Sabbath, when the Lord's Supper was to be celebrated in the congregation to which he belonged, there being some strangers in the house, he discovered himself not quite well pleased with their conversation, and read to them a passage from an old practical work, describing, in very rich and fervent language, the ordinance under the emblem of a feast. The passage appears to have impressed his mind, and it is obvious that he was thinking of the peculiar services of that Sabbath. He was early in the habit of paying particular attention to the discourses which he heard. I remember him speaking distinctly of discourses which he had heard in 1811, before he was twelve years of age; and from circumstances, which I need not specify, I had it in my power to know well the correctness of his apprehension and of his memory. How important is it early to feed the kids beside the shepherds' tents! The pleasures and advantages connected with early attention to religion are unspeakable, and the hazard incurred by the loss of this precious period of life, is dreadful beyond description.

Besides the important subject of his personal religion, Mr. Halliday's attention was directed particularly to his Christian profession. He did not adopt this as a matter of course, or as the religion of his father. Being furnished with means of information, he applied himself sedulously to "prove all things," and to be "fully persuaded in his own mind." He occasionally agitated the subjects in dispute among different denominations. At one time when his father gave him a book to read on a particular point, he said to him, "That is only the one side: I wish to see what is said on the other side too;" and he would not come to a determination without reading the opposite writings. He pursued the investigation of the claims of the different denominations with great diligence, and did not embrace the religion of his father, but in the full persuasion of his own mind. The advantages accruing to him from this diligence appeared in the perspicacity of his views, the decision of his sentiments, and his undeviating steadfastness. With these conscientious preparations, after much difficulty in his own mind, he became a communicant at the Lord's Supper, in the year 1819.

This part of our narrative supplies two important remarks. 1. There is advantage connected with an early attention to the observation of the Lord's Supper. Danger is incurred by a precipitate approach to this ordinance; and parents and church riders contract great guilt, if, by their indolence and neglect, they are accessory to this evil. But the danger is not all on one side. There is much peril in undue delay. After a certain period the mind becomes more indifferent and callous. It is of great advantage to be laid under a necessity to think, both on the subject of personal religion and of a Christian profession. Too often is the former of these things treated as a future concern, and the latter viewed as a matter of unimportant and interminable controversy. Early attention to this ordinance is calculated to make the young person feel the one as a present concern, and the other as a duty in which he is called to decide and to act for Christ. Without a judicious decision here, we are in danger of substituting the generalities of religious decency for the life of godliness, and of being carried away, in general speculation and skepticism, from due attention to important parts of the will of Christ. This remark applies with peculiar strength to students of Divinity. Their submission to the will of Christ in the practical observation of the Supper, and their adoption of a particular profession, should not appear to devolve upon them as matters of propriety, from being students of Divinity, contemplating the work of the ministry; but the study of Theology should flow from their practical submission to Christ, and be prosecuted with the special advantages which are derived from this connection. The second remark we had in view, is, the great propriety of embracing opportunities of religious conversation with youth and others. Much evil is done by imprudence here, and no good can be derived from the language of mere cant on these things. But some benefit and much comfort may be lost by an undue reservation. The vicissitudes of the present state, and our constant liability to death, teach us to do with all our might what our hand finds to do. How often are omissions of this kind matter of regret among surviving relatives! The words that may prudently be elicited from the youthful lips will, in some cases, relieve the mind in its future distress, and in others be useful to the living. On fit occasions even the day of health should be thus improved. Views of Divine truth and illustrations of the Scriptures, in Christian conversation, are sometimes remembered with peculiar advantage and comfort by survivors, when death has given to them its solemn sanction. They are taken up like the mantle that fell from the translated prophet, and may be useful in dividing the waters through which we are to follow those who have gone before us. Often do parents and near relatives express regret on the subject of their omission here. In other cases they have consolations that soothe their minds in the moment of trial. In this way we may, without our knowledge, be preparing consolation for ourselves, or for those who shall survive us.

We are next, to view Mr. Halliday as a student of Divinity. With the preparation of a regular education and fixed habits of mental application, and with the special preparation arising from the close application of his mind to the business of personal religion, as well as of the public avowal of the name of Christ, he now entered upon his most favorite study. At this time the Rev. John Macmillan, of Stirling, Theological Professor, in the connection to which Mr. Halliday had acceded, was removed by death.[2] By this lamented event our young Divine was left in a great measure to private study, under the direction of the ministers in whose vicinity he resided. A successor to Mr. Macmillan was appointed in May following, but there was no regular course of prelections that season. In the autumn of that year, (1820,) Mr. Halliday presented himself at Paisley, along with the other students of divinity, and delivered his first homily. He attended the sessions in 1821, and 1822; and the greater part of the following one, although by this time he had received license and was preaching every Sabbath.

As a student of Divinity, Mr. Halliday

---

[2] He died October 20, 1819, at Edinburgh, on his way home from Hath, whither he had gone for his health. He was in his 68th year, and in the forty-second of his ministry.

manifested the most eager attention to the business of the Theological class, and appeared to take a deep interest in everything that was going on. He read Greek and Hebrew correctly —the examinations proved that he was digesting well the arguments under discussion —his critical observations on the performances of others were judicious and acute—his own compositions showed a vigorous and expanding mind—and the devotional exercises always manifested humility, piety, and deep impression of the importance of the work of the class, and of the necessity of personal religion and the influences of the Holy Spirit.

His private deportment was consistent with his appearance under the eye of the teacher. "As a student," says his most intimate companion to me, he showed remarkable diligence. We were never well into our lodging till he was at work some way or other; and he seldom, or I might say never, lost time unnecessarily at meals, continuing reading or writing till the last moment, and beginning again as soon as obstructions were removed. Nothing almost could disturb him. He seemed quite abstracted, and often he would reply to anything said to him without appearing to have his mind in any degree withdrawn from what was engaging it. Joking he exceedingly disliked, in company or in private. He had a considerable vein of humor when he chose to open it. This was seldom, and he speedily stopped it, with some expression of regret that he had indulged himself too far. His whole soul seemed bent on his work, and he had no relish for anything that did not bear on mental improvement. He was very unfond of interruptions in his study. I have seen the announcement of a tea party almost put him out of humor. He liked rational society, but the common-place routine of fashion and gossip he could not endure. The unction of piety that characterized his pulpit ministrations appeared in the whole of his studies, in the solemnity and zeal with which he prosecuted them, and the manner in which he subordinated them to the interests of religion, and in his habitual dependence on the Divine aid and blessing."

It appears also from his manuscripts that the intervals between the meetings of the hall were well occupied. Besides his preparation of the exercises that were prescribed, his other papers give evidence of great diligence. He has large notes of the Theological Lectures written in a fair hand. He has one hundred and seventy close quarto pages of translations from Turretin's *Institutio Theologia Elenctica,* and his *Disputations.* He has an epitome of Butler's *Analogy*—of Chalmers *On the Divine authority of the New Testament*—of Owen *On the Spirit*—Brown's *Letters* on the controversy between Presbyterians and Independents—and full Contents of the Protestant. He has also large Annotations on the Book of Genesis and the Epistles to the Romans and Hebrews. The two last of these and a part of the first had been read from the original, in the Theological class, and it had been recommended to the students to write a digest of the argument as the reading proceeded; which he appears to have done, and to have corrected and enlarged afterwards. His reading was in the first instance, select and careful, rather than general. He digested well in study what he read, and committed the substance of it to writing. Habits of reading, close thinking, and careful writing, so essential to successful prosecution of study, are recommended to the young theologian by the example and the success of Mr. Halliday. By these means his mind was furnished, his faculties, by regular discipline, were trained to activity and prepared for further successful application. And in all this exertion, he still continued humble, was not impatient of obscurity, but, was always courting retirement, till a period arrived when he could not be hid.

Having finished the usual preparatory studies, he was recommended to the Presbytery, and was put upon trials, and acquitted himself to the great satisfaction of the Court. He was licensed to preach the everlasting Gospel, on the first of April, 1823. There being a greater call for preaching than could be supplied, the Presbytery had rather accelerated Mr. Halliday's trials. He proceeded with considerable reluctance, and his feelings on the occasion may be estimated from the last Sermon in the volume, which was his second public discourse, and was delivered at Paisley, April 27, 1823. Everyone who heard it will bear witness that the appearance of the preacher was altogether becoming the matter of the discourse. He exemplified the well known description of a preacher, which I find he has prefixed to the volume from which the greater part of the following sermons have been taken.

> "*The Preacher such as Paul, were he on earth, would hear, approve, and own, is simple, grave, sincere. In doctrine uncorrupt, in language, plain, and plain in milliner, decent, solemn, chaste, and natural in gesture; much impressed Himself, as conscious of his awful charge, and anxious mainly that, the flock he feeds may feel it too: affectionate in look, and tender in address, as well becomes a messenger of grace to guilty men.*"

Mr. Halliday's services as a preacher were universally acceptable. His composition was correct, his style perspicuous, his scripture proofs and illustrations apt, and his reasoning conclusive; and the whole, tending to a practical improvement, was calculated to leave an impression on the heart of the hearers that they had a concern in what was spoken. His appearance in the pulpit was grave, indicating thoughtful impression; his delivery was distinct, but rather monotonous, and tending to rapidity. He had no gesticulation, and obviously paid little attention to the niceties of elocution; but this want was compensated by the excellence of his matter, and the unostentatious solemnity of his manner. The excellence of his ministrations, and the uniform humility and prudence with which he conducted himself, procured him universal respect.

Our preacher had not itinerated long as a probationer, when he received calls from different congregations to take the pastoral charge of them. The vacant congregations of Whithorn, Kilmalcolm, and Airdrie, gave him most harmonious and urgent calls to become their pastor. The congregation of Kilmalcolm had very lately become vacant by the decease of their faithful minister, the Rev. Thomas Henderson[3], and would not, in ordinary circumstances, have solicited a moderation so early; but having conceived a high respect for Mr. Halliday's talents and character, they could not forego the opportunity. In their petition to the Presbytery, they thus apologize for soliciting a moderation, while the wound inflicted by their recent bereavement still bled.

Our young preacher was now placed in much difficulty. One invitation was sufficient to impress his thoughtful mind, but competing calls increased his embarrassment. When I wrote to him the issue of the moderation at Kilmalcolm, in which I had been appointed to preside, he says, in his reply to me, I had heard a report that the moderation at Kilmalcolm was to take place some weeks ago, and as no tidings of it

---

[3] The Rev. Thomas Henderson died Oct. 21, 1823, in the fiftieth year of his life, and 37th of his ministry.

had reached me, I had almost drawn the conclusion that some other person had been the object of the choice of that congregation, I think I utter nothing but the real sentiments of my mind, when I say that both for my own sake, and that of the congregation, and my fellow-laborers, I was sincerely glad at this. Men's thoughts, however, are but vanity, and your letter put an end to my idle speculations, and should perhaps also administer a reproof to my rashness, in indulging such thoughts without better evidence. I now feel myself in the perplexing situation of being surrounded with three congregations wishing me as their pastor, and all, so far as I have learned, perfectly unanimous. I wish my heart may be suitably exercised in my present circumstances, and that I may be directed by the great Head of the church himself in that delicate duty which, according to ordinary human probability, will soon devolve on me." In another letter, he says, "Even one call to take the charge of immortal souls, must awaken solemn considerations in every serious mind, and still more must a plurality of calls do so." Pressed with the personal importunities of individuals, and the urgent entreaties of the delegates from the respective congregations, he felt the difficulty of his situation, and it was desirable for all parties that he come to a decision. The calls were laid on the table of Synod, May 12, 1824, and after commissioners from the congregations were heard, and members delivered their sentiments, they were, without any influence whatever, presented to him for his choice. After a few appropriate observations, Mr. Halliday with great Christian simplicity and dignity, accepted the call from Airdrie, filling the hearts of the people there with joy, and those of the other congregations with disappointment and grief. Only one of them could he accept. The people of Airdrie had been four times disappointed in their attempts to obtain a minister. This circumstance had some weight on Mr. Halliday's mind. His decision, while it was received with peculiar satisfaction by the successful congregation, did not, it is believed, in any degree, diminish respect for the candidate, in the congregations that were disappointed.

The next prominent event in Mr. Halliday's life was his ordination. After the usual preparatory trials, this was appointed for Monday, August 23, 1824. The Lord's Supper had been dispensed in the congregation on the preceding Sabbath, and after one sermon, and the usual conclusion of the services, the Presbytery constituted, and repaired to a field on the north side of the town, when the solemn work was proceeded in. The Rev. William Anderson of Loarthead, (Lasswade,) preached from 2 Cor. iv. 7, and the writer put the questions of the Formula, offered the ordination prayer, along with the laying on of the hands of the Presbytery, and delivered addresses to the young minister and the congregation. Nothing could be more agreeable than the harmonious procedure of the congregation in this matter, and the solemnity and gratitude which appeared to possess their minds on receiving a pastor, after having been several times frustrated in this laudable endeavor. On the following Sabbath, the writer of this, at Mr. Halliday's request, introduced him to his congregation, delivering a discourse from Acts x. 33, "thou hast done well that thou art come. Now therefore we are all present before God, to hear all things that are commanded thee of God." Mr. Halliday followed in the afternoon by a sermon from 2 Cor. iii. 5. "Not that we are sufficient of ourselves to think anything as of ourselves, but, our sufficiency is of God." In this discourse he viewed the insufficiency of the Gospel minister, and the sufficiency of God for him, manifesting his characteristic solemnity and humility of mind, and in the conclusion spoke, in a very affecting manner, of the importance of the relation and his uncertainty. Never could ministers be received with greater cordiality. It might be said, he was received among them as an angel of God, and, may I add? even as Jesus Christ. If there could be an error in excess here, so far as the messenger is concerned, for there can be none in the other, they were in danger of it. This cordiality continued and increased; nor was I here occasioned to say, as the great apostle said, "Where is then the blessedness ye spake of?"

I shall here introduce two extracts from a book in which Mr. Halliday had preserved a journal of his travels; the one showing the correctness of his habits, and the other the impression of his mind, at this era of his life.

"From the time of my license to that of my ordination, there were a year and about 20 weeks. In that period there were 73 Sabbaths. The two first of these I did not enter upon any public service. The two following I delivered a single discourse, and on the 3d sabbath of May and 1st of June, 1823, I only preached the half of the day. I was never a week unemployed until the 3d sabbath of August, 1821; immediately before my ordination. In the course of my probationary labors I delivered 150 discourses, including a few which I was called to deliver on weekdays—assisted at 10 sacramental occasions— and travelled 3150 miles."

"To this interesting period of my life I will ever look back with pleasure. It put an end to my sedentary career as a student, and introduced me into the service of the church. It was of comparatively short continuance, and as new and important prospects were always presented to my mind, I got no time to become languid or weary. I sometimes feel inclined to wish it had been continued a while longer, yet such a feeling may arise from an unfair view of the subject. In reflecting on the past, imagination generally seizes on the fair parts of the picture, and overlooks those of an opposite description. I find myself now in a very different situation, more settled no doubt, and affording more leisure for study. At the same time its duties are more arduous, and its responsibility greater. Let me not forget Him who has brought me hitherto, and made my way more prosperous than I could have allowed myself to expect when I entered the busy scene."

Such were the circumstances in which Mr. Halliday entered upon his duties of the ministry; and as was his entrance, so was his short course, acceptable and happy to all that were connected with him. He applied himself assiduously to the functions of his office. His copious notes give evidence of his careful and conscientious preparations for the pulpit. Besides a course of sermons, regularly dated in succession, and most of them pretty fully written, till the time when his health did not admit of the wonted application, there are large notes on the 1st Epistle of John, and the Epistle to the Ephesians, and on the Psalms. He had also delivered monthly, on sabbath evenings, a series of discourses on the Divine perfections. There are 14 discourses arranged as follows: 1. The Existence. 2. The Self-existence. 3. Spirituality. 4. Omnipresence. 5. Omnipotence. 6. Wisdom. 7. Holiness. 8. Justice. 9. Goodness. 10. Patience. 11. Mercy. 12. Truth. 13. And Sovereignty of God. 14. A concluding discourse, as a general improvement of the whole. These discourses had excited a considerable interest, and were gradually attracting an intelligent auditory. Many expressed a wish to see them from the press. This the modest author uniformly declined. I mentioned to him, not long before his death, the wishes of the people on the subject, when he replied, that there were many volumes on these subjects far better already. He added, with a slight feeling of fretfulness, "If I thought they would attempt to print them I would burn them; but at any rate the thing is impossible, as they are not in a state in which they can be printed." I find that this is the case, and that it will be impossible to gratify the wishes of the hearers. Those who hear the gospel should be, careful to improve sermons in the hearing, for excepting by the remembrance, they may never have any other opportunity of profiting by them. Never should the present improvement be delayed in the hope of a future.

Mr. Halliday took a deep interest in the prosperity of his congregation, and abounded in those other labors of love, comprehended in the pastoral care. He persevered also in his habits of application to close study. In a small volume, which he has called, "A Memorandum of Studies in the Heading department," I find mention made of books which he read. It had been his practice after reading a book carefully, to write a short account of it, and to give his opinion of its merits. This book begins with Dec. 1821, and is continued so late as Nov. 1826, within a short time of his death. I find observations of this kind on Dr. Edwards against Chauncy on the Salvation of all men—on Home's introduction to the critical study and knowledge of the Scriptures, Dr. M'Crie's Lives of Knox and Melville, Brown's Lectures on the Philosophy of the human mind, Fuller's Gospel its own Witness and Essays, Erskine on the Internal Evidence for the truth of revealed Religion; and on Mr. Haldane's Letter to the Geneva Professors, Gethsemane, Johnston's Commentary on the Revelation, &c. His reading must have been extensive, and it appears to have been very careful. His observations on the above and other works are exceedingly judicious. I submit the following specimen. Of M'Crie's *Life of Knox*, he says, "Read over this work in the course of the last two weeks. Had read the first edition some years ago, but never till now the more enlarged one in two volumes. The high opinion I had entertained of the work from my former perusal, and from the praises I uniformly hear bestowed upon it, is not at all diminished by the present reading. Dr. M'Crie does justice to his subject to a degree rarely paralleled. Knox was worthy of such a Biographer, and the wisdom of Providence is to be gratefully acknowledged in raising up one to vindicate his memory. In the perusal there is nothing with which I was more struck, than the extraordinary research and acquaintance with the history of the period that the author discovers. He seems to have read every remaining fragment of the history of that age, both domestic and foreign, the writings of Papists and the Reformers, ancient MSS, records of courts, civil and ecclesiastical. The materials are ample, and the arrangement luminous and happy. Knox is the main subject, yet it is almost a history of the period, and is likely to be the guide to future students of Scottish history, in their inquiries into that period. The style is luminous, masculine, and well adapted to the subject. The notes are copious and cannot be expected to be always interesting, yet in general they will well repay a perusal. In this work Dr. M'Crie has done an eminent service to his generation and to posterity; and it is doubly valuable from its tendency to bring our long-neglected *Reformation* into view, and to revive its interest among us." His remarks upon the Life of Melville, and on other works, are equally judicious and striking; and the man who united such diligence and penetration, in select and regular reading, could not fail soon to enlarge his knowledge, and to invigorate his mental powers. His mind, already furnished, was in a process of high cultivation; and his humility and piety continued to maintain their ascendancy, and to adorn his character. The church had much to expect from him. His congregation were becoming riveted in their attachment; and, in the expectation of enjoying his valuable services, had made an effort to erect a neat and comfortable manse for him in the vicinity of the town, when, alas! death was marking him for the narrow house. His hidden worth was coming gradually into view, and the prospects of the congregation were of an agreeable description; but they suddenly changed, as when a cloud overcasts the sun, after it has risen with all the tokens of a bright shining day. Our narrative must now change, and instead of a fulfillment of the anticipations which the character and circumstances of our young minister have excited, we must relate the mournful tale of his declining health, and of his death.

Early in 1826, Mr. Halliday exhibited symptoms of declining health. He felt weakness, but from his disposition to be reserved, and also from his native resolution and fortitude, he made almost no complaint. When engaged, by appointment, of Presbytery, in the spring, visiting families in a vacant congregation, he had felt much exhausted, and he was obliged once, in the time of prayer, to pause a little. He did not soon recover from his fatigues at this time, and his countenance began to indicate more unfavorably for his health. On the Sabbath of the communion in his own congregation, the first Sabbath of July, after he had preached the Sermon, and was engaged in the other preparatory service, he was obliged to stop, and he partially swooned. After receiving a little wine and water, he recovered, and resumed and finished the services, he had delivered a long discoursel, and the day was pretty warm. In this way we were pleased to find a satisfactory explanation of the occurrence, which had almost petrified the large assembly at the time; but his friends never recovered from the alarm about his health which this occurrence excited. He assisted, very shortly after this, at the dispensation of the Lord's Supper at Kilbirnie, and at Paisley. At both of these places, when preaching on Monday, he discovered a tendency to faint, and it was necessary to give him a little water. From Paisley he went to spend a few days at Rothesay. He was earnestly recommended to desist from public work; but even there, he seemed unhappy till he had made a promise to preach a little on the Sabbath. His eagerness to preach manifested something like a strong presentiment that his period of service was to be short. He always said, when spoken to on the subject that he was not the worse for preaching; and he was almost at the point of fretting, when any person advised him to desist from it. It was thought that an apprehension that he would be interdicted his delighted labor, was a reason why he did not sooner apply for particular medical advice. Although he had the benefit of professional advice, he rather manifested a reluctance to call medical aid, and it appeared that he was not altogether conscious of the danger attending his ailments. Young people, and persons who have never experienced indisposition, expose themselves to danger by neglecting necessary precautions, and treating them as something indicative of weakness.

In the end of August, Mr. Halliday took a journey to the south country, to visit his friends, breathe his native air, and to attend the ordination of his esteemed companion, the Rev. Gavin Rowatt, which was to take place at Whithorn, on the 13th of September. He remained in the south, during the whole of September. He performed the journey from Penpont to Whithorn on horse-back, attended the ordination, and returned in the same week. This was quite beyond his strength. On the way back he complained considerably, and could only permit his horse to walk slowly the whole journey. He preached on the last sabbath of September, and first of October, at Eskdale-muir; and although he did not faint, he was obliged to pause occasionally, and take a little water. He left Farthing-well on the 11th of October, to "return no more, nor see his native country." Although he had received no benefit from his journey, he resumed his labors, on his return to Airdrie. Ascribing his failure of strength when preaching more to his standing, than to his speaking, he thought if he had a proper seat, he might still preach without doing himself any injury. A seat of proper elevation was procured, and for some time he sat and preached. His strength continuing still to decline, he was advised to desist from his public labors for a time. In the end of November, he came to the west country, to spend a few days with some friends; and particularly to visit a medical friend, under whose hospitable roof he enjoyed professional attendance and advice, and the pleasure of agreeable and Christian conversation. This gentleman, with his characteristic kindness of heart, entered into his case, with all the feeling of a brother, and was sedulous in his attentions to him. But the dictates of the warmest friendship, guided by the soundest science and extensive observation, and executed by the most skilful hand, could not now avail the much-valued patient. Disease had struck its roots into his constitution, and they could not be eradicated. It is our duty to use "all lawful endeavors to preserve our own life, and the life of others," and to call in the aid of medicine when accessible; but it is impossible to impart immortality to the human body, or to extend the term of existence here beyond the determined bounds. Mr. Halliday left us now for the last time, and some friends who saw him to the coach, when he left Paisley, feared the farewell to be, what, alas! it proved, final for earth; and returned sorrowing because they would see his face no more. He returned to Airdrie and resumed his work. He began now to abbreviate his discourses, but appeared still resolved to continue his labors, and to live and die in the service of his loved Master.

He complained considerably of the fatigue of this journey, and his views may be gathered from an extract from a very affectionate letter, which the writer received from him a few weeks after his return:

"I reached home safely the evening of the day I left you. But as the coach from Glasgow to this was very crowded, I was considerably fatigued. Whether it was owing to the journey altogether or riot, I cannot say, but I was scarcely so well for eight or ten days after my return—rather more languid than ordinary, and my bowels a little more disordered than usual. From this I have been a little more recovered, and the general state of my health is much the same as when you saw me. In some respects I am rather better of late, but the cough for some weeks has been rather more troublesome than formerly. It is worst at night, and sometimes my rest is very much broken by it. I have been endeavoring to walk according to the Surgeon's directions, and the thought at times arises, Am I not beginning yet to reap advantage? In the use of all means, natural and moral, we must wait patiently, and remember whose the event is. I have preached a little every sabbath since I was your way, and by keeping the seat pretty constantly, and making The services short, I have got through without particular fatigue or difficulty. My infirmities are trying to me more from their lingering nature than their severity, and I would be thankful that there is so much mercy mingled with judgment. I am still able to go about through the week, and endeavor to do a little on sabbath in the service of Christ. As I am not employed in any ministerial duties except preaching, and as I do not think it proper to confine myself to close study, I have a good deal of leisure time, which I am sensible I ought to turn to some profitable account. When passing sleepless hours on bed, I have felt that the Psalmist's example, who remembered God in the night watches, had its call to imitation. But in such exercises I am a slow scholar."

Mr. Halliday endured his affliction with exemplary patience and fortitude. He was far removed from his friends, and his situation would appear to some to be lonely. However trained by his previous habits of study to solitude, his present circumstances required the attention of a friend. The members of his congregation paid all the attention in their power; and formerly, and now, seemed to vie with one another in the duties of kindness and sympathy. One would have thought the presence of a mother, or of a sister, if there had been one, was much needed; but Providence supplied this lack. The hand of God is often seen in preparing and fitting instruments to be the mediums of its kindness to us, when we are, by distance or otherwise, deprived of the natural channels. Of this Mr. Halliday often expressed his sense, in his present situation. But the time approaches, when neither the embraces of affection, nor the hand of skilful care, no, nor the cry of earnest prayer, shall be able to detain him here; and it was so appointed that, till the last day of his life, he was never closely confined.

When things appear to be hastening to a solemn crisis, the reader, from higher motives than curiosity, may be inclined to ask, what are now the views of Mr. Halliday himself respecting his situation? He was sensible of the decline of his health, and he could not fail to perceive that apprehensions were entertained by his friends; still he does not appear to have been fully aware of the extent of the insidious disease, and of the immediate approach of dissolution. The wishes of his friends might incline, even them, to entertain some hope; and their tenderness and delicacy might prevent them from expressing their fears. We believe that Mr. Halliday lived in habitual preparation for death, but that he did not enter fully into all the apprehensions of his friends, and that the end came more suddenly than he anticipated. We have abundant evidence, however, that he was in the holy fear, and also in the calm hope, of the issue. This appeared from the subjects upon which he preached, and from his letters, and from the tenor of his prayers. On the sabbath after his return from Dumfriesshire, he preached from Psalm xxxix. 4. "Lord, make me to know mine end, and the measure of my days what it is, that I may know how frail I am." Not long before his death, he appears to have preached two discourses on Matt. ix. 10, "They that be whole need not a physician, but they that are sick." About a month before his death, he had "called for the elders of the church," and they assembled in his house, for the purpose of special prayer, in the present aspects of Providence toward him and the congregation. They had severally engaged in prayer, and Mr. Halliday himself concluded the social exercises, in a strain of humble sweet submission to God, and of holy fervor, making a deep impression upon all the members, which they shall not soon forget. His last sermon was from Prov. xvi. 19. "Better it is to be of an humble spirit with the lowly, than to divide the spoil with the proud." This was on the 2nd sabbath of January 1826. It had been agreed to observe a day of fasting in the congregation on the following Tuesday, and this discourse may be viewed as preparatory. I cannot omit to observe his train of thought, as expressed in his notes. His plan was to give reasons for being of an humble spirit, and to shew the excellency of his spirit. His first observations are—1. Our formation from the dust, and speedy return unto it—2. The utter uncertainty of everything we enjoy below; strength, riches, beauty, health, connections, mental talents, &c. 3. The afflictions and adversities to which we are exposed— 4. Our deep sinfulness in the sight of God. From these he proceeds to take a view of—the sufferings of Christ for us—our misimprovement of the means of grace—the imperfect manner in which we perform our duty—the wickedness of the generation— and our responsibility to God. The notes contain only an outline; and even this, like many of his other MSS. has an intermixture of stenographic character, which prevents its correct transcription. I mention the above merely to show what place death and eternity were now holding in his mind, and in the view of his engaging in humiliation.

The following Tuesday was observed as a public fast in the congregation, and the services were conducted by the writer. Mr. Halliday attended all day, but presented obvious indications of languor and debility. In the evening, however, he was able to engage in conversation with the writer, and another brother who had come to visit him and to wait over the night. The conversation which I have related above took place on the following day. It was designed as an introduction to a regular correspondence on the subject of personal religion, in which we would have an opportunity of expressing our thoughts with confidential freedom. At this time, and in his previous letters, Mr. Halliday manifested in his friendship that peculiar tenderness which is induced by affliction, and the prospect of separation, he accompanied me to the coach, when I was parted from him, fearing that I might never see him again, and partly hoping that there might yet be an opportunity. I indeed saw his face no more, till his kind nurse afforded me a melancholy gratification, by removing from his countenance that part of the shroud which covered it, when, "Like blossomed tree o'erturned by vernal storm, Lovely in death the beauteous ruin lay."

He went to the pulpit on the sabbath after I left him, gave a discourse on the Psalm, and lectured, in his ordinary course, in Ephesians. It was observed that he ascended the pulpit with difficulty, and while he sat and spoke, he was obliged to support his head with his hand. He was unable to proceed to the other discourse. His congregation were pained at his appearance, and wept as he said to them, that it was not "choice but necessity" that caused him dismiss them, and lifted up his trembling hands, for the last time, to bless them in the name of the Adored Three.

On the following sabbath he attended public worship, when one of his companions in study, who was itinerating in the bounds, preached for him; but he made his way to the place of worship with much difficulty, and left it for the last time. He felt himself becoming worse, and wrote to his friends on the 1st of February, as follows:—

"My very dear Friends, I shall boldly write a short letter at this time, but I am sorry that it must give you more uneasiness than any I have yet written to you.

Since I wrote last, my health has got considerably worse, and for near two weeks now I have been in a feebler state than I have been at all since my present infirmities came upon me. My bowels for some days got into a very bad state, which weakened me considerably, and though by proper means I got that removed, my ailments continue to operate upon me in such a way that I feel it a fatigue to walk up and down the stair, and put off and on my clothes. On sabbath eight-days I was in a very unfit state for preaching: but as the congregation expected sermon, and were assembling for it as usual, I went and gave them a short preface and lecture, and dismissed them between 1 and 2 o'clock. Sabbath week I fell in with Mr. Ferguson, who preached all day. On Sabbath first we are to be without sermon: but on Sabbath eight days I expect Mr. Mason. By that time I will have got three Sabbaths rest, and will see what providence brings about. Till of late I kept up my spirits well, and under the favour of the Almighty cherished hopes of recovery when his time should come. I now find matters somewhat altered. My great bodily weakness keeps my spirits dull, and as trouble increases, the call of the Most High becomes louder and louder, to be in readiness for the great change."

"When I was not so poorly as now, I used to rest ill at night. For some time past, I have used a little laudanum, which has given me greater ease and tranquility, and made the night pass away more pleasantly. I sit up the greater part of the day, but generally go to bed two or three hours in the afternoon for a rest. I cannot attempt a more particular description of the way I am in. I assure you I wish to make no concealment nor exaggeration, but just to state the matter as it stands. It is matter of thankfulness that I have been attacked with no new complaint, and that there are no symptoms as yet materially different from what they were formerly, only greater weakness. Be not then unduly anxious, any of you. All is in good hands. Many a one worse has recovered. I shall conclude with saying that I would like much that some of you would come this length before long and see me."

He then makes some specification respecting a brother, who had been purposing to visit him in spring, requests that he might, on his account, come soon, asks them to write him immediately, and affectionately concludes, specifying, "Dear Father, Mother, and Brothers." This letter was received by his friends as the summons of death, and his brother forthwith repaired to Airdrie, with very different feelings from those with which he had anticipated the intended visit in spring.

The disease continued to gain strength. On the 7th of February, Mr. Halliday wrote to me employing his brother as his amanuensis. After an apology for not writing on the previous week, and some things respecting his increased debility, and some medical advice which he had received, he adds:— " With regard to the state of my mind under my present infirmity, I could wish to say something, and yet know not well what to say. My bodily infirmity hath greatly impaired my mental activity, and I feel much inclined to fall into a dull and languid state of mind. Amid the multitude of thoughts to which my present situation cannot fail to give rise, I trust I am not an entire stranger to God's comforts sometimes delighting my soul. Fixing the anchor of my hope on Christ, and relying on his blood for pardon and peace, I will hold fast the beginning of my confidence to the end. Since I saw you, the call has become louder, "Set thy house in order." Yet I fear I have made little preparation. To the hand of the Almighty I would commit myself whether for death, continuance in trouble, or recovery to health. I much need an interest in the prayers of Christian friends, in my present situation, and hope to a certain extent that I enjoy this privilege. O that these prayers of others were accompanied with believing supplications of my own, and the whole enforced by the intercession of our great High Priest. The consequences then could not fail to be glorious."

"It is not altogether necessity but ease that, has caused me to employ the hand of a brother, who happens to be with me on a family visit at present, in scrawling these lines. I expect my mother here soon, to stay with me a little, till we see what Providence brings about." The above is in the hand of his brother. He concludes the letter very affectionately with his own hand, requesting an early reply.

He continued still gradually to decline, but the symptoms did not indicate, in the view at least of those around him, that his dissolution was just at hand. He felt himself a little relieved, and his brother left him on Thursday morning. His mother arrived on Saturday evening. He had, by this time, reclined on his bed, but seemed revived when informed that his mother was come, and expressed, very tenderly, a wish that his attendants would not alarm her about his situation. And to lessen the shock which he feared his changed appearance would produce on her feelings, he rose, and prepared himself to receive her.

He was very restless during the night, and his language occasionally manifested that his recollection was a little impaired. Next day (Feb. 11th) the Sabbath, his last on earth, he became obviously much weaker. Excepting for a little time when, with some assistance, he dressed himself to rise, he was in bed all day. He early remembered that it was the Sabbath, and made some remarks lamenting his stupidity, and unfitness to sanctify it. To a female friend who had attended him through the night, and who, at his request, had gone to prepare for attending church, he said, on her return before the public worship began, "I had little thought of this." He was by this time sensibly worse, and expressed his consciousness of it with some feeling of surprise. To a friend, on the evening before, who had said to him, "whatever be the issue, I hope all will be well;" he replied, "we cannot be too well prepared for death." He had also said, "whatever be the event, it is always best to be going on in the way of present duty." His mother continuing with him, he insisted on other friends to go to church; but he became on one occasion so very weak, that it was judged proper to send for them. In his last letter to Farthingwell, he had spoken of provision being made for the pulpit on this Sabbath, thus caring and providing for his flock to the last day of his life. He had also said, that "by that time he would have rested three Sabbaths, and would see what Providence would bring about." It was to bring about to him, a rest from all his labors. Most probably this was not anticipated so soon; but the anticipations of Divine providence, in its dispensations, have often a merciful, as well as a castigatory, or judicial character.

At the dismission of public worship, the elders of the congregation, and other members, called to inquire for him. He was able to give them his hand, and spoke affectionately to them. One said, "Mr. Halliday, there was much joy in this part of the church militant when you came to Airdrie, and I hope there will be joy in the church triumphant on your admission there." He replied, "If I be a saint, and if I am to be removed at this time, I have no doubt of that," but these are important if at on one occasion, when a friend was aiding him in washing his hands, he said, "You are washing my hands, and the Master washed the disciples' feet." At another time he gave some orders respecting the servant attending to her catechism, and expressed a religious care about her. To a member of the congregation, who had said, speaking of the loss which the congregation were about to sustain, that they must submit; he said, "we not only must submit, but it is our duty to submit well pleasedly." Those in attendance remarked, also, that what little he did say occasionally in the course of this day, he spake with an unusual dignity and sweetness of manner. He was visited in the afternoon and evening by the venerable father who had been officiating in his pulpit; but he regretted deeply that he was not more able to profit by his conversation and prayers, weakness frequently overcoming him. Prayers continued to be uttered up by visiting friends. In the evening, he was raised on his bed, and partook of a little tea, officiating at the conclusion in the giving of thanks, with his usual sedateness and accuracy, blessing God that the mercies were provided, although some were not able to partake largely. After this, he sunk into a kind of slumber, and at 11 o'clock, breathed, to breathe no more; his spirit returning to God who gave it. His natural life had now reached the bounds which it could not pass, and his soul, we have every reason to hope, made a happy transition from the unfinished Sabbath on earth, to the unwearied employment of the eternal "sabbatism that remains to the people of God." How interesting the moment which terminates our relation to time, and introduces us fully into infinite duration! How different the state lately and now occupied by the immortal spirit, and the circumstances of the society which the spirits of the just leave and join, at the solemn moment of death! We are more ready to sympathize with the sorrows of the bereaved on earth, than with the joys of the emancipated spirit, and the satisfactions of those who have welcomed it into their happy fellowship.

It is unnecessary to say what deep sensations of grief this event produced in the relatives, in the congregation, and in all who knew him. On Friday following the mortal remains were committed to the tomb. A mournful feeling reciprocated in the hearts and countenances of all who attended, while they carried him to his burial, and made great lamentation over him. He was interred in New Monkland church-yard; and his congregation are about to erect a tomb-stone, to mark the spot where his remains repose.

It devolved on the writer of this to address the congregation on the Sabbath following. In the first part of the service, the translation of Enoch was the subject of a discourse, founded on Gen. v. 21—24, and the Sermon in the afternoon was founded on Mat. xiv. 12. "And his disciples came and took up the body, and buried it, and went and told Jesus." After some observations on the extraordinary circumstances of the case referred to in the text, the attention was directed more generally—to the death of the Ministers of Christ—to the respect due even to their mortal remains, in the decent interment of them—and to the duty, after this, of betaking to Christ. The mournful congregation was directed, after the burial of their minister, to go to Christ himself, as—the Sum of the Christian ministry—the glorious Sovereign by whose will his servants were removed in times and circumstances as it pleased him—the exceeding Great Reward of the faithful minister— the Support and Comfort of the mourning survivors—the Abiding and ever-living Head of the church—the Source of that grace by which alone the living can be prepared to follow those who have had the rule over them, and spoken unto them the word of God—the Resurrection and the Life—and, the Glorious One before whom ministers and people shall soon stand to give an account. To this Lord they should go and tell—all their surprise at this appointment of his providence—their grief under their loss—their trouble under an apprehended frown—their fear in anticipation of the future—and all their wishes and desires respecting themselves and others. Very different indeed were the circumstances in which they were addressed at this time, and on the occasion of the introduction of their young minister two years and a half before. Their gladness was turned into mourning. They may remember the affecting references that were made, even on the former of those occasions, to death and judgment, making their gladness to partake of a deep solemnity. And now that their joy is turned into mourning, they must beware of giving indulgence to a kind or an excess of sorrow that is inconsistent with submission to God, and with continued hope in Him for themselves and for his church. In our present state, it, were well that our joy and grief wore at all limes, moderated, by each participating a portion of the other to chock its excess; our joys having in them something of trembling, and our griefs of joyful hope; and neither of them having that exclusive and unmingled character which they too often assume on occasions exciting them, and admitting their indulgence. The Lord liveth, and it is witnessed of our great High Priest that he liveth, and that he is the same yesterday, and today, and forever. In all our adversity we have a refuge, and it always becomes us to think and feel and act, not only like those who know "whither to flee for help," but who have "tied for refuge to lay hold on the hope set before them."

Thus died, in the twenty-seventh year of his life, and third of his ministry, the Reverend Thomas Halliday, Minister of the Reformed Presbyterian

Congregation, Airdrie. As Christians, believing in the divine revelation, we cannot entertain a doubt of his having lived his appointed time, and having finished the ministry which he had received of the Lord Jesus. The full admission of these things is perfectly consistent with marking the proximate causes of his dissolution. His complaints began with a deranged state of the digestive organs, which ultimately affected his lungs. The complaint in his bowels, and the pulmonary complaint induced by it, acting in concert, overcame his natural strength, and carried him to his grave. The disease which carried him off is not unfrequently induced by too close and intense application to study, and the omission of that attention to diet, clothing, and exercise, which is necessary to counteract the evil effects produced by confinement and close mental application. The writer is not without fear, that in the present case, these things had a part in inducing a disease into a constitution naturally healthful and vigorous, and that the subject of this Memoir, in his eagerness for study, from the absorption of his mind in if, and from his natural resolution of character, might neglect that attention to his health, and delay those corrective applications to the first symptoms of disease, which, in other cases, might be means, under Providence, of prolonging him. We indulge in no reflections. Health and disease have a master who says to the one, "Go, and it goeth," and to the other, "Come, and it cometh." The dear subject of our Memoir had accomplished his day. At the same time, we must remember our obligation to use lawful endeavors to preserve our natural lives; and young persons particularly, who have not had experience of disease, are too apt to be neglectful, and to feel as though they were invulnerable, and equal to every exertion. Students preparing for the ministry, or entered upon its labors, should be admonished of the danger resulting from inattention to a proper regulation of diet and exercise, and of the propriety of an early attention to check the first symptoms of disease; for by slow and gradual progress, it may assume a character which places it beyond the control of all ordinary means. In many cases, we have regrets, and these are often as insubmissive to the will of Providence, as they are in themselves unavailing. As the parent who has lost a dear child will sometimes look with a too suspicious eye on the health of those that remain, while cleaving to them with an increased tenderness, we must be indulged in introducing those admonitions to youth, convinced that in this, as in other more important things, the grave of Halliday speaks a voice which should not be disregarded.

Unable now to recall him from the grave, as we were unable to prolong his days, it only remains that we cherish his memory, and improve the dispensation of Providence in his early removal.

In his person, Mr. Halliday was a little above the middle stature, of slender make, and of fair complexion. His countenance showed that paleness which indicates delicacy or confinement and study, rather than vigorous health and exercise in the open air. His countenance indicated a peculiar sweetness, blended with composure and humility. In his natural disposition, as I have said above, he was reserve, and rather retiring than obtrusive. In conversation he presented often an appearance, of absence, and would speak as if rather hesitating what to say. Although much abstracted in his own thoughts and studies, he was no ascetic, but by his conversation and his letters showed himself alive to the pleasures of society, and to the tenderest sympathies of friendship. His understanding was sound and discriminating, and his taste was correct. Both were cultivated with all the advantages derived from a perseverance, that nothing almost could divert from its object. Were we to specify any particular prominence in his mental character, we would fix upon the soundness, discrimination, and comprehension of his intellect. He was cautious in forming his opinions—decisive, after adopting them on proper evidence—and discovered great independence of mind, he was unambitious of worldly greatness, always conducting himself with humility; and in all that he did he was distinguished by a prudence that not only rendered him inoffensive but attractive. In friendship he was unostentatious, true, steady, and unforgetful.

But, *Christian* is the more exalted view which we should take of his character; and the preceding narrative supplies agreeable evidence that this had been superinduced upon what was merely natural. When engaged in the exercises of devotion, in private or in public, he uniformly showed the presence of a rational, scriptural, humble, calm, and fervent piety. Humility and self-denial, dependence upon the Spirit of God, great conscientiousness, and practical holiness, with the other features of Christian character, were combined in him. No amiable dispositions of nature, no cultivation that is merely human, can impart unto the character of man that life, and spirit, and finish, which it derives from Divine grace. How is human nature elevated and ennobled when a Divine image is reimpressed upon it by the Spirit of the living God!

It is as a preacher that we have been led to take our deepest interest in Mr. Halliday and to lament his death as a public loss. In his public labors as a Minister, he supported the character which he had acquired as a Preacher. He selected subjects of the deepest interest and affording scope for scriptural argumentation. He distinguished correctly between the Arminian and Calvinistic systems. He put the impress of the cross upon every subject, and always made it to bear, in the end, on the interests of practical godliness; and exhibited, in proper connection, the privileges of the gospel, and the obligations of holiness. He showed also a judicious and zealous attachment to the Reformation, and cherished a lively interest in the cause of the kingdom of Christ in the, world. Inditing "good matters," he sought out "acceptable words," and fed the people with knowledge and understanding, manifesting an earnestness for their spiritual good, and seeking in their spirituality and holiness, and not in their noisy applauses, the tokens of the acceptance of his labors, with his heavenly Master. As a Pastor, he abounded in the more private duties of his office. In these his congregation attest that he was diligent, affectionate, and persevering. His flock seemed to be much upon his heart; but when projecting labors for their good, and devoting himself to them, he was called away, and they are again as "sheep having no shepherd."

This event must bear immediately and heavily upon the congregation, and their circumstances call for the sympathy of the church. In the bitterness of their grief, let them not forget their obligation to be thankful for what they have enjoyed, nor conclude that all has been in vain, because the time has been short. While they lament their loss, let them remember "how that, for the space of two years and a half," the young servant of Christ "ceased not to warn them with tears." Of those of whom he took the pastoral charge, some were fallen asleep before him; and we know not what reasons they may have had to bless the Lord for the ministry under which they closed their relation to the church on earth, and which, though short to the survivors, was long enough to them. Mr. Halliday's ministry was a sowing time, and there was scarcely time for even the blade to spring up; but God who giveth the increase, may yet cause it to yield much fruit. The saints of God, it may yet appear, have been edified and comforted, and the precious seed may have entered the hearts of others, and yet spring up unto everlasting life; and when the servant has rested from his labors, his works may follow him. God can, by a special blessing, make his short labors as effectual, or more effectual, than those extended to a much longer period. We know not what good work may have been begun in the hearts of youth, and though another enter into the labors, "both he that soweth, and he that reapeth, may rejoice together." Let his congregation "remember the word of the Lord," which their young minister spake unto them, and which must be "the savor of life unto life, or of death unto death." Let them cherish his memory, and while they humble themselves under the mighty hand of God, let them betake to Him who has the care of all the churches, and who has received gifts for men, that he may bless the honors of other servants among them, and send to them, in his time, a pastor according to his heart, for their good, and the good of their children after them.

The talents and Christian character of the deceased made him a valuable acquisition to the church of his connection, and his early death is felt as no ordinary calamity. The event loudly admonishes the ministers of Christ to prosecute their labors of love under solemn impressions of the sudden coining of their Lord, and the people who enjoy their ministry "to know them who labor among them, and are over them in the Lord, and admonish them, and to esteem them very highly in love for their work's sake." It calls the young minister presently to occupy his talents with fidelity, without depending upon a protracted period of service, and the people who enjoy his labors, to prize them presently, and not to procrastinate the improvement in the anticipation of many future opportunities. When a congregation receives a young minister, and feel themselves happy under his ministrations, some may be more ready to dwell on the agreeable prospect before them, than to make that present improvement which, alas! his decease may soon show to them, or their decease to others, to have been "the one thing needful." The servants of Christ who have, had a longer period of labor allotted to them, and the people who have enjoyed more lengthened opportunities, are admonished to inquire how they have severally occupied, and to prepare for the account, which must soon be given. The event we deplore has a special voice to the church, and calls upon her members to pray fervently to "the Lord of the harvest to send forth laborers into his harvest." Of what essential consequence to the prosperity of the church is a succession of ministers deeply imbued with fervent piety, endowed with gifts well cultivated and sanctified of God, animated with zeal in the cause of Christ, nobly disinterested in devoting themselves to his service, and bringing into it the ornament and influence of holy character? To the youth of his congregation, and others into whose hands this account of Mr. Halliday may come, his death tenders a solemn admonition of the uncertainty of life and the importance of early piety. To his companions in study and labors, it has been an occasion, we doubt not, of much solemn reflection; and to them may this brief sketch of his *Life,* and the following specimen of his compositions, by perpetuating this reflection, be made profitable; as we presume, for the sake of the deceased, they will be acceptable. The event, in itself and all its circumstances, is calculated to inspire the mind with an awful reverence of the sovereignty of God. While it proves our faith in the wisdom and rectitude of the Divine dispensations, may we obey the voice, "Be still and know that I am God," and patiently anticipate that hereafter in which the mystery of Providence shall be unveiled, and all the Divine procedure fully approved.

In closing this Memoir, we experience the mournful feeling of one who is under necessity of parting from an esteemed friend, without the prospect of soon or ever enjoying his society—a feeling which makes him linger ere he takes his leave. Part we must. Parted we already are, never to resume society on earth. Mr. Halliday has indeed been cut out in the bloom of life and in the commencement of useful labors; but he has neither lived in vain, nor died in circumstances of unmitigated sorrow, or of doubtful comfort to his survivors. In our views indeed, his death was too soon for his friends, for his flock and for the church of God; but it was not too soon for himself, and it was the work of him who does nothing prematurely. Let those regrets which imply the infirmity, and selfishness, and in subjection of our minds, be suppressed in dutiful submission to God, and in a profitable improvement, of the event. That very death, which so soon terminated acceptable labors, and anticipated others, may itself, by the seal which it sets upon the character, and by the solemn reflections to which it leads, become a gain to us, fully compensating our loss. And must we part? Part we cannot. The character and labors of Mr. Halliday shall dwell in our remembrance. The following sermons will be a memorial of him, and in perusing them the silent dead will yet speak to us and to others. And we shall follow his immortal spirit, cherishing the hope, that it is employed in more exalted services than those which it loved so much in the sanctuary on earth. "To the spirits of just men made perfect," let us come, by coming to "Jesus the mediator of the new covenant, and to the blood of sprinkling," and united with them to the same living Head, by lofty thoughts and anticipations of their felicities and employments, we may enter into their rest, and "in part" resume their fellowship, join them in their blessed work, and taste their celestial pleasures. Recall them we cannot, but follow them we may; and by delighting in those services which were their greatest pleasure on earth, we shall be prepared to rejoin them in congenial, but more exalted employments and satisfactions in the eternal world.

SERMON I:
The First and Great Commandment

"Thou Shalt Love The Lord Thy God With All Thy heart, with All Thy soul, and with all thy mind. This is the first and greatest commandment"—Mat. xxii. 37, 38.

THE essence of true religion consists in a proper state of the affections. However extensive be our knowledge, or amiable our character, in the sight of men, if the heart is not right with God, the very root of the matter is awanting; and all our other attainments will go for nothing. Whatever a man's character be in other respects, if the feelings of his heart be in such a state that he can contemplate the infinite holiness and moral excellence of God's nature without loving him, or reflect upon his goodness without feeling grateful to him; if he is so hardened under all the sin that he has committed, that he is never melted into godly sorrow on account of it, and feels no transports of holy joy excited in his mind at the prospect of being restored to the Divine favour, he is evidently destitute of the very essence of true piety, and has no claim to the character of a saint of God. Religion has been correctly defined to consist in thinking rightly—in feeling rightly—and in acting rightly, with relation to God; and of these distinct things it is easy to see that the second, or a proper state of mind, with respect to fueling, is the most important. It is the only one which never goes unaccompanied by the other two. In the present corrupted state of human nature, accurate conceptions of God and Divine things may exist in the understanding, without exercising any sanctifying influence either on the heart or conduct. A religious education, too, and a desire to have a respectable character in the sight of men, may train up an individual, whose heart has never experienced the sanctifying influence of Divine grace, to such a regularity of external deportment, as will entitle him, in the estimation of his fellow creatures, to rank among the genuine saints of God. But it is an evident impossibility for any to have the affections of the heart rightly exercised, without also possessing the other features of the religious character. A proper frame of mind, with respect to feeling, necessarily implies correct conceptions of God and Divine things, as its foundation; and it universally leads to a proper course of acting, as its consequence. No attainment in theological knowledge, no regularity of external deportment, no amiableness or respectability of outward character, are sufficient to satisfy a man's conscience that he is a genuine saint of God: But grant that the affections of his heart are rightly exercised, that he loves God supremely on account of his infinite moral excellence, that he is truly grateful to him for all his goodness, that he is humbled to the dust in godly sorrow when he offends him, and that his soul gladdens with a holy pleasure when he enjoys the smiles of his reconciled countenance, and no doubt can remain that he is possessed of that spirit of genuine piety with which God is well pleased.

This idea, so obvious and reasonable in itself, and of such fundamental importance in practical religion, is set before us with great plainness and frequency in the holy Scriptures. When we are told that the fear of the Lord is the beginning of wisdom, and that to fear God and keep his commandments is the whole duty of man, we are certainly given to understand, that a heart impressed with reverential feelings, and actuated by a religious fear of God, is such an essential trait of true religion, that there can be no real piety where it is awanting, and that wherever it is possessed, there true piety exists. When it is said that "love is the fulfilling of the law;" that "charity or love is the greatest of all graces;" that "the end of the commandment is charity out of a pure heart," and of "a good conscience," and of "faith unfeigned;" we are no less plainly told, that a heart drawn out in the habitual exercise of love to God, is so connected with the life and power of godliness in the soul, that these can never exist apart. When Moses says to the ancient Israelites, and through them to the people of God in every age, "And now, Israel, what doth the Lord thy God require of thee, but to fear the Lord thy God, to walk in all his ways, and to love him, and to serve the Lord thy God with all thy heart, and with all thy soul," he plainly inculcates a supreme fear and love of God in the heart as a duty of such great importance, that all true religion is summed up in it. What, indeed, are the numerous exhortations to the love and fear of God, occurring throughout the Scriptures, but so many proofs of the doctrine, that religion has its chief seat in the heart? Why is the want of the fear and love of God so frequently represented in Scripture as the universal character of unrenewed men, if these feelings do not constitute the very essence of true religion? What, in short, is the whole book of Psalms, and the other devotional parts of Scripture, but a description of religion, as having its chief seat in the feelings of the heart, and consisting mainly in the spiritual exercises of love and fear, and hope and joy, and the breathings of holy affections after God?

But of all the passages of Scripture in which this truth is set before us, there is none so remarkable as the one which we have chosen for our text, "Thou shalt love the Lord thy God with all thy heart, with all thy soul, and with all thy mind. This is the first and great commandment." Numerous are the duties which are incumbent upon man in his present state; but the first and most important of them all is, that he love the Lord his God. Many are the precepts of which the Divine law consists, numerous are the exhortations to duty which the holy Scriptures contain; but they are all of a subordinate nature to this one. We are expressly required to love our neighbor as ourselves; but this is only the second precept of the law. It is our imperious duty to make ourselves acquainted with the character and counsels of God, so far as he has been pleased to reveal them, and to enrich our minds with stores of useful knowledge. We are expressly required to attend with the utmost circumspection to our external deportment, and to maintain a walk and conversation becoming the Gospel. But a more important precept than any of these is that which requires a supreme love unto God in the heart. These are all but secondary; this, however, is the first and great commandment.

All that is proposed in the present discourse, is to make a few remarks with a view to explain the duty required in the text; and then to consider the supreme importance of this duty, by stating a few reasons why it is called the first and great commandment.

I. We are, then, in the first place, to make a few remarks, in order to open up the nature of the duty of loving the Lord our God. 1. The first and great commandment requires us to exercise a certain kind of affection to God—to love him. A short explanation of what love to God is, is the design of our first remark.

That love which mankind exercise to one another, may be said to consist of the following distinct elements:— 1. An esteem of the person beloved, on account of his good qualities. 2. Gratitude to him for what goodness he has shewn to us. 3. A desire of intercourse with him; and, 4. An anxiety to please him; or, which comes to the same thing, a desire to see, and make him happy. We do not say that each of these elements enters into the feeling of love in every instance; but it is evident that they all may, and often do, form part of that affection. That love which we are required to exercise to God, differs in degree and certain necessary circumstances, rather than in nature and kind, from that which we feel towards our fellow creatures. The Supreme Being is infinitely more excellent than any creature, and, of course, entitled to a proportionally higher place in our esteem. If, however, we make due allowance for this, and keep out of view everything that implies deficiency in the object of affection, we may warrantably describe the love which we owe to God, as consisting of similar elements, and involving similar feelings with that which warms our hearts towards such of our fellow creatures as are the objects of our particular attachment.

That love, then, which the first and great commandment requires us to exercise to God, includes, in the first place, a high esteem of him, on account of the infinite excellencies of his nature. The belief of excellence in an object, is absolutely necessary in order to our loving it. The feelings of that man must be strangely perverted, who can regard with a complacent affection and esteem, an object which possesses no good qualities. In proportion, as an object rises in excellence, so is it entitled to our love; and our own consciences convict us of doing what is wrong, if we do not feel for it a degree of esteem proportioned to its excellencies. In the character of Jehovah every excellence is united, and that, too, in absolute perfection. Infinite excellence, without any alloy, characterizes him; so that if our love of an object ought to rise in proportion to its excellence, it can never rise high enough when directed to Him. When we fix our attention, indeed, on the incommunicable attributes of his nature, his eternity, his immensity, his omnipotence, his omniscience, and his immutability, these alone shed such an awful dignity over his character, as at once must tend to fix the mind in astonishment, or rather, perhaps, to overwhelm it with awe, than to awaken its esteem and love. In connection with these, however, contemplate him as possessing every moral excellence. View him, also, as infinitely holy, and wise, and just, and good, and you will see his character to be infinitely more excellent than your highest conceptions can reach, and worthy of far greater love, and far higher admiration, than your most expanded affections can bestow. "Who," says the Psalmist, "can utter the mighty acts of Jehovah? who can shew forth all his praise?" The greatest love of which the exalted faculties of angels are capable, falls infinitely short of his excellence; much more must that of imperfect sinful man but our inability to love God as we ought, must by no means prevent us from loving him as much as we can. On the contrary, the very fact that his excellence so far exceeds our comprehension, ought rather to stimulate us to persevering and redoubled exertions to have our minds more and more enlightened in the knowledge of his perfections, and our hearts more and more impressed with his glory. If, even in human characters, we esteem what is virtuous and excellent, if we admire the man whose heart glows with a disinterested benevolence, which is unweariedly employed in relieving the wants, and increasing the happiness of his fellow creatures, whose mind exhibits that firm independence and unbending integrity which neither frowns nor caresses can seduce from the path of duty, whose talents and influence are all exercised in the best of ways, and to the best of ends, whose purity of affection is such, that he reddens at the tale of guilt, and shrinks with abhorrence from the very appearance of evil, much more ought we to love and admire the great Jehovah, before whose uncreated glory all created comeliness is turned into corruption: and compared with whose infinite excellencies, the brightest human virtues diminish as the glimmerings of a sickly taper, before the brightness of a summer's sun in his meridian splendor.

This esteem of God, on account of the intrinsic holiness and excellence of his nature, is the fundamental and most important part of that love which the first and great commandment requires us to cherish towards him. The other ingredients just to be mentioned, seem more of a secondary nature; and are, perhaps, consequences or accidents, rather than parts of love, strictly so called. This much, at least, we may affirm with safety, that if we do not love God principally for what he is in himself, but cherish only a selfish affection for him on account of what he is to us, we are not feeling towards him as we ought, and the genuine love of God is awanting in our hearts.

The second thing included in that love which we owe to God, is gratitude on account of his goodness. Gratitude and love are, no doubt, in the strict sense of the terms, distinct feelings. They appear, however, to be seldom or never separated. The love of benevolence, or a desire to communicate happiness, may exist in circumstances where gratitude is impossible. God, for example, loves his creatures so as to desire their happiness; but it were blasphemy to say, that he feels any gratitude to them. Seldom, however, do creatures feel a complacent esteem for one another, on account of their virtues, without also feeling in some measure grateful to them. Love, no doubt, frequently exists between equals, who are under no particular obligations to one another to be a ground of gratitude: but even in this case, I apprehend, the pleasure which they have derived, and expect to derive, from each other's society, and their consequent importance to one another's happiness, are viewed by them as benefits which give rise to feelings between them very nearly allied to, if not altogether identified with, gratitude. But it is needless to have recourse to nice distinctions of this kind, in speaking of that love which we owe to God. The obligations, on account of benefits received, which we are under to him, are so inconceivably great, and so strongly pressed upon our notice, by every circumstance in our lot, that it is scarcely possible for us to regard him as deserving of our esteem, without also feeling that he is entitled to our gratitude. Instead, then, of viewing God as he is in himself, abstractly from what he is to us, and attempting to make his intrinsic excellence the solo ground of our love, it is much more agreeable to the weakness of our nature, and must be equally well-pleasing to him, that we view him in both these relations together, and unite the mingled feelings of gratitude and esteem into one great affection of love to the Lord our God. The Scriptures, which ought to be our guide in all our religions exercises, while they require us to love God primarily for what he is in himself, also authorize us to love him for what he is to us. It is said, to the commendation of Mary Magdalene, that "she loved much, because she was forgiven much," Luke vii. 47. "We love God," says the Apostle John, "because he first loved us," 1 John iv. 7. "I love the Lord," says the Psalmist, "because, he heard my voice and my supplications," Psal. cxvi. 1.

The obligations lying on every rational creature, and particularly on every believer, to love God, on the score of gratitude, are inconceivably great. "He made us, and not we ourselves." He formed those bodies, whose structure is so admirable; and those souls, whose faculties are so noble. All the enjoyments which have cheered us in the journey of life, from our birth to the present moment, have been showered down upon us by his bountiful hand; it is his air which we breathe, it is at his table that we are daily fed: Yet our unworthiness is great. We are less than the least of all the mercies, and of all the truth which he has shewn unto us. Neither our unworthiness, however, nor even our sins, numerous and aggravated as they have been, have provoked him to discontinue his goodness, or write bitter things against us. Even in our low estate, sunk in the mire of sin, and when we had no eye to pity, he has thought upon us, because his mercy endureth forever. He has sent his own Son to save us, and delivered him up for us all; and in the glorious Gospel, he offers us all the sure mercies of the everlasting covenant, "without money and without price." Think, Christians, on these things; reflect on all the great and unmerited goodness which God has "caused to pass before you since you had a being until now." Think particularly on the riches of his redeeming love—the grace which he has provided for you here, and the glory that awaits you in eternity; and then you will see abundant reason for uniting with the Psalmist in calling upon your souls, and all that is within you, "to bless his holy name;" then you will see it to be no unreasonable thing that you are commanded to "love the Lord your God, with all your heart, with all your soul, and with all your mind."

A third thing included in genuine love to God, is a desire to be much in his presence, and to enjoy much intercourse with him. A desire of intercourse with the object of our attachment is a feeling which always accompanies genuine love. Every man courts the society of the object of his love with the same earnestness that he shuns that of the object of his aversion; and it is impossible to conceive either love or hatred to exist, without producing these effects. Having formerly discovered the amiable qualities of an object, and experienced the pleasures enjoyed from its presence, we are naturally led to seek frequent intercourse with it, that these pleasures may be renewed. If it does not disappoint our expectations, new excellencies are discovered, as our acquaintance with it increases, our attachment to it grows stronger and stronger, and the pleasures we derive from it are proportionally enhanced. In numerous instances, these effects are, in some measure, experienced; but it is only when our love has God for its object, that they are realized to their full extent. The Divine perfections are the only unfailing source of felicity to an immortal soul. The believer who has once obtained a spiritual discovery of the incomparable beauties of his character, and tasted the sweets of communion with him, ceases not, thenceforward, to make him the object of his supreme attachment, and to thirst after intercourse with him, that he may have his soul satisfied from the rivers of pleasure that are at his right hand. He knows and feels it to be a good thing for him to draw near unto God; and unto God, yea, unto God, his exceeding joy, it is his habitual exercise to go. To God, in whose favour there is life, his longing eyes are at all times directed, and in him all his expectations of happiness are centered. "The desire of my soul," it is his exercise to say with the Prophet Isaiah, "is to thy name, and to the remembrance of thee. With my soul do I desire thee in the night; and with my spirit within me, will I seek thee early," Isa. xxvi. 8, 9. "O God, thou art my God; early will I seek thee: my soul thirsteth for thee, my flesh longeth for thee in a dry and thirsty land, where no water is; that I may see thy power and thy glory, as I have seen thee in the sanctuary," Psal. lxiii. 1, 2.

This thirsting of heart after God—this desire of communion with him, which is felt by every man that loves him in sincerity, produces important effects upon the believer's character. It is this principle which leads him to frequent the ordinances of Divine grace, and to attend conscientiously upon all the means which God has appointed, and in the use of which he has promised to meet with his people. It is this principle which leads him to read the Scriptures, and to study their sacred contents. It is here that he is told of God. It is chiefly by the instrumentality of the word, brought home to the heart by the Holy Spirit, that communion with God is enjoyed. It is the same principle, which more than any other consideration, raises his affections above the world, and makes it his great delight to meditate on God and Divine things. Were the things of this life to be the portion of his soul, he might well set his heart upon them; for however poor a portion they would be, he must be content with it, as if there was no better. The fountain of his happiness, however, lies in a different quarter; and where he knows his treasure to be, there his heart is also. From the same principle he can retain his joy and peace of mind in the day of affliction and adversity; and even glory, as the Apostle says, in tribulations. Temporal comforts not being the source of his felicity, the want of them cannot destroy his happiness. No poverty nor outward adversity can shut him out from communion with God; and while he enjoys the manifestations of his love to his soul, he is truly happy, be his external circumstances what they may. The existence and exercise of this gracious principle in the heart, then, is an important part of true religion, and an essential element of a genuine love to God. Unless we feel in our heart a strong desire after communion with God here, and the full enjoyment of him hereafter, we cannot be yielding obedience to the first and great commandment.

The only other thing which we mention, as included in a genuine love to God, is a desire to please him—a willingness and alacrity to obey all his commandments. We mentioned as one of the parts of that love which we exercise to our fellow creatures, a desire to promote the happiness of the object of our attachment. Without this, all professions of love are justly charged with insincerity. To say that you love a person, while, at the same time, you are indifferent whether he be happy or not, and are unwilling to do what in you lies to promote his happiness, is one of the grossest inconsistencies with which any man can be chargeable. Our love, however, must not exert itself in this way, when it has God for its object: for it were blasphemy to suppose that the happiness of the independent Jehovah admits of augmentation, or can deceive the least increase from any exertions of ours. There is a feeling, however, very nearly allied to this, and which, indeed, may be said to be the very same feeling, only exercised in a different way, and directed to a different object, which always accompanies genuine love to God; and that is, a desire to please him, a readiness to obey all his commandments. When we love a person, we are ready to do everything in our power to promote his happiness; and the means which we use for this purpose, is the doing of those things which are pleasing to him. In like manner, if we love God in sincerity, we will feel the same anxious desire to please him, by doing all that he commands us; as if, by doing so, we were shewing kindness to a friend whom we love, and contributing to his happiness. Hypocritical indeed, then, must the professions of that man be, who says that he loves God, and yet lives in the willful neglect of any known duty, on that habitual commission of any known sin. "If ye love me," says our Saviour himself, "keep my commandments," John xiv. 15. This is the great test of the reality of true love. When weighed in the balance, if it be found wanting in this, alas! how little will it avail us? The apostle John speaks to the same purpose, and in language, if possible, still more striking, "This is the love of God, that we keep his commandments:" and, "He that saith, I love God, and keepeth not his commandments, is a liar, and the truth is not in him."

We have thus endeavored to shew what love to God is, by stating that it consists, 1. Of a high esteem for him on account of the intrinsic excellence of his nature, 2. Of gratitude for his goodness to us, 3. Of a desire after intercourse with him, and, 4. Of a desire to please him, by keeping his commandments. What has been said in the illustration of these remarks, may be considered as an explanation of the first expression in the text, "Thou shalt love." But the object whom we are called to love, next claims our attention, "the Lord our God." This brings us to the second remark, illustrative of the duty required in the text.

2. Our love to God must proceed from knowledge, and be founded on correct views of his character. It is the true God, the Lord our God, whom we are required to love; and it is indispensably necessary that we love him as such, and do not found our affection to him on false views of his character.

There is reason to fear there are many in the world who cherish a kind of love to God, which is very deficient in this respect. Conceiving him to be a Being all mercy and goodness, without either holiness or justice—believing that he neither regards their sin, nor will punish them for it—esteeming him to be very kind to them here, and hoping that he will receive them into heaven when they die; they entertain, and can scarcely but entertain, a kind of love to him similar to what they feel for any generous benefactor. The idea of loving him for what he is in himself, never enters their minds of his moral character they are entirely ignorant, and they would be just as ready to love the devil as God, provided he were equally good to them. A love of God, founded on such false and partial views of his character as these, is so far from being acceptable to him, that he regards it with little less abhorrence than the hatred of an avowed enemy. Nor is it unreasonable that he should. I refer the matter to yourselves. What would any of you think of that man who, being himself a murderer, an adulterer, or some notoriously wicked person, and thinking you to be a person of a similar character with himself, should love you on that account? Would not you reject with abhorrence, all love that was professed for you, when you knew it to proceed from such a cause. Equally good reason has the great Jehovah to detest the love of all those who take up false views of his character, and make these reasons of their love to him. Observe in what menacing language he himself speaks to all such persons: "These things hast thou done, and I kept, silence; than thou thoughtest that I was altogether such an one as thyself: but I will reprove thee, and set them in order before thine eyes," Psal. 1.21. I will not, indeed, go so far as to say, that real love to God may not exist in the hearts of some whose knowledge of God is but small, and whose views of his character are not altogether correct. The Holy Spirit, I believe, may work a saving change in the heart of a sinner, and implant in it a principle of true love to God, before he fully dispels those erroneous views of his nature which he previously entertained. This much, however, I will confidently say, that you must have some correct know ledge of God, before you can truly love him; and that your love to him must be founded on what you do correctly know concerning him, and not on those mistaken views of his character that we suppose you still to entertain. I may love a person who I believe is, in the main, a good man, and though I may observe several blemishes in his character, my love to him not being on account of these blemishes, may be still sincere and honorable. Suppose, however, my heart were so depraved as to make his bad qualities, and not his good ones, the reason of my love to him, the state of the matter is entirely altered. My affection no longer deserves the honorable name of love: it has degenerated into that perverted feeling of attachment that unite devils to devils, and wicked men to their wicked companions.

In order, then, that we may observe the first and great commandment aright, we must make ourselves acquainted with God, so far as he has been pleased to make himself known. In his works, and particularly in his word, we must study his character. There only we can attain that knowledge of "the only true God, and of Christ Jesus, whom he hath sent, which is eternal life." We must keep his whole character constantly in our eye, and love him on account of the perfections which he in reality possesses. Nothing is more obvious, then, that if we take up false views of God, and make these the reasons of our love, we are not paying homage to the true God at all, but falling down to an idol of our own imaginations. Our corrupted hearts are particularly inclined to overlook the holiness and justice of God, and even to hold these in aversion. In making him the object of our love, therefore, we must be sure that this feature of his character is not overlooked. In no respect is there so marked a difference between the love which renewed and unrenewed men may have to God, as in the sentiments which they entertain respecting his holiness. Unrenewed men may feel a kind of love to God, but they do so only because they think he is good and merciful, ready to pardon their sins, and to make them happy. His moral character, consisting in holiness and justice, they not only overlook, but were it properly impressed on their minds, they would see nothing in it but ground of terror, and their love would instantly vanish. The renewed soul, however, loves God principally on account of his holiness. Beholding an inconceivable beauty in the character of a Being so transcendently holy as God is, his whole soul is drawn forth in admiration, and he is grieved that his affections are not more elevated in love to an object so infinitely worthy. The angels around the throne are continually exclaiming, "Holy, holy, holy, is the Lord of hosts." In this song every believing heart concurs. The infinite greatness and almighty power of God may strike us with awe; his universal dominion and glorious majesty may affect us with admiration; his goodness to us may call forth our gratitude: but it is principally his moral excellence that must excite our esteem, and attract our love. It is chiefly when they attain enlarged discoveries of the holiness of God that the saints are made to see the King in his beauty. It is then, particularly, that they are led to exclaim, *How great is his goodness, how great is his beauty!* It is then, too, that they are enabled to reduce to practice the Psalmist's bountiful exhortation, "Sing unto the Lord, O ye saints of his; and give thanks at the remembrance of his holiness."

3. Our third remark, illustrative of the duty required in the first and great commandment, is, that in loving the Lord our God, we must view him in his new-covenant character, and be enabled to contemplate him as a reconciled God and Father in Christ. This idea seems plainly suggested by the words, "the Lord thy

God." This appellation obviously refers to a covenant relation; and there is no other medium by which God ever exercises his love to sinners, or through which sinners are ever brought to love him, than the covenant of grace.

While man remained in innocence, the interposition of a Mediator was not necessary to enable him to love God. His unclouded faculties were naturally capable of discerning, and his lively affections of esteeming, the excellencies of the Divine character. While untainted with pollution, and free from guilt, there was nothing in the character of a Being infinitely holy, and inflexibly just, to give him alarm. Now, however, when sin has perverted our moral powers, and destroyed the happy relation which originally subsisted between us and our Creator, circumstances are mournfully changed. Our understandings have become so darkened, that they cannot discern, and our affections so perverted, that they will not esteem the excellencies and beauties of the Divine character. Nor is this all. We have provoked God against us, and he is become our enemy. All his perfections are armed against us, and demand our destruction. To sinners, a God encountered apart from salvation in Jesus Christ is a consuming fire. Even though there were no backwardness on our part, then, even though we were both able and willing to love God, still the relation in which as guilty sinners we stand to him, is such as renders this impossible. Should we, in our present guilty and polluted state, attempt to approach God in his essential character, and to lift up our souls in admiration of his holiness, the thought that he is a Being of purer eyes than to behold iniquity, and that he will allow no unclean thing, and therefore no polluted sinner, to stand before him, must instantly occur to us, and repel us from his presence. Should we, in like manner, attempt to contemplate the glories of his character, by thinking upon his justice, the guilt of our sins must stare us in the face, and we must tremble with terror at the thought, "that this is a Being who will by no means clear the guilty." Such forever must have been the issue of all our attempts to love God, had he been revealed to us in no other character than that of an absolute Deity. Blessed be his name, however, he is revealed in another character, a character in which the guilty sons of men may approach him with safety, and still adore and love him. In the everlasting Gospel the glorious discovery is made—Christ has died—God is reconciled—his anger is turned away, and he is become the God of salvation. In the wonderful scheme of man's redemption, the Lord Jesus Christ, the eternal Son of God, and God equal with the Father, descended in human nature into our world, became his people's Surety, undertook to bear the punishment due to their sins, and to remove every ground of the Divine displeasure against them. Being both God and man in one person, he was fully qualified for the high undertaking, and could not fail in his work. By his obedience and sufferings in our nature, accordingly, he has finished transgression, made an end of sin, and brought in an everlasting righteousness. With the whole of his work the Father has declared himself well pleased; and on account of it he has exhibited himself as willing to pardon our sins, and to save us with an everlasting salvation. To sinners of every class, and every name, the most guilty and polluted not excepted, his gracious language is, *Believe* on the name of my Son, place your dependence upon the merits of his blood, and flee for refuge to his righteousness as your only shelter in the day of wrath, and I am pacified to you for all that ye have done. Here, then, is a safe; and open way of access for sinners into the Divine presence. Crediting the declarations of the glorious Gospel, and viewing God in his reconciled character, we have every encouragement to draw near into his presence, and to make him the object of our confidence and love. Approaching near, with an eye of faith directed to the mercy seat, placing all our dependence upon the Mediator's atoning blood, and drawing near under the cover of his righteousness, we may contemplate God not only in his love and mercy, but in his holiness and justice, without being afraid that that holiness will banish us from his presence, or that justice rise against us to our condemnation. On the contrary, believing in his own infallible promises, and complying with his own gracious invitations, our minds may be kept in perfect peace, while we deliberately survey his character, and contemplate his glory; in this way we may even draw near with true hearts, and full assurance of faith.

In order that we may love God in the way required in the first and great commandment, we must be brought into a new covenant relation to him, and be enabled to view him as a reconciled Father in Christ. There is no other way in which a sinner can ever come to contemplate the Divine character with comfort. Saints themselves can approach God in no other manner. To say nothing of their former sins unrestrained by the fear of wrath, and on account of which, a believing view of the blood of Christ is continually necessary, their holiest frames have still so much corruption cleaving to them, and they fall into so much sin in all that they do, that were they to address a single prayer, or present a single offering, any other way than through the Lord Jesus Christ, the insulted Majesty of heaven must instantly cast their sacrifices in their faces, with the challenge, "Who hath required these things at your hands?" In all your religious exercises, then, Christians, you must keep the blood of Christ before you. It would have been death for the high priest, under the law, to have gone into the holy of holies, or approached the symbols of the Divine presence, without the blood of sacrifice; equally hazardous is it for you to come before God, or present an offering upon his altar, any other way than through faith in the blood of Christ. It is only by the new and living way which Christ has consecrated for us, through the veil, that is to say, his flesh, that you can come into the holiest with acceptance; and blessed be God, this way is always open, and no sins of yours can shut it. Think not, then, of approaching God on his throne of justice; for if he enters into judgment with us, no flesh can be justified. Approach him not on his throne of essential glory; for there he dwells in light that is inaccessible: but draw near to him on his throne of grace; for there only can you find acceptance there only will he be inquired of by his people. On Christ Jesus, our New Testament altar, present all your offerings; in his name present all your prayers. Thus, let it be your daily exercise to live lives of faith in the Son of God, and "to come boldly unto the throne of grace, that you may obtain mercy, and find grace to help in time of need."

4. The first and great commandment requires us to love the Lord our God with a supreme and ardent affection. This is evidently a leading idea in file text, "Thou shalt love the Lord thy God with all thy heart, with all thy soul, and with all thy mind." It is of little consequence whether we consider these several terms as nearly synonymous, and added principally to express the idea more strongly, or view them as having a reference to the different powers of the soul, all of which it requires to employ in the duty of loving God. In this last view of the passage, loving God "with all the

heart," may refer to the sincerity and voluntariness; loving him "with all the soul," to the ardor; and loving him "with all the mind," to the intelligent nature of our affections. We love God with all our heart, when we have sincere delight in contemplating his moral excellencies, and when it is our real desire and supreme study to be constantly devoted to the duties implied in loving God. Drawing near unto God with the heart, in opposition to drawing near unto him with the mouth, means the sincerity of the individual, and the reality of an exercise of the heart in the duty, in opposition to mere formality. Something of the same kind may be remarked concerning loving God with the heart. We must love, as the apostle John says, "not in word, neither in tongue, but in deed, and in truth." On beholding a sublime or beautiful object, we are sometimes struck instantaneously, and, in a manner, involuntarily, with a feeling of love. In loving God, however, we must exercise a deliberate choice; it must be the real and prevailing bent of our inclinations to love him, and to think upon, and adore his perfections. We love God with all our soul, when the whole strength of our affections, as it were, is drawn forth in love to him, when lively impressions of the excellencies of his nature, and of our infinite obligations to love him, are constantly present with us, stimulating every faculty, and awakening every affection to the love and admiration of his glorious character. When the soul, or the whole soul, is said to be engaged in this exercise, great earnestness, intentness, and devotedness, are meant; and such seems to be the meaning of the expression here. We love God with all our mind, when we have enlarged conceptions and enlightened views of the Divine nature and perfections, and when, along with our knowledge, our hearts are properly impressed, and our affections suitably exercised, respecting the object of worship. The term, mind, has generally a reference to the intellectual character of the soul, and, in this instance, seems to imply, that the understanding must go along with the heart in the duty of loving God. It is not the character of the Christian that he worships he knows not what: his devotion does not consist in ignorant raptures, or the blind impulse of a heated imagination. No; he is one that can give a reason of the hope that is in him. He sees God to be supremely excellent, and therefore he loves him; he knows that he is laid under stronger obligations to love him than tongue can express; and therefore he calls upon his soul, and all that is within him, to bless his holy name.

But without insisting on the distinctive meaning of these terms, it is obvious to the most superficial reader, that the first and great commandment requires us to employ all the faculties with which we are endowed in loving the Lord our God. Even our bodily members which were formerly employed as instruments of sin, must now be yielded as willing servants of righteousness unto holiness, and we must be ever ready to exercise them in any way in which they can be serviceable to our higher powers in the performance of this great duty. The powers of the understanding must be vigorously exercised in making ourselves acquainted with the character of God, and collecting all we can learn of him from every source of information to which we have access. The works of creation and providence ought to be carefully observed, and above all, the sacred volume must be attentively studied. No branch of knowledge must be esteemed so important, none pursued with so much ardor as that which has God for its object. Our affections must be scrupulously guarded against the debauching influence of sin, or undue attachment to worldly objects, and preserved pure and uncorrupted for this great duty. We must allow no worldly pursuit, however honorable or important, to engross our attention and esteem, so much as to be inconsistent with the exercise of a supreme love to God. We must bring our susceptibilities of being struck with what is grand, of admiring what is glorious, and of being delighted with what is beautiful; and fix them on the perfections of Jehovah, as objects on which to exercise themselves with unrestrained scope. Upon him and the enjoyment of his Divine perfections, our desires must be supremely fixed; to him all our expectations must be directed; on him our hopes must centre; nor must our fears be excited by anything so much as him and his righteous displeasure. When we enjoy the manifestations of his favour, our joys may flow profusely; that when he testifies displeasure because of our sins, godly sorrow must fill our hearts.

Nor is it unreasonable that all the faculties of our mind should in this manner be supremely fixed upon God, and employed in that way which the first and great commandment requires. They were not given us by God for the very purpose of loving and serving him; and we cannot surely employ them in a better way, or for a better end, than that for which our Creator designed them. The unbounded perfections of his nature also, together with his great and unmerited goodness, lay us under such strong obligations to love him, that if we keep back from this holy service any of the faculties which he has given us, we withhold from him a part of that homage which is his due, we are justly chargeable with base ingratitude; nay, with direct rebellion against him. Never too can our faculties be employed in a way so beneficial to ourselves, or calculated to bring us so much delight and satisfaction, as when they are fixed upon God, and intimately engaged in loving him. Justly then may we unite with the Psalmist, "in calling upon our souls, and all that is within us, to bless the holy name of God." Justly may we place every other exercise, after the great duty of loving the "Lord our God with all our heart, and with all our souls, and with all our mind."

II. But from this rather lengthened illustration of the duty of loving the Lord our God, we proceed to consider the supreme importance of this duty, stating a few reasons why this is called the first and great commandment.

1. The injunction, "Thou shall love the Lord thy God," may be called the first and great commandment, because it is the first duty which, in the nature of things, is incumbent upon the rational creature. All our other duties are dependent upon a greater variety of circumstances, and result less necessarily, and less directly, from the relation subsisting between God and his rational creatures, than the one under consideration. A person may be placed in such circumstances as to be under no obligation to love his neighbor, for he may not have a neighbor to love. Adam, immediately after his creation, was in this situation; but no rational creature can be in such circumstances as to be under no obligation to love God. This became the duty of Adam the moment he was created; this is the duty of angels in heaven as well as of man upon earth. Some of our duties are not necessarily obligatory on us as rational creatures, but result from a positive command of God. This however is not of a positive but of a moral nature; it flows necessarily from the moral nature of God, and is binding on every rational creature, whether they have received an express injunction requiring it or not. Many of the duties incumbent upon man in his present state, were not originally obligatory on him, but have become so in consequence of the entrance of sin, and introduction of

the scheme of grace. The duty of loving God however has a higher origin. It was as incumbent on man in innocencey, as it is now when he has sinned; it is equally the duty, and ought equally to be the exercise of sinners on earth, and of saints in glory. It is thus easy to see that while most of our other duties result either from positive institution, or have a reference to relations and circumstances of a secondary nature, this great duty of loving God is incumbent on us antecedently, to any positive injunction, is dependent upon no other circumstance, and results from no other relation than that of our being the creatures of God's power, endowed with faculties capable of knowing and loving their Creator.

2. The injunction requiring us to love God, may be called the first and great commandment, because our obligations to perform this duty, are paramount to those of every other. In consequence of the ever varying circumstances and numerous relations in which we exist in this world, it frequently happens that duties interfere with one another, and that we are obliged to omit one duty for a time, in order to attend to another; and in all such cases, the rule is, that the less duty give place to the greater. It is the duty of a son, for example, in all ordinary circumstances, to obey the command of his father; but should he be commanded to do what is sinful, his duty to obey is in that instance at an end, because it interferes with the greater duty of obeying God. Now, viewed in this light, the duty of loving God is of paramount importance, and rises superior to every other. It is incumbent upon man in every diversity of circumstances, and no excuses, no interference of other duties can justify him in acting inconsistently with its strict moral obligation. It is, obviously, the duty of every man to engage in some lawful occupation, and to prosecute it with diligence. "For he," says the apostle,

"that provideth not for his own, and especially for those of his own house, hath denied the faith, and is worse than an infidel," 1 Tim. v. 8. But this duty, important as it is, must not engross our affections, so far as to be inconsistent with the higher duty of loving God. For, "Love not the world," says another apostle, "nor the things of the world; for if any man love the world, the love of the Father is not in him," 1 John ii. 5. To honour and obey our parents, and esteem our earthly relations is a duty evident from the light of nature, and expressly enjoined in Scripture. Yet even this must be kept in subordination to the love of God: "For," says our Saviour himself, "he that loveth father or mother more than me, is not worthy of me," Mat. x. 37. "Nay, if any man come not me, and hate not father and mother, and wife and children, and brethren and sisters," in comparison of me, "he cannot be my disciple," Luke xiv. 20. The strongest feelings of the human heart unite with the precepts of the Divine law, in leading us to value life, and to use every means in our power to preserve it. But if even the preservation of life come into competition with love to God, we must not hesitate for a moment, but lay it down for his sake. He that cometh to Christ, "and hateth not father and mother, yea, and his own life also," in comparison of Him, cannot be his disciple, Luke xiv. 26.

3. Love to God. is called the first and great commandment, because it is a necessary prerequisite to the acceptable performance of every other duty. Without a genuine love to God in the heart, the principle of acceptable obedience is awanting. Unless the first and great commandment be observed, no other precept of the Divine law can be acceptably obeyed. "He that is not with me," says Jesus, "is against me; and he that gathereth not with me, scattereth abroad." All who are destitute of true love to God in their hearts, are

actuated by a principle of enmity against him; and whether their character be externally decent, or openly profane, he accounts them among his enemies. They may make a profession of religion, and maintain a fair show in the flesh; but they have only a name to live, while they are in reality dead. They may attend upon ordinances, and engage in religious duties, but they only offer strange fire upon God's altar; they may perform many works externally good, but they are only the "sacrifices of the wicked, which are an abomination to the Lord." Their heart is destitute of the love of God, and in nothing that they do, can they be actuated by a pure regard to his glory. The power of sin reigns unsubdued in their souls, and all that they do is polluted. When they present an offering on God's altar, it is only the torn, the lame, and the. sick, which they bring, and this he has declared he will not accept at their hands. "Cursed," says the prophet Malachi, "be the deceiver, which voweth and sacrificeth a corrupt thing." Observe in what strong language the apostle Paul proclaims the vanity of the most splendid acts of human virtue which do not proceed from a principle of true love to God in the heart, 1 Cor. xiii. 1, 2, 3. "Though I speak with the tongues of men and of angels, and have not charity, I am become as sounding brass, or a tinkling cymbal. And though I have the gift of prophecy, and understand all mysteries, and all knowledge; and though I have all faith, so that I could remove mountains, and have not charity, I am nothing. And though I bestow all my goods to feed the poor, and though I give my body to be burned, and have not charity, it profiteth me nothing." Destitute of this heavenly principle of charity, then, our very best works are both unprofitable to ourselves, and unacceptable to God. It is only when the Saviour has been embraced by faith, and the gracious principle of love implanted in the heart by the Holy Spirit, that a foundation is laid for the performance of duties which shall come up with acceptance before the throne of God.

4. The injunction, "Thou shalt love the Lord thy God," may be called the first and great commandment, because the observation of it naturally produces obedience to all the other precepts of the Divine law. Love to God is not only an essential prerequisite to the acceptable performance of other duties; but wherever this love exists, all other duties will be conscientiously attended to. "Love," it is expressly said, Rom. xiii. 10, "is the fulfilling of the law." And it is easy to see, that if there be a supreme love to God reigning in the heart, it will effectually counteract the workings of every corrupt principle, and exert a sanctifying influence over the whole conduct. It is abundantly obvious, that if a man be actuated by a sincere and a strong affection for a friend, he will scarcely fail in discharging any of the duties which he owes to that friend, or in using every means in his power to promote his happiness; and it is equally certain, that if we have a supreme love to God in our hearts, we shall shew it forth by keeping his commandments. As soon might a man maliciously attempt to thrust a dagger into the heart of a friend whom he daily loves, as a believer who is actuated by a true love to God, deliberately indulge in the commission of sin. Under the constraining influence of this delightful principle, the believer cannot but study to do the whole will of his heavenly Father. He has seen, and been convinced of the evil nature of sin; he has read its demerits in the Redeemer's sufferings, and he knows it to be exceedingly displeasing to God. Because God hates it, therefore, he cannot but hate it also; shun it as his mortal enemy, and strive against it in every part of his conduct. The beauty and excellence of holiness, he has in some measure discovered; he has

contemplated it as it was exemplified by the Son of
God in our nature; he has beheld it shining forth in all
its glory, in the character of God himself; and he has
heard the command issuing from his exalted throne,
"Be ye holy, for I the Lord your God am holy." Can he
therefore but make holiness his constant study, strive
to know more and more of its power, of its power in his
heart, and to shew it forth in "all holy conversation and
godliness?" Is there, a single precept of the Divine law,
which a person under the influence of a supreme love to
God can knowingly transgress? No: the love of Christ
constrains him, that he should not henceforth live unto
himself, but unto him that died for him, and rose again.
Corruption, no doubt, cleaves unto him, and he is often
falling into the commission of sin; but this is his
burden, not his delight. So long as the love of God rules
and reigns in his heart, he may truly say, concerning
every sin that he commits, "It is not I that do it, but sin
that dwelleth in me." Nor is the constant struggle
which he is called to maintain with indwelling
corruption, without its benefits. It teaches him
humility and self-denial, leads him to faith and trust in
God; and stirs him up to constant and fervent prayer.
Finding that it is not in himself to keep his feet in the
way of God's commandments, or to subdue the
corruptions that rage within him, he commits the
whole work into the hands of God, supplicates the
sanctifying influences of his Holy Spirit, and trusts in
him, who has begun the good work in his soul, to carry
it on, and bring it to perfection. Acting in this manner,
the power of corruption within him is gradually
weakened, he gains daily victories over sin and Satan,
and advances rapidly unto a perfect man, unto the
measure of the stature of the fullness of Christ. Such
being the native fruits of the principle of a supreme love
to God, is it not strictly true, that love is the fulfilling of

the law? And may not the injunction, requiring us to love God with all our hearts, be with the greatest propriety, designated the first and great commandment?

A few inferences shall now conclude this Discourse.

1. From this subject we may infer, that the only effectual way of introducing holiness of heart and morality of conduct amongst mankind, is by teaching them to love the Lord their God. It seems to be the opinion of many in the present day, that the duties of morality may be taught apart from those of religion; and that man may be brought to perform aright the duties which he owes to his neighbor and himself, while he neglects those which he owes to his God: as if it were a thing both consistent and reasonable, that obedience may be given to the Divine law in the conduct, while the principle of obedience is awanting in the heart, as if it were possible to teach men obedience to the other commandments of God, while the first and great commandment stands neglected. As the essence of human depravity lies in the heart—as this is the corrupt fountain from which all the streams of iniquity that desolate the world proceed, the sanctification of the heart must, in the order of things, precede the reformation of the life. The fountain must first be purified, else the streams can never be made clean. You know how vain a thing it is to think of drying up a stream of water by merely damming the current. In this way you may indeed stop its progress for a time, but as the stream above continues to flow, it must gradually swell higher and higher, till it either break down the barrier that has been opposed to it, or else burst over it, and pursue its course as before. Equally vain is it to think of making men pious and moral, and teaching them to be regular and

conscientious in obeying the law of God, while the natural pride and enmity of the heart remains unsubdued. By the force of rational motives, indeed, such as the respectability and honour attaching to a virtuous course of life, and the shame and disgrace attending a vicious one, the corruptions of the heart may be kept considerably in check, and a good deal of outward integrity of character acquired. But all this is only obstructing the current, not drying up the fountain. So long as a man is destitute of an inward principle of love to God, of a sincere desire to please him, and a real delight in his service, obedience to the Divine law must be all uphill work with him. He has no heart for religious duties, and no delight in them. It is only because his inward lusts are laid under restraint, dammed up, as it were, by considerations directly opposed to their natural tendency, that they do not manifest themselves in his conduct: take these restraints away, and he will soon shew what manner of man he is. Does a forced and heartless obedience of this kind come up to the spirituality of the Divine law, or can it be accepted by God? No: he commands us to give him our hearts, and to be actuated by a supreme love unto himself, when we engage in his service; and when this gracious principle of love is awanting, the best works that we do are but as "sounding brass, or a tinkling cymbal." It is vain, then, to think of teaching the doctrines of morality apart from those of religion, or of making men wise unto salvation any other way than through faith in the Lord Jesus Christ. It is only by discovering unto a sinner his lost and ruined state by nature, convincing him of the awful guilt and misery into which he has been brought by sin, then exhibiting to him the riches of redeeming love, making known the Lord Jesus Christ in his ability and willingness to save, and inviting him to repair to his blood and righteousness as his only refuge in the day of wrath, that his heart would be savingly changed, or a principle of love to God implanted. By the blessing of the Holy Spirit, the preaching of those doctrines has been made effectual, in every age, in sanctifying the hearts and reforming the lives of thousands. All other methods of attaining those important ends, however, are but inventions of men, and have never yet been honored to save a single soul, or even to teach an individual to perform a single duty which God will accept.

2. This subject informs us where the essence of true religion lies, and hence furnishes an important test for trying whether we be genuine saints of God or not. Is it the first and great commandment that we love the Lord our God with all our hearts? And is it, in the exercise of a supreme love to God that the essence of true religion lies? Then it must be a matter of the utmost importance to every individual of us, to ascertain whether we are possessed of a supreme love to God or not. And here, my brethren, I must be permitted to use great plainness of speech, for the eternal welfare of your immortal souls is at stake. Is it then, indeed, your exercise to love the Lord your God, could you, at the close of this day, enter into your closets, when there was no eye of man to observe you, and there, as in the presence of that God, before whose eye all things are naked and bare, lay your hand upon your heart, and solemnly say unto him, "Thou, Lord, who knowest all things, knowest that I love thee?" Would not your face redden with conscious guilt, while you made such a declaration? Would not your conscience within you give the lie to your lips, and convict you of the aggravated sin of deliberately appealing to the Majesty of heaven for the truth of a falsehood? Alas! my hearers, are there not some of you who must plead guilty to this charge? Are there not

some of you whose own consciences bear you witness, that God is seldom in your thoughts? That the things of the world engross your whole attention? That you seldom pray to God in secret, or do so only in a cold and formal manner? That you have no delight in meditating on God and Divine things, and as for the duty of loving him with all your hearts, you know nothing whatever of the matter. It appears strange doctrine to you to be told, that you ought at all times to be impressed with a reverential fear of God—that even in the intervals of your worldly business you ought to be thinking of him and that you are commanded to love him with all your heart, and to esteem him above every other object. You account it a great bondage to be obliged to be always thinking of God, and loving him with your whole hearts. You have a strong aversion to engage in this duty at any time, and would gladly be excused from it altogether. Nay, it is well if the wickedness of your hearts is not so great that you sometimes entertain a wish that there were no God at all; for then you would be at liberty to pursue your sinful courses without any danger of being called to account. To all persons of this description—to all whose own consciences bear them witness that they have no true love to God in their hearts, but love the world more than him, I must plainly say, that they know nothing of the life and power of true religion, they are still in the gall of bitterness and the bond of iniquity, and that if they live and die in this state, they can expect nothing else than to be punished with "everlasting destruction from the presence of the Lord, and the glory of his power." Your own hearts, my friends, bear you witness that you have no love to God; how then can you expect him to have any love to you! You habitually disregard the precepts of his law, and particularly, you trample his first and great commandment under foot; what hope can you then have of escaping the punishment which he has threatened against all the workers of Iniquity? The habitual language of your heart concerning God is, "We will not have thee to reign over us;" "Depart from us, for we desire not the knowledge of thee nor of thy ways." Will it not then be but the strictest justice though he should in his turn say unto you, "Depart from me, ye cursed, into everlasting fire, prepared for the devil and his angels?" "Be not deceived," my dear hearers, "God is not mocked; for whatsoever a man soweth, that shall he also reap: He that soweth to the flesh, shall of the flesh reap corruption; and he only that soweth to the Spirit, shall of the Spirit, reap life everlasting." They that spend their lives in the service of sin, and neglect to love God bore, shall never enjoy him hereafter. The heavenly inheritance is prepared for none but those who have been previously made holy and prepared for it. Within the sacred walls of the New Jerusalem, no unclean thing, no unsanctified sinner, shall ever enter. "The wicked shall be turned into hell, and all the nations that forgot God." As sure as God is in the heavens, and his throne established forever; so sure it is, that all who do not meet with God in mercy now, shall meet with him in wrath and judgment hereafter. For all who spend their lives in the service of sin, and in the pursuit of the pleasures, and profits, and honors, of the world, and neglect the great duty of loving the Lord their God, there is prepared a place of misery and woe, where their worm shall never die, nor their fire be quenched. Be wise, then, before it be too late. While the day of your merciful visitation lasts, oh, attend to the things of your everlasting peace. God is still waiting to be gracious with you. This very day, by the mouth of the unworthy instrument who is now addressing you, he is saying unto every individual of you, "Seek ye the

Lord, while he may be found; call ye upon him, while he is near: Let the wicked man forsake his way, and the unrighteous man his thoughts, and let him return unto the Lord, and he will have mercy upon him, and to our God, for he will abundantly pardon." Despise not, then, his offers of mercy. Seal not your own condemnation, by adding the sin of unbelief to all your other sins. When Jesus is saying to you in the Gospel, "Come unto me, all ye that labor and are heavy laden, and I will give you rest;" be it your reply unto him, "To whom shall we go but unto thee, Thou alone hast the words of eternal life." Sensible of your need of salvation, supplicate it of God in prayer. Ask of him, in particular, his Holy Spirit to renew your hearts and change your natures; to implant and maintain in your souls the principles of faith, and love, and hope; and to renew you in the whole man, after the image of God. Thus shall ye be fitted for loving and serving God here, and enjoying him through eternity hereafter.

3. There is an extreme degree of wickedness and ingratitude implied in a total want of love to God. There are many ways that I might take to illustrate and enforce this remark: its truth seems so obvious, that nothing need be said to prove it. In the first place, is God infinitely excellent? does every possible perfection, every moral attribute adorn his character? And is he thus infinitely more glorious, lovely, and excellent in himself, than any creature? Then there must be a strange incongruity, nay, a gross and wicked perversion of feeling and loving any other object more than Him. Of all who see no beauty, and behold nothing worthy of being loved in the Divine character; it may, with the greatest truth, be said, "the God of this world hath blinded their minds." They behold no beauty where the very perfection of beauty is; they see nothing worthy of being loved or esteemed, where everything glorious and

amiable exists. They love the world more than God. Alas! how literally true of them, are the apostle's words, "They change the truth of God into a lie, and worship and serve the creature more than the Creator, God over all, blessed forever!" That God whom angels worship, and glorified saints adore, has no beauty in their esteem; their hearts are without a single impression of His glory. Alas! my friends, may we not say of you, as Moses did of the ancient Israelites, "The Lord hath not given you an heart to perceive, nor eyes to see, nor ears to hear, unto this day?" But, secondly, there is also the basest ingratitude implied in the want of love to God. God, my hearers, is ever mindful of you; but are there not some of you who are thus unmindful of him? He formed you at first, he spares you from day to day, he is ever scattering unnumbered benefits around your habitations, yet you never think of thanking him for all his unmerited goodness. You express thankfulness to your fellow creatures when they do you the smallest favour, but you have scarcely a spark of gratitude in your minds for your bountiful Creator. He gave you your beings at first, your soul with all its faculties, and your body with all its members, that you might spend them in his service, and employ them in promoting his glory; but, alas! you devote them all to the service of sin. He renews his goodness to you from day to day, he grants you food for your nourishment, and sleep for your refreshment, that he may strengthen you for farther work in his service, and furnish you with additional reasons for praising him; but, alas! You are still obstinate and disobedient. His goodness, as fast as you receive it, you consume as food for your lusts; his benefits, as fast as he showers them down, ye convert into instruments for carrying on your impious rebellion against him. Such is the way in which you despise and abuse his temporal goodness. But, alas! the worst of the tale remains still untold. You also trample under foot his spiritual mercies. At an infinite price, and in the exercise of his infinite love, he has provided a way of salvation for your perishing souls. Of this salvation, you are in infinite need; and in the Gospel you have it offered to you freely; nay, you have the most pressing invitations given you to come and receive it. Yet such are the pride and rebellion of your hearts, that you set all these offers and invitations at nought, and say unto God, when he sets before you the most precious blessings which Heaven itself has to bestow; "Thy gifts to thyself, and thy rewards to another." Christ Jesus is offered to you in the Gospel, as an all sufficient Saviour; but by your deliberate and willful neglect to improve this offer, you make a near approach to the crime of treading underfoot the Son of God, counting the blood of the covenant, wherewith he was sanctified, an unholy thing, and doing despite unto the Spirit of grace. O my friends, is there not the vilest ingratitude, the basest wickedness in all this? "Do ye thus requite the Lord, O foolish people and unwise?" "Of the Rock that begat thee, why art thou unmindful? Why hast thou forgotten the God that formed thee?" "Is it a small thing for you to weary men, but will ye weary God also?" But, thirdly, there is an extreme wickedness in the want of love to God in the heart, because it is a direct violation of his own solemn and express commandment. Not one of you will deny that it is your duty to observe the other precepts of God's law. When God says unto us, "Thou shalt not kill, thou shall not commit adultery, thou shalt not steal," you own it would be great wickedness to break any of these commandments. But, my friends, the very same God who is the author of these commandments, also says unto you, "thou shalt love the Lord thy God with all thy heart." Disobedience to this command, then, must be as criminal as the transgression of any other precept of his law; nay, if there be more guilt in the violation of one commandment than another, the highest degree of it must attach to this, for it "is the first and great commandment." Beware then of deceiving yourselves with a name to live, while in reality dead. Beware of thinking that because your lives are outwardly regular, and stained with no gross violation of the laws of God, you can be in no danger. If you are destitute of a supreme love to God in your hearts, let your characters be as respectable as they may, ye are habitual transgressors of the first commandment of the law, and all your outward sobriety of conduct, and respectability of character, will avail you nothing in the end. Think, my friends, on these things. Be impressed with the extreme wickedness, the base ingratitude, and direct rebellion that is implied in the want of a supreme love to God in the heart. Be alarmed at your danger, before it be too late. Under a deep impression of your guilty and lost state, as of yourselves, repair to the throne of grace, and entreat God to fulfill on your behalf his gracious promises: "I will take away the stony hearts out of your flesh, and give you hearts of flesh." "The Lord thy God will circumcise thine heart to love the Lord thy God with all thine heart, and with all thy soul, that thou mayest live."

4. Sinners have the greatest encouragement to turn from their evil ways unto the Lord, and to make him the object of their confidence and love. It is an idea, my friends, which we should never lose sight of, that it is the Lord our God whom we are required to love, that it is not to an absolute Deity, but to a God in covenant, a reconciled God in Christ, that we are invited to look. Had God exhibited himself to us in no other character than that of an absolute Deity, how deplorable might have been our situation.

Omnipotence hath unsheathed its sword, and the offended Majesty of heaven is in arms against us. Alas! whither shall we flee for refuge, or how shall we escape? Shall we too gird on our armor, and go with sword in hand to meet the Almighty in the contest? Ah! foolish creature, wilt thou indeed presume to contend with thy Creator. With infinitely greater ease than we can crush the feeblest creature that crawls upon the ground, Almighty God will dash our armor from our hands, and crush us to pieces with a single stroke of his terrible vengeance. In open resistance then there is no hope. But may we not try to flee? Can we conceal ourselves under the darkness of the night, or flee to a distant land, and there live in some obscurity, where the Almighty shall not behold us? Infatuated mortal! can such a thought once enter thy mind? God's eyes are on every place beholding the evil and the good: the darkness and the light are alike unto him; and from the remotest corner of the universe, he will send his angels after thee to drag thee forth to punishment. Living thus, we cannot be safe. But may we not find refuge in death? Will we invite the grave to open its mouth and swallow us up, and call upon the rocks to fall upon us, and the mountains to cover us from the wrath of God? Equally vain is it to think of escaping in this manner. The mountains and the rocks prove deaf to our entreaties, and that same inflexible justice which forbids us to live in happiness, demands our continuance in existence, that we may live in misery. All other refuges then are cut off. But may we not cast ourselves on the mercy of God, and humbly implore his forgiveness? This on the whole, no doubt, were our wisest course. Yet, alas, how terrible is our situation! It is a fearful thing to fall into the hands of the living God. A holy God, in his essential character, is necessarily a consuming-fire to guilty sinners. The criminal who has imbrued his hands in innocent blood, in vain implores mercy at the hand of his judge. Justice must be administered; the laws of the country must be put into execution. Equally vain would it have been for sinners to look for mercy at the hands of the righteous Judge of all the earth, had he been revealed to us in no other character than that of an absolute Deity. Blessed be his name, however, the glorious gospel has brought glad tidings of great joy to our ears. Jesus has died upon the cross, the justice of God is satisfied, and a safe and patent way into the Divine presence, is opened up to the guilty sons of men, through the Redeemer's atoning blood. Behold! then, sinners, what glorious encouragement there is here? Christ hath quenched in his own blood the vengeful flames which Divine justice was sending forth to consume you. God's anger is turned away, his countenance smiles with love and benignity, and his words are words of peace and consolation. "Look unto me, and be ye saved, all ye ends of the earth; for I am God, and besides me there is none else." Are there any of you, my friends, who are afraid to look upon God? He is so holy, and you are so sinful, that you think it would be presumption to come into his presence, or engage in the duty of loving him. Dismiss your apprehensions; they are unscriptural, and proceed from unbelief. Contemplate by faith the Savior's atoning blood, and be no more afraid. Look at the rainbow of the covenant which surrounds the throne of God, and fear not to approach it. Greater encouragement than what is set before you in the gospel, it is impossible to desire. To God in his new covenant character, we invite you to draw nigh, and "pray you in Christ's stead, be ye reconciled to God."

5. We may learn from this subject, the reason why Christians are so often languid in the exercise of grace, and so lifeless and indifferent in the duties of

religion. They have little love to God in their hearts—they are careless and remiss in yielding obedience to the first commandment of the law, and therefore it is little wonder that they are cold and formal in their obedience to the rest. A supreme and ardent love to God in the heart, my friends, is the animating principle of all obedience: without it, duty must soon become burdensome, and religious exercise tiresome. Be sure, then, that you not only have this principle in existence—that is, be not satisfied with knowing that you ever possessed it, but study at all times to maintain it in lively exercise. It is only in this way that you can persevere with cheerfulness and zeal in the discharge of your duties, and find real delight and satisfaction in the exercise of religion. It is only in this way that you can enjoy the sweets of communion with God in this world, and find wisdom's ways to be indeed ways of pleasantness, and all her paths to be peace. Believers themselves are subject to many decays in religion: they often become cold and languid in the exercise of grace, and are barren indeed in the fruits of holiness and righteousness. Would you guard against this most unbecoming and disagreeable frame of mind, and have the graces of the Holy Spirit maintained in lively exercise in your hearts; then let me exhort you to give yourselves much to the duty of loving the Lord your God. Be much employed in contemplating the glorious excellencies of the Divine character, meditate often on the great and unmerited goodness which he has shewn to you, and be much impressed with the high obligations under which you are thus laid to love him. By being often employed in this manner, and keeping these things continually in view, the corruptions of your nature will be kept in perpetual check; and such powerful motives to holiness will be set before you, as cannot fail to make you zealous and earnest in religion, and cause you to grow rapidly in grace and every spiritual attainment. Waiting in this manner upon the Lord, you will renew your strength—you will mount up with wings as eagles—you will run and not be weary, you will walk and not faint.

6. The obligations lying on Christians to love the Lord their God are inconceivably great. Our God, Christians, speaks from heaven, and will we not Hear? He commands us to love him, and will we not obey? That glorious Being, who is infinitely exalted above all blessing and praise, and whose unbounded perfections are the only source of unfading happiness to our immortal souls, requires us to place our affection upon Him, and still we refuse them. Our Creator, our Preserver, our Redeemer, calls us to love him, and will we turn a deaf ear to his expostulations? Have we faculties capable of esteeming what is excellent, of loving what is beautiful, and admiring what is grand? And shall we contemplate the glorious perfections of the Divine character with a heartless apathy? Have we felt the most delightful emotions rising in our minds, when we surveyed the beauty and sublimity of external nature, and shall we never raise the pious feelings of love and admiration to the infinitely grander attributes of Nature's God? Are we delighted with the charms of literature and science? Do our hearts glow with admiration of the enchanting scenery around us, when we tread the paths of knowledge? When Philosophy unveils to our eyes the sublime objects which she discloses to her votaries, do we stretch out our arms, and pant after a still farther acquaintance with what she discovers? And has that God who formed the heavens to declare his glory, who hangs the earth upon nothing, and guides the planets in their courses, no glory in our esteem? Can we survey the bright effulgencies of uncreated majesty that surround his

throne with a frigid indifference? No. With all these inconsistencies, and many more, worldly men are daily chargeable. But the feelings of your hearts, Christians, are not so grossly perverted. The standard of all excellence occupies the highest place in your esteem. Your hearts are glowing with love and admiration of the inconceivable grandeur and excellence of the Divine character, and swelling with gratitude for his unbounded goodness to you. Feeling this to be a duty of indispensable obligation, considering it as the noblest exercise in which you can engage, and looking forward to the endless recompense of reward that awaits it, you have called upon your souls and all that is within you, to bless the holy name of God. The emotions of your hearts are too big for utterance. You feel the Divine glory an object too dazzling for your feeble eyes to contemplate. Still you desire to love God. You lift up your souls with devout admiration of his glorious Majesty: you prostrate yourselves before his throne, and devote yourselves wholly to his service. Grieved that you can love him so little, and anxious to love him more, you look forward with rapturous anticipation to that happy period, when the sinful imperfections of the present state shall be done away, and when you shall employ the whole strength of your then enlightened faculties, in singing eternal *Hallelujahs* to your redeeming God. Now you only see, as through a glass, darkly; but then you shall see God's face, and know even as you are known. Happy indeed are you, my friends, if these are your exercises. Persevere in the good ways of the Lord, in which it is so evident you are already walking, and entertain no doubt of all your hopes being in due season fully realized. "The vision is yet for an appointed time, but at the end it shall speak and not lie; though it tarry, wait for it, because it will surely come: it will not tarry." Meanwhile, as you travel on through the wilderness of this world, with the eye of your faith directed to heaven, you must be careful to walk in the path of commanded duty. All the precepts of the Divine law must be scrupulously observed; but you must be particularly careful to yield obedience to the first and great commandment, by loving the Lord your God with all your hearts, with all your souls, and with all your minds.

SERMON II:
On Regeneration.

"Verily, verily, I say unto thee, except a man be born again, he cannot see the kingdom of God."—John iii. 3.

THE circumstances in which these words were uttered, are strongly calculated to impress the mind with a sense of their importance. The Saviour of mankind, God manifest in the flesh, had lately appeared on our world, and was just commencing his public ministry. Feelingly alive to the wants of immortal souls, he eagerly embraced every opportunity of publishing the joyful messages of grace to the lost sheep of the house of Israel. Nicodemus, a Jewish ruler, of the sect of the Pharisees, struck with the astonishing miracles, by which this Divine teacher demonstrated the authenticity of his doctrines, seems to have been convinced by them, that he was indeed a teacher come from God, but had as yet obtained no accurate knowledge of the nature and design of his extraordinary mission. Anxious to acquire farther information on this important point, and afraid at the same time of exposing himself to reproach and persecution, by shewing any open respect for one whom the generality of his countrymen, and particularly those of his station and sect, regarded as a low impostor, he embraced an opportunity of repairing to Jesus by night, when there was no eye to witness their interview. While the shades of evening, then, are spread over the world, and the generality of mankind he drowned in sleep, the Jewish ruler and the Divine Saviour meet, and hold a conversation on one of the most important subjects that can occupy the attention of the human mind. Nicodemus begins the conversation with stating his belief of our Savior's Divine mission: "Rabbi, we know that thou art a teacher come from God, for no man can do those works which thou doest, except God be with him." In these words, though he asks no question, nor mentions any particular subject which he wished to have explained, yet he obviously intimates a desire that Jesus would communicate to him some information, concerning either the purpose of his mission, or the doctrines he was commissioned to reveal. Jesus accordingly takes no notice of his complimentary language, but immediately introduces to his notice a doctrine of fundamental importance to his everlasting salvation: "Verily, verily, I say unto thee, Except a man be born again, he cannot see the kingdom of God." The Jewish ruler was so ignorant, that he understood these words in a literal sense, and was accordingly not a little startled at the supposed absurdity of being born a second time: "How can a man, said he, be born when he is old? can he enter the second time into his mother's womb, and be born?" Pitying and reproving the ignorance of one, who, though a master in Israel, and a teacher of others, still needed to be himself taught the first principles of the oracles of God, Jesus renews and confirms his assertion, but adds, at the same time, such explanatory observations as might render it intelligible, introduces the doctrine of his own Divine mission, the astonishing love of God in the gift of his only Son, and inculcates at some length the necessity of faith in him, in order to salvation. What the effects of this conference upon Nicodemus were, the Evangelist does not inform us; but as we find him afterwards opposing the Sanhedrin, when raging against their officers for not apprehending Jesus, though they had sent them out for that very purpose, and taking part with Joseph of Arimathea in burying the Lord's crucified body, there is reason to hope that he became henceforth a true disciple of Jesus, and realized in his own experience the felicitous effects of that second birth, which, at its first proposal, appeared to him so strange. "Except a man be born again, he cannot see the kingdom of God."

On turning our attention to these words, the solemn and all important truth which they announce, ought to be deeply impressed upon our minds. It is not a question of speculative curiosity which we are about to discuss—our subject is not one which may be approached with a spirit of levity and unconcern: the very mention of it, if rightly considered, is sufficient to banish every vain thought and every listless feeling, and to produce emotions of a deep and solemn anxiety. "Verily, verily, I say unto thee," are the words in which the Son of God himself addresses us, "Except a man be born again, he cannot see the kingdom of God." It is the testimony of the faithful and true witness himself—of him who taught as never man taught—of him who, being the only begotten of the Father, possesses an intimate acquaintance with all his counsels, and has been commissioned by him to reveal these to man, so far as respects the method of his salvation, that unless we are "born again"—regenerated in our souls by the Holy Spirit—we have no interest in himself as the Saviour of sinners—no share of the blessings of his spiritual kingdom—no title to that inheritance which is incorruptible, undefiled, and that fadeth not away. On the contrary, we must remain through life the slaves of sin and Satan, enemies to God in our minds and by wicked works, liable every moment to be overtaken by the sword of his avenging justice; and when this life comes to an end, to be excluded forever from the presence of God, and shut up in that place whom his mercy is clean gone. Since regeneration, then, is a change on which consequences of such infinite importance depend, ought we not to approach the subject with seriousness? Ought not till that fixedness of attention, and solemnity of emotion, which the thought of happiness and misery, of heaven and hell, of judgment and eternity, is calculated to produce not within our minds while this subject is under our consideration? To every individual of us, as well as Nicodemas, does our Lord address the emphatic words, "Verily, verily, I say unto thee, Except a man be born again, he cannot see the kingdom of God."

In the discussion of this subject, I propose, I. To make a few remarks illustrative of the nature of regeneration, II. Mention some reasons why regeneration may be compared to a birth, or called a being born again; and—III. State some reasons why regeneration is indispensably necessary to salvation.

I. "We are then, in the first place, to make some remarks illustrative of the nature of regeneration; or, which comes to the same thing, to shew what being born again is. Nothing can be more obvious, than that the language of the text is figurative. The idea into which a literal acceptation of the words led Nicodemas, namely, that in order to be born again, we must enter the second time into our mother's womb and be born, is so grossly absurd in itself, and is so plainly rejected by our Lord in this very passage, that I need not spend a single moment in refuting it. Of what nature then is that change of which Jesus inculcates the necessity, when he says, "Ye must be born again?" This question I shall endeavor to answer by a few observations.

1. Regeneration is a spiritual change. It does not consist in admission into the visible church, or the enjoyment of any external privilege; but is a change of a purely internal and spiritual nature. This remark may be thought so obvious, as scarcely to require any illustration. Since regeneration is a figurative term, and

cannot be literally a second birth, it seems impossible to fix on any other change of an external kind, as intended by our Saviour in the words of the text. His reply to the question of Nicodemus, "How can a man be born when he is old?" places this beyond a doubt. Jesus answered, "Verily, verily, I say unto thee, Except a man be born of water and of the Spirit, he cannot enter into the kingdom of God. That which is born of the flesh is flesh; and that which is born of the Spirit is spirit." Without inquiring at present into the particular meaning of these expressions, it is obvious their express design was to correct the gross misconception of Nicodemus, in understanding our Lord's words in a literal sense, and to assure him that regeneration was not a change in external circumstances, or anything connected with the flesh, but was a spiritual renovation of the heart, effected by the agency of the Spirit of God.

So obvious does it seem that the change of which our Lord here inculcates the necessity, refers entirely to the internal state of the heart, and not to any external rite or privilege, that we would have judged the present remark altogether unnecessary, had it not been for the extensive prevalence of the doctrine, that water baptism is regeneration. This opinion, which has received the sanction of the Church of England, and is taught in the instituted language of her ritual, in a manner calculated to have a most delusive influence on the souls of men, is at once so irrational in itself, and so directly opposed to the current doctrines of Scripture, that it is truly surprising it should ever have been adopted by any who bear the Protestant name. Is it at all reasonable to suppose, that our Lord, in the very solemn address which he bore makes to Nicodemus, means only to inform him that he must be baptized? If this is what is inculcated under the metaphor of being born again, how was Nicodemus worthy of reprehension for his ignorance on the subject? Baptism, in the New Testament sense of the term, was at that time a rite of very recent institution; its necessity is no where taught in the Old Testament, and might therefore be still unknown to Nicodemus, without his being culpable for his ignorance. If, however, it be the spiritual renovation of the heart of which the Lord here speaks, this was a doctrine amply taught in the Old Testament scriptures, so that for his ignorance of it, the Jewish ruler justly deserved the reproof which he received, when it was said to him, "Art thou a master in Israel, and knowest not these things?" Besides, the intention of our Lord in this passage, plainly, is to state an essential requisite to salvation. Except we are born again, he assures us, we cannot see the kingdom of God; and between these two things, it is a fair and obvious inference from his words, there is an inseparable connection. But what such connection is there between baptism and salvation? Are there not thousands in every country where Christianity is generally professed, who have experienced all the regeneration that baptism can give, of whom it is nevertheless true that they live and die in their sins. Simon Magus, we are assured by the authority of inspiration itself, professedly believed and was baptized, and yet was all the while in the gall of bitterness and in the bond of iniquity. And at the last day, the Evangelist Luke informs us, chap. xiii. 26, 27, there shall be found many who have been admitted to the most solemn ordinances of the Christian church, to whom the real Judge will nevertheless declare, "I know you not whence you are; depart from me, ye workers of iniquity."

But should it be said that baptismal regeneration is not always followed by salvation, it is only necessary to it: this opinion is equally untenable.

The design of the institution of baptism is not to confer faith on the recipient, for it requires the previous possession of it. "He that believeth and is baptized shall be saved." "See here is water," said the Ethiopian Eunuch to Philip, "what doth hinder me to be baptized?" "If thou believest with all thine heart," was Philip's reply to him, "thou mayest." An individual, then, may have faith, and, of consequence, be in a state of salvation before he is baptized, and should death cut him off in that situation, his eternal happiness will not be prevented, for the end of faith is infallibly the salvation of the soul. In the case of infants, we know there is such a thing as sanctification from the womb: it must be as unscriptural, therefore, as it is uncharitable, to suppose that of all the infants who die unbaptized, none are the objects of God's electing love. But it is needless to multiply arguments against a doctrine that bears its own refutation on its face. The opinion that baptism is either indispensably necessary to salvation, or that it is always followed by it, is so nearly allied to the Popish doctrine, that the mere external observance of a sacrament is of saving nature, and confers grace on the recipient, independently of faith and holiness on his part—a doctrine which disconnects religion altogether from the state of the heart, and places it wholly in external ceremony— that it can never gain for a moment the assent of any unprejudiced and well-informed mind.

But as the opinion under consideration is not the dogma of any obscure or exploded sect, but an authorized doctrine of one of the most celebrated churches of the present day for numbers and learning, it would be scarcely fair to dismiss it without taking some notice of the evidence adduced in its support. There are two texts of scripture, then, on which the doctrine that baptism is regeneration is principally founded, and these are, verse 5 of this chapter, "A man must be born of water and of the Spirit," and, Tit. iii. 11, "Not by works of righteousness which we have done, but according to his mercy he saved us, by the washing of regeneration, and the renewing of the Holy Ghost." Now what, we are asked, can be meant by being born of water, and by the washing, or, (as some of them translate the word,) the laver of regeneration, but being baptized with water? In reply to this objection, we remark, that as we have proved the absurdity of baptismal regeneration, and as these passages are susceptible of an explanation, which gives no countenance to that doctrine, they must be totally insufficient to support the conclusion deduced from them. It is a common idiom in scripture language, to designate an object by two different expressions, the one literal and the other figurative, the former being explicative of the latter. Thus, Isaiah xliv. 3, "I will pour water upon him that is thirsty, and floods upon the dry ground." Here are figurative expressions, and they are explained by the more literal language that follows: "I will pour my Spirit upon thy seed, and my blessing upon thine offspring." So, Ezek. xxxvi. 25, "Then will I sprinkle clean water upon you, and ye shall be clean." Here is a figurative expression, and it is explained more literally in the following clause of the verse: "From all your filthiness, and from all your idols will I cleanse you, and I will put my Spirit within you," &c. A similar phraseology occurs in the New Testament. Thus, Mat. iii. 11, "He," viz. Jesus, "shall baptize you with the Holy Ghost and with fire." These two terms, the Holy Ghost and fire, evidently refer to the same thing; and the figurative expression is used along with the literal, to point out more fully the nature of that change, which Jesus, by the instrumentality of the Spirit, effects upon the souls of men. The application of this principle furnishes, we presume, a satisfactory explanation of the expressions under consideration. "A man must be born of water and of the Spirit," that is, he must undergo that spiritual renovation of heart, of which cleansing with water may be a faint symbol, but of which the Holy Spirit alone is the author, before he can see the kingdom of God. So, in Titus iii. 5, "The washing of regeneration, and the renewing of the Holy Ghost," are just two expressions of the same thing: the one is literal and the other figurative; the literal explains the figurative; and the two together express the idea more fully than one of them could have done. It were perhaps going too far to assert, that there is no allusion to baptism in these expressions. Regeneration is the thing signified, of which baptism is the sign; and it is quite consistent with the idiom of scripture language, that expressions having an allusion to the one of these two things, should be employed in describing the other. But this can never warrant us to distort these figurative expressions, to the support of a conclusion which is contradicted by the whole tenor of the word of God. We might just maintain, that the promised influences of the Holy Spirit to refresh and sanctify the souls of men, mean no more than the sending of dew and rain to fructify the earth, because they are often expressed in language borrowed from these natural phenomena, as confound regeneration with water baptism, on account of a similarity of language employed to describe them.

But leaving an error, on which, however important it be in itself, it was perhaps scarcely necessary to have dwelt so long before my present audience, let it apply our present remark to a purpose of more practical importance. Since regeneration is a change of a spiritual nature, and has no necessary connection with baptism, or any external privilege, it must be most foolish to build any part of our hopes for eternity upon our enjoyment of external privileges. In countries where the Christian religion is generally professed, there are numbers of individuals who, because they were baptized in their infancy, have become members of some visible church, upon whose ordinances they regularly wait, and are guilty of no flagrant transgressions of the Divine law, build themselves up in the hope that their state in the sight of God must be perfectly safe. They do not, perhaps, regard their external privileges and profession alone as equivalent to regeneration; but out of these, along with their general sobriety of conduct, they form an imaginary holiness, which they substitute in its room. Such individuals cannot be too often nor too solemnly warned, that the only regeneration which secures admission into the kingdom of God, is a spiritual renovation of the heart; and that for the want of this, no regularity of deportment, no membership in any visible church, even though it were the purest on earth, can do anything to compensate. Let hypocrites in Zion, then, who, instead of using the ordinances of the church as means for the cultivation of heart religion, deduce from their enjoyment of them an encouragement to neglect it, be alarmed! It is to the heart alone that God looks: it is in the heart that all true religion has its seat; and if this be not right in his sight, no other attainment will be of any avail. Beware, then, of trusting in your enjoyment of the external privileges of grace, as if these alone gave you any security for salvation. At the great day of judgment, when the mask of hypocrisy shall be forever torn off, and the secrets of all hearts disclosed, many shall discover, when it is too late, that they have made these the objects of a delusive confidence. Then shall they begin to say, "Lord, we have eaten and drunk in thy presence, and thou hast taught in our streets. But he shall say unto them, I know you not whence ye are;

depart from me, all ye workers of iniquity," Luke xiii. 26, 27.

2. Regeneration is n supernatural change. It is not a mere reformation of external conduct, nor the acquisition of virtuous habits by our own exertions, but a radical change of the affections and dispositions of the heart, effected by the supernatural agency of the Spirit of God. It is the doctrine of a numerous class of theologians, and the opinion, we fear, of vast numbers who call themselves Christians, that when our Lord says we must be born again, all that he means is, that we must lay aside or subdue our vicious habits and passions, cultivate virtuous and benevolent affections, and attend carefully to our various duties, and that if we persevere in the doing of this, we shall not fall short of everlasting happiness. Now we do not deny that external reformation of conduct, and the cultivation of virtuous habits, are included in regeneration, that is, that regeneration cannot be real without them; but these are by no means the whole of the change that is required. There are numbers of individuals of the most amiable dispositions, and externally virtuous characters, and therefore possessed of all the regeneration which the above doctrine requires, who are nevertheless destitute of the love of God in their hearts, and entire strangers to the love and power of true religion. That, regeneration inculcated in the text is of a much deeper nature than the above language represents it. It is nothing less than a radical and universal renovation of the actions and dispositions of the heart, effected not by our own feeble exertions, but by the supernatural agency of the Holy Spirit.

In proof of this position, may we not safely appeal to the language of the text itself? "Ye must be born again." Why is such language used? why such a strong figure employed, except to intimate that the change of heart, of which it inculcates the necessity, is of a deep and radical nature? Our hearts must surely be greatly disordered, nay, totally depraved, when they need not merely to be slightly rectified, or partially reformed, but to be totally regenerated—to be born again. Intending afterwards to make some remarks illustrative of the figure in the text, we shall not at present anticipate them; *but it must be obvious, on the slightest inspection, that it represents regeneration as a change, of which we are the passive subjects, and not the active cause.* It is not said we must regenerate ourselves, but we must, be regenerated—we must be born again. We must undergo a spiritual renovation of heart, which we are as little able to produce in ourselves, as the child unborn can be the cause of its own birth. The context also contains decisive evidence of the same doctrine. When our Lord repeats the declaration of the text to Nicodemus in other terms, to make it more intelligible to him, he not only continues to use the passive voice, but ascribes the change of heart of which he speaks to the Holy Spirit as its only author: "Except a man he born of water and of the Spirit, he cannot enter into the kingdom of God." By the Spirit here, we are undoubtedly to understand the Holy Spirit, that glorious person in the Godhead, whose work in the economy of redemption it is to apply the purchased salvation to the soul. Now, if regeneration be a change which we are able to work in ourselves, why is it said, "Ye must be born of the Spirit?" Why is the agency of another, yea of a Divine person, represented as necessary to produce it? The true and the only reason is stated in the following verse: "That which is born of the flesh is flesh; and that which is born of the Spirit is spirit." By the flesh in scripture, is commonly meant human nature in its sinful corrupted state. By the expression, then, "that which is born of the flesh is flesh," we are given to understand, that all the efforts which the flesh (that is, corrupted human nature,) can make to regenerate itself, will still leave it in the flesh, that is, in its original state of sin and corruption. We must be born of the Spirit; we must experience a renovation of soul, wrought in us by the powerful influences of the Holy Spirit, before we can attain that holiness of heart, which will secure us an entrance into the kingdom of God. It is only that which is born of the Spirit that is spirit.

From other places of scripture, abundance of evidence might be adduced in proof of the same doctrine, but we can only refer to a very few passages. The character of the sons of God, as drawn by the Evangelist, in the first chapter of this book is, that "they are born not of blood, nor of the will of the flesh, nor of the will of man, but of God." If language is capable of conveying an idea, this strong declaration puts it beyond a doubt that regeneration is not a human but a Divine work. "They were born not of the will of man but of God." The change inculcated in the text is represented in other places of scripture as a new creation. "We are his workmanship, created in Christ Jesus unto good works," Eph. ii. 10. "If any man be in Christ Jesus he is a new creature," 2 Cor. v. 17. "In Christ Jesus, neither circumcision availeth anything, nor uncircumcision, but a new creature," Gal. vi. 15. Or as the expression, in both these texts, might with propriety he rendered, "a new creation." Now this language is calculated to mislead, rather than to instruct, if a man be able to regenerate himself. No man, it is undeniable, can create himself, or be the author of his own existence in a natural sense. As little, these expressions plain imply, can he create himself anew, or be the author of that spiritual life which is necessary to fit him for the enjoyment of God. Man's spiritual condition, by nature, is represented as a state of death, and the change which delivers him from that state *as a* quickening of the dead, and restoring them to life. "You hath he quickened," or as the original word literally signifies, you hath he caused to live, "who were dead in trespasses and sins," Eph. ii. 1. "Verily, verily, I say unto you, the hour cometh, and now is, when the dead shall hear the voice of the Son of God, and they that hear shall live," John v. 25. "As the Father raiseth the dead, and quickeneth them; even so the Son quickeneth whom he will," verse 21. "It is the Spirit that quickeneth," or causeth to live; "the flesh profiteth nothing," chap. vi. 63. Now it is surely beyond the power of a dead body to recall the departed spirit, and restore itself to life. As little, it is plainly implied in these expression, can the spiritually dead soul deliver itself from the dominion of sin, and convenience, without supernatural aid, the practice of genuine holiness. The regeneration of the heart is frequently ascribed in scripture to the immediate agency of God, in such emphatic terms, as imply it to be his peculiar work. "Of his own will," says the apostle James, "begat he us with the word of truth," James i. 18. "I," says Jehovah himself, "will sprinkle clean water upon you, and ye shall be clean: from all your filthiness, and from all your idols, will I cleanse you. A new heart also will I give you, and a new spirit will I put within you; and I will take away the stony heart out of your flesh, and I will give you an heart of flesh," Ezek. xxxvi. 25, 26. "No man," says our Redeemer himself, "can come unto me, except the Father who hath sent me, draw him," John vi. 14. "Without me ye can do nothing," chap. xv. 5. "Can the Ethiopian change his skin, or the leopard his spots? then may ye also do good, that are accustomed to do evil," Jer. xiii. 23. Experience, in short, unites with scripture in proving that as mankind are naturally in a

state of moral estrangement from God, and slaves to
their sinful lusts, so they have neither inclination, nor
ability to throw off their spiritual chains, and return to
the ways of holiness. Occasional awakenings the
unrenewed mind may undergo. A person may resolve,
and re-resolve to abandon the practice of sin, and
commence a religious life in good earnest. He may even
make considerable proficiency in the cultivation of
moral virtue, and gain an irreproachable character for
piety and good works in the sight of men. But after all,
unless Divine grace interpose to work a saving change
upon his heart, his own conscience must bear him
witness, that his endeavors at self-sanctification are in
reality unsuccessful; his natural enmity to God
remaining unsubdued. He has no love to God in his
heart, nor real delight in his service, no single eye to his
glory, nor interested desire to please him. He accounts
the exercises of religion a burden, rather than a
pleasure, and would willingly return to his sinful
courses, could he hope to do it with safety. His proud
ungodly dispositions, in short, remain unmortified; and
notwithstanding all his fair outside attainments, "he
has only a name to live, while he is dead." But it is
needless to multiply arguments, in proof of a doctrine
which is as clearly revealed, as the word of God can
make it. If there is one truth more frequently, or more
strongly inculcated in scripture than another, it is, that
men in their natural state, are the subjects of a
depravity too deep for themselves to eradicate; that
sinful and worldly pursuits engross the whole of their
affections; that notwithstanding the amiable temper,
and respectable character which they may sometimes
possess, they are without a vestige of a supreme love to
God in their hearts; that if left to themselves, they will
go on in their career of rebellion, without ever once
thinking of returning to their duty; and that unless

Divine grace interpose to change their hearts, and restore the Divine image to their souls, they will remain forever strangers to the genuine fear and love of God, and to that deep humility of heart, and holiness of affection, which are necessary to an admission into his kingdom.

The doctrine which represents regeneration as merely an external reformation of life, as the cultivation of virtuous habits in our own strength, is of an extremely dangerous tendency. Considering the natural blindness of the human mind in spiritual matters, its readiness to put its trust in refuges of lies, and its strong propensity to prefer any system which allows man to share in the glory of accomplishing his salvation, to the humiliating doctrines of the gospel, it must be strongly calculated to encourage sinners to rest in a form of godliness, while strangers to its power. If the depravity of human nature be as deep and extensive as scripture represents it, those who teach such doctrines, and recommend such partial remedies, are certainly chargeable with healing the hurt of the daughter of God's people slightly, and may be eventually guilty of crying peace, peace, when there is no peace. You must beware then, hearers of the gospel, of deluding yourselves with the idea, that because your characters are externally virtuous, and stained with no flagrant vices, you possess all the regeneration which is necessary to the enjoyment of the kingdom of God. It is something more than reformation of life, or the cultivation of virtuous habits of which our Lord inculcates the necessity, when he tells you, "Ye *must* be born again." The ruling propensities of your hearts, so far as they respect God and Divine things, must be entirely changed. You must have the old heart taken away, and new hearts given you, else you can never meet with God in peace. Nothing less than this, be assured, is sufficient to secure you an entrance into the kingdom of heaven. The corruption of your natures is so deep, and the alienation of your hearts from God so great, that nothing short of a supernatural and radical renovation is sufficient to rectify them. Renouncing then, all dependence upon your own exertions, and betaking yourselves wholly to the promised grace of the Gospel; let it be your exercise to supplicate with earnestness the gracious out-pouring of God's Holy Spirit, that he may regenerate and sanctify you, and so produce in you a meetness for the inheritance of the saints in light.

3. Regeneration is, in this life, an unperfected change. It is not the complete sanctification of the heart, but the production in it of such, principles of vital holiness, as render the general bent of the affections, and the general tenor of the conduct, holy, and conformed to the Divine law. When our Lord tells us, "we must be born again," he does not mean that we must be completely sanctified, while we are in this world. Had this been his requirement, the attainment of salvation must have been altogether hopeless, "for there is not a just man upon earth, that doeth good, and sinneth not." The imperfections attending the best services of believers, and the numerous sins, some of them of a very aggravated nature, into which they daily fall, are melancholy proofs that regeneration does not altogether destroy the power of sin in the soul. There is still a body of corruption within them, with which they are to maintain a perpetual struggle. "There is still a law in their members, warring against the law of their mind, and bringing them into captivity to the law of sin which is in their members."

But though regeneration is not the complete sanctification of the soul, it is still a deep and permanent renovation of it, extending to all its faculties. It is the conversion of the heart from sin to holiness, from the world unto God. It is a change which allows its subject to indulge no longer with the full consent of the will in the commission of sin, but makes obedience to the law of God, the leading desire of the heart. The power of corruption is not totally subdued, but the bent of the inclinations is changed; the alienation of the heart from God is removed; communion with him is now accounted the greatest happiness, and his favour the source of all true felicity. That, deep-rooted indifference about God and their spiritual interests, which so generally characterizes worldly men, gives place, in the renewed man, to a strong concern about salvation, and a holy diligence to make his calling and election sure. An interest in Christ, he esteems of more value than the whole world, and so deeply convinced is he of his need of this, that he is willing to make any sacrifice in order to attain it. Those superficial views of the evil nature of sin, and that high opinion of his own powers, which universally lead the natural man to think himself also to do something to recommend him to the favour of God, give place to an humbling sense of guilt, and a heart-felt conviction that of himself he can do no good thing whatever, but must he a debtor to free grace, for the whole of his salvation. Jesus Christ he no longer regards as a partial Saviour, for whose righteousness he sees no other need, than to supply a few deficiencies of his own; but so deeply sensible is he of the universal corruption of his nature, and the pollution attending his best works, that he sees he must stand wholly on the ground of the Savior's righteousness, else he can never be saved. Encompassed as he is with infirmities, and surrounded with temptations, he may frequently give way to the commission of sin. But this is not his delight but his burden, the best desires and resolutions of his heart are against it, and on every such failure, if he is acting a part at all consistent with his character, he can use the apostle's distinction, and say, "It is not I that do it, but sin that dwelleth in me." The whole bent of his renewed nature, indeed, leads him to hate sin, and to follow holiness; so that while such a principle remains within him, that habitual and deliberate indulgence of his sinful lusts, which characterized him in his unrenewed state, is altogether impossible. "He that is born of God," says the apostle John, "doth not commit sin, for his seed remaineth in him; and he cannot sin, because life is born of God," 1 John iii. 9,

Regeneration, then, though it is not the complete sanctification of the heart, is still a great and an important change. Its effects on the external conduct generally are, and always should be, visible in a life of increased holiness: but it is not in this that it mainly consists. The characters of a refined hypocrite and of a real saint, of those who have experienced this change, and those who have not, may sometimes appear equally excellent in the view of men, but between the states of their hearts in the sight of God, there is a mighty difference. However nearly their external character may approximate., there is in the heart of every real saint a deep and genuine hatred of sin, a sincere and heart-felt love of holiness, an humble sense of his own vileness and unworthiness in the sight of God, and of his utter inability to do many things really good, an habitual dependence upon the ill-sufficient grace of the Redeemer, and a single eye to the glory of God; feelings, to which, in the midst of all his refinements, the hypocrite is an entire stranger, but which give their possessor a preciousness of character in the sight of the Searcher of hearts, which he could never receive from the highest external accomplishments of human virtue. In declaring, then, that those who have been born again, shall be admitted into the kingdom of heaven, and that those who have not, must be excluded, God does not arbitrarily make a difference where there is none: the division extends only to those whose depraved state of mind disqualifies them for the enjoyments from which they are excluded. Yes, the principles of grace in the renewed soul, give their possessor a meetness for the inheritance of the saints in light, of which unrenewed men, however amiable their characters, are totally destitute. To the renewed nature, the exercises and enjoyments of heaven are exactly suited; to unregenerated men, these would only prove wearisome and disgusting, nay, a burden too heavy to be borne.

Should it be inquired, why God only introduces his people into an imperfect state of holiness in this world, or in other words, why he does not make their regeneration their complete sanctification, it is sufficient to reply, that such is the will of Him who giveth not account of any of his matters. He has, for wise and sovereign reasons, appointed that they should maintain a perpetual struggle with remaining corruption while in this world, and await their complete deliverance from it in heaven. In this appointment of his, it becomes them cheerfully to acquiesce, and to acknowledge with adoring gratitude, his goodness in the grace which he has been pleased to communicate, instead of repining that he has not communicated more. The change which he works upon them in the day of regeneration, is sufficiently great to stamp upon their hearts a character specifically different from what it was before; and to enable them, if they properly improve their privileges, to recognize themselves to be the objects of his redeeming love; and has, therefore, not without reason, been appointed the first step in that process which conducts the soul to glory, and the door of an admission into the kingdom of God. On this subject, too, it is deserving of remark, that the partial sanctification of the saints in this world is not owing to any imperfection in the nature of the principle implanted in their souls at regeneration, but only to its weakness and the imperfect degree of its exercise. This principle, so far as its operation extends, aims at nothing less than a holiness absolutely perfect, and it is only because its operations are checked and opposed by other principle, that it does not accomplish all that it aims at.

When we arrive at perfect holiness in heaven, accordingly, it does not appear that any new principle will be implanted, but only that those already implanted in regeneration will be strengthened and brought to perfection. Thus the saints in this world are represented in scripture as being only in part; but in heaven that which is in part is done away: here they are only children, but there they arrive at full manhood. If this idea be correct, we seem to be warranted in saying, that the change which takes place on the souls of believers when they leave this sinful world, and enter into a state of perfect holiness in heaven, great and glorious as it is, is not so great as that which they undergo at regeneration. That is only bringing to perfection the work which this begins: this is the bringing of the children into existence; that is only the carrying of him forward to manhood.

The doctrine, that regeneration, while it implants principles of abiding holiness, does not by any means completely sanctify the soul, strongly reproves the delusion of those who talk about the goodness of their hearts, and encourage themselves in the hope of salvation from the imagined fewness and trivial nature of their sins. There are numbers in the world who seem to think that their state in the sight of God must be safe, because they are better than many of their neighbors, they are religiously disposed, well-meaning people, and their hearts are in the main good. Such sentiments, we decidedly maintain, are the very opposite of those of a genuine saint: so far from being a mark of regeneration, they are an evidence of the contrary. They discover a mind which has never been awakened to the evil nature of sin and the desperate wickedness of the heart, rather than one that has been delivered from its power. The real saint is not at all disposed to boast of the goodness of his heart. He has seen so much of the awful depravity of his nature, and still feels so much of the workings of corruption within him, that he is even led to think that scarcely any man can have a worse heart than himself. The language of the apostle Paul he is always ready to use, for it is an exact expression of his feelings, "I know that in me, that is, in my flesh, dwelleth no good thing." Instead of feeling the least disposition to say with the Pharisee, "God, I thank thee that I am not as other men;" it is his habitual exercise to prostrate himself in the dust before God, acknowledging his utter unworthiness of the least mercy, and adopting the humble supplication of the publican, "God, be merciful to me a sinner."

Our present remark is no less full of encouragement to those who, on account of the guilt and aggravations of their sins, and the dreadful depravity which they feel working within them, are ready to exclude themselves from an interest in the mercy of God, and to think that they cannot be among the number of those who have been born again. That regeneration, my friends, which connects with the enjoyment of the kingdom of God, is not a perfect, sanctification. The holiest men that ever lived, have had to complain, as well as you, of the wickedness of their hearts, and the power of indwelling corruption. Listen to the language of the apostle Paul himself, and examine if his feelings did not bear a near resemblance to your own: "I find then a law, that where I would do good, evil is present with me. I see a law in my members, warring against the law of my mind, and bringing me into captivity to the law of sin, which is in my members. O wretched man that I am, who shall deliver me from the body of this death." A deep sense of the evil nature of sin, and of the dreadful corruption which works within you, so far from being a matter of discouragement, you ought rather to interpret as an evidence in your favour. It is a feeling, you may be assured, to which the unrenewed mind is almost a total stranger. Maintain, then, a constant struggle with your corruptions, and endeavor to the utmost to have them mortified: but be not discouraged. Trust in the all sufficient grace of the Redeemer to strengthen you for the contest, and to enable you to persevere. Live in the renewed actings of faith upon him, and doubt not that he will in due time, bring to perfection the good work which he has begun in your souls.

4. Regeneration is an intelligent and rational change. Though this change be supernatural, and in many respects mysterious, it is effected by the instrumentality of motives, and in a manner perfectly consistent with man's rational nature. This remark I think of importance to introduce here, with a view, in the first place, to stop the mouths of the enemies of evangelical religion, who are continually exclaiming against its doctrines as absurd and irrational; and, secondly, to reprove the deluded notions of those who mistake the workings of a natural imagination, and an excited state of feeling, from whatever cause these originate, for those holy affections and enlightened emotions inspired by true religion. The gospel, throughout all its parts, is a rational system. Its

doctrines may often surpass the powers of reason to comprehend or unfold, but they are never in contradiction to its sacred and enlightened dictates.

It is a saying of the apostle James, "Of his own will begat he us with the word of truth;" and of the apostle Peter, "Being born again, not of corruptible seed, but of incorruptible, by the word of God which liveth and abideth forever." These expressions plainly intimate, that it is by the instrumentality of the word, that is, of the truths and doctrines of the gospel, that the regeneration of the soul is affected. The Holy Spirit is indeed the supreme agent in the work, and without his influences, the truth, with all the powerful motives which it presents, could never accomplish it. Still the truth is the great instrument by which he conducts his operations. It is by applying and bringing home the truths and doctrines of the gospel with power to the heart, and impressing it deeply with those views of God and Divine things which the gospel presents, that he withdraws its affections from the love and practice of sin, and inspires it with the love of universal holiness, or in other words, that he regenerates it.

So long as a man has not experienced the renewing influences of the Holy Spirit, whatever knowledge of the truths of the gospel he may possess, he receives from them no sanctifying impression. They may exercise his natural faculties while he investigates and endeavors to explain them, but they neither affect his heart, nor influence his practice, but leave him just as really the slave of sin and corruption, as if he were totally ignorant of them. Now, the work of the Holy Spirit in regeneration, consists in bringing home these truths with such power to the heart, that they are no longer treated as matters of mere speculation, but become active influential principles, exercising a transforming efficacy upon the soul, subduing its depravity, purifying its affections, and renewing it in all its faculties after the image of God. The first part of the Spirit's work in accomplishing this great change generally is, the applying the law to the conscience, and impressing the sinner with such views of the depravity of his nature, and the wickedness of his life, and cause him to feel that he is a guilty and a miserable creature, necessarily the object of abhorrence to an infinitely holy God, and deserving nothing but his everlasting displeasure. He sees the justice of God to be an avenger of blood in arms against him, and seeking his destruction; he becomes seriously concerned about the welfare of his soul, and looks out with earnestness for a way of escape from the danger to which he sees himself exposed. Having thus convinced him of his sin, and made him sensible of his need of salvation, the Spirit's next work is to lead him to the Saviour. By exhibiting to him the atonement made for sin by the Lord Jesus Christ, and the forgiveness that there is with God for guilty sinners through the one Mediator between God and man, he shews him away by which his sins may be pardoned, and the salvation of his soul secured. His apprehensions of misery are now succeeded by the hope of mercy; and he longs for an interest in that salvation, without which he sees he must perish forever. In all probability, however, he is not yet fully enlightened in the nature of the gospel system: his disposition to trust in his own righteousness is not yet wholly subdued; and instead of casting himself on the Savior's mercy, simply as a sinner, without merit or excellence of his own to recommend him, he thinks of uniting his own righteousness with that of the Savior's, and betakes himself to amendment of life, to prayer, and religious duties, in order, as he thinks, to contribute something towards his salvation, and to qualify him for receiving those blessings which Christ has purchased for his people. Thus, going about to establish their own righteousness, many continue unwilling to submit to the righteousness of God, and not a few perish in their delusion. Where God has a purpose of mercy, however, the work is not left to stop here. By renewed applications of the law to the conscience, and fuller discoveries of the infinite holiness of the Divine nature, and the strictness and spirituality of the Divine law, the Spirit convinces the sinner that he is altogether an unclean thing in the sight of God, that his very best works proceed from such an impure and wicked heart, and are accompanied with so much sinful imperfection, that they are an abomination in the sight of Him who is of purer eyes than to behold iniquity, and that in spite of all he can do to repent and reform his ways he is every day sinking deeper in guilt in this situation, he is not unfrequently the subject of deep menial distress. The terrors of the Lord thicken around him, and he sees no way of escape. He sees himself to be a wicked rebel against the Majesty of heaven, —that his whole life has been a continual course of sinning, and is afraid that his guilt is therefore so great, that it can never be pardoned. Now, however, the happy time for his being visited with the cheering light of the gospel is arrived. The Holy Spirit opens up to him the riches of redeeming love, and his fears are at an end. He discovers to him the Saviour in his ability and willingness to save, shews him that the greatest guilt is no objection with him, and that he invites the very chief of sinners to come to him for salvation; and he is encouraged to venture his guilty soul into his hands. Now, the gospel scheme of salvation is opened up to his mind in all its beauty, and he cordially acquiesces in it. He sees, that as sinners possess no good quality to recommend them to the Savior's mercy, so his mercy needs to be attracted by no goodness of theirs, but that all the blessings of salvation are offered to them "without money and without price." Hence, guilty and polluted as he is, he sees that there is hope in Israel for him, he trusts in sovereign grace for every blessing, learns to rely implicitly on the Saviour for all that he needs; and thus, in due time, comes to find joy and peace in believing.

I by no means assert, that those who are born again are always sensible of having been brought to the Saviour by a process of this kind. The Holy Spirit has various ways of working, and can accomplish the same end by a diversity of means. It is sufficient for my present purpose, if it is admitted that something of this description often takes place, and that a work of the law always precedes, in the nature of things, and generally, too, in the experience of the individual, the faith of the gospel. Now, concerning this change, in all its parts, what part of it, I would ask, is not completely rational? Are not the individuals who are its happy subjects treated, from first to last, as rational creatures; actuated by rational motives, and never driven by a physical compulsion, of which they are involuntary subjects? Surely when a man is made to see himself to be a condemned criminal in the sight of God, and prevented by nothing but the brittle thread of natural life from being immediately subjected to a punishment, at once indescribable in severity, and endless in duration; nothing can be more reasonable than that he should be alarmed, and stirred up to such concern about salvation, that, he can give neither sleep to his eyes, nor slumber to his eyelids, while he remains in that state, but flees with haste to the gates of mercy, that he may be delivered from it. The deep concern and dejection of mind which frequently accompany the work of regeneration, may be imputed by irreligious men, who know nothing of these matters, to a gloomy and disordered imagination; but it is all in perfect consistency with the soundest reason, for it proceeds from a cause amply sufficient to produce it. When a man, in like manner, sees all his own righteousness as filthy rags, and is assured by the holy scriptures that salvation is attainable no other way than through faith in the Lord Jesus Christ, he surely acts a most rational part in renouncing all dependence upon his own good works, and placing his whole reliance on the all sufficient righteousness of Christ as the ground of his acceptance before God. So highly rational, indeed, is his conduct in all this, that to act otherwise would be in the highest degree irrational. So far is the Spirit's work in regeneration from being inconsistent with man's rational nature, that it only stirs him up and enables him to do that which his own reason should lead him to do, and which indeed it would do, were it not that his understanding is darkened by sin, and his mind so blinded by the god of this world, that he loves darkness rather than light, and will not come unto the light, lest his deeds should be reproved. It is not by any physical operation affecting the substance of his soul, it is not by any compulsion, of which he is the involuntary subject, but by being enlightened, convinced, and persuaded, that a man is born again. It is with cords of a man, and with bands of love, that Jesus draws sinners to himself. It is by convincing them of their need of salvation, and shewing them the richness and suitableness of that salvation which he has purchased with his own blood, that he makes his people willing in the day of his power, and allures their hearts into a cordial acquiescence in that scheme of salvation which the gospel makes known.

In maintaining the rationality of that change which is wrought on the heart in regeneration, I by no

means wish to deny that there is something in it too
mysterious for reason to explain or comprehend.
Jehovah's ways are said to be in the sea, and his path in
the great waters, and his footsteps are not known. If his
works of creation and providence are often veiled in
darkness, and inscrutable by our feeble powers, much
more may we expect his operations on the human soul
to be mysterious and inexplicable. Our Saviour, in this
very passage, compares the work of the Spirit in
regeneration, to one of the mysterious phenomena in
nature. "The wind bloweth where it listeth, and thou
hearest the sound thereof, but canst not tell whence it
cometh, and whither it goeth; so is every one that is
born of the Spirit." Perhaps the most inexplicable thing
in this work is how the Spirit makes the truths of the
gospel effectual to the production of so great a change
as regeneration. How is it that a man is brought by the
instrumentality of any motives, to give an unreserved
acquiescence of heart, in a method of salvation which
he formerly contemned—to love a God whom he hated,
and to trust in a Saviour whom he despised? Such an
extraordinary change is not effected by a mere
illumination of the understanding; there is also some
secret influence conveyed along with the word, which
causes it to impress and change the heart. When the
carnal mind is said to be enmity against God, we
cannot suppose that this enmity arises solely from
ignorance or incorrect views of the Divine character; for
if it did, its object, would be a mere idol of the
imagination, and it would not be in reality enmity
against God at all. It consists chiefly in a depraved state
of heart, which views those very attributes of holiness
and justice, which render God the proper object of love,
with hatred and dislike. Now since the want of correct
knowledge is not the reason why unrenewed men hate
God, and cherish feelings of enmity against him: the

mere correcting of these views can never bring them to love him. Daily experience sufficiently confirms this, for there are numbers of men in the world, whose views of evangelical doctrine are perfectly orthodox, whose hearts are nevertheless destitute of every religions impression. Now since in other instances the most correct ideas in the understanding, are not inconsistent with a depraved state of the heart, how is it that the Holy Spirit so works with these discoveries of the truth which he opens up to the subjects of his regenerating influences, as to effect by them a removal of the depravity of the heart, and a thorough change of its inclinations and leading propensities? How is it that views of God and Divine things, which would otherwise have floated as idle speculations in the head, are so powerfully impressed upon the heart, as to transform it in its whole character, and to bring it to hate what it formerly loved, and to love what it formerly hated? These are questions to which it does not appear any satisfactory answer can be given. There the work of the Spirit is written in a mystery which reason can never explain—is covered with a darkness too dense for the human mind to penetrate. "The wind bloweth where it listeth, and we hear the sound thereof, but cannot tell whence it cometh, and whither it goeth; so is every one that is born of the Spirit." But the mysteriousness attaching to the manner of this work, can be no objection to its truth, nor even militate anything against its rationality. There is no subject in science or philosophy, any more than in theology, which does not involve difficulties, surpassing our comprehension, and baffling our utmost efforts to explain them.

The remark, that regeneration is effected by the instrumentality of the truths of the gospel acting as motives on our rational nature, strongly reproves the deluded enthusiasm of those who imagine religion to consist in a certain succession of deep convictions and enraptured joys, without any regard to the cause by which their affections are excited, or the effects which they produce on the life and conversation. In periods noted for revivals of religion, in particular, when the agitated state of men's imaginations renders them an easy prey to the delusions of Satan; it has been a prevailing opinion, that all who are brought under deep convictions on account of sin, and afterwards transported with lively emotions of joy from the hope that they are become children of God, and heirs of heaven, have certainly been born again. Now, though it is by no means denied, that a saving work of the Holy Spirit generally commences with deep convictions of sin, and is often followed by peace of conscience and joy in the Holy Ghost; still a mere experience of these successive feelings, cannot be interpreted as a certain evidence of regeneration, it is not so much the liveliness of our affections, or the order in which they are excited, as the views of Divine truth from which they originate, and the sanctified state of mind in which they terminate, that is to be regarded. If our affections be the ignorant ebullitions of an excited imagination, if our distresses arise from any other cause than scriptural views of the evil nature of sin, and the wickedness of our hearts in the sight of God, and if our joys are of such a nature that we cannot trace them to distinct, and comforting views of the riches of Divine grace, and the excellence and suitableness of the gospel scheme of salvation, we have more reason to suspect our emotions to be a delusion of Satan, than to conclude them to be a saving work of the Spirit of God. Remember, then, hearers of the gospel, that it is by the instrumentality of sound and scriptural discoveries of Divine truth, that the Holy Spirit regenerates the soul, and that it is only by bringing our affections to the test of the written word, that we can know them to be his genuine work. In all your attempts at self-examination, take this principle along with you, and conclude not that you have been born again, from the mere fact that you were once distressed, but are now comforted. Examine rather by what views of Divine truth your affections are excited, and what sanctified effects upon your heart and conduct they produce. In respect of religions affections, as well as opinions, the saying holds true, "To the law and to the testimony: if they speak not according to this word, it is because there is no light in them," Isaiah viii. 20.

5. Regeneration is a believing change. It prepares the mind for, and is immediately followed by, the exercise of faith. In 1 John v. 1, it is expressly said, "Whosoever believeth that Jesus is the Christ, is born of God." To believe that Jesus is the Christ, is not only to believe the doctrines of his Divinity and Messiahship as abstract truths, but to yield an acquiescence of heart in all that the gospel testifies concerning him. It is in short, nothing less than to receive Christ himself into the heart, and to rest upon him for salvation as he is offered to us in the gospel. Now, when it is said, that "whosoever believeth that Jesus is the Christ, is born of God;" we are plainly informed, that between a saving faith in the Lord Jesus Christ and regeneration, there is an inseparable connection; every one that believeth has been born again, and every one that has been born again believeth. In John i. 12, 13, also, faith and regeneration are mentioned together in such a manner, as plainly implies that they can never exist separately, "But as many as received him, to them gave the power to become the sons of God, even to them that believe on his name; who were born not of blood, nor of the will of the flesh, nor of the will of man, but of God." We have

scripture authority, then, for saying that believing in
Christ, and being horn again, are two things which
imply one another, and can never be separated; and
were I called upon to explain in a few words what
regeneration is, I would say, it is a work of the Holy
Spirit, disposing and enabling the mind to exercise
faith in the Lord Jesus Christ. To regenerate a sinner's
heart, and to enable him to believe, I consider as little
else than two ways of expressing the same thing.
Regeneration is the work of the Holy Spirit enabling
the mind to believe; and faith is the act of the mind in
consequence of that work. In the order of nature,
regeneration goes before faith; for until the soul be
renewed by the Holy Spirit, it, is spiritually dead, and
unable either to believe or do anything truly good.
Faith, however, is such an immediate consequent of
regeneration, that if it can scarcely be said to be
posterior to it in the order of time. As no assignable
portion of time elapses between a person's opening his
eyes, and his seeing any object that may be before him;
so no sooner are the eyes of the spiritually blind soul
opened by the Holy Spirit, than it beholds by faith the
Lord Jesus Christ. As a dead body upon being
quickened and restored to life, immediately begins to
breathe, and move, and act; so the dead soul is no
sooner quickened by Divine grace, than it begins to
exhibit symptoms of spiritual life, by putting forth an
act of faith on the Son of God. As in regeneration, the
Spirit discovers to the soul its lost and hopeless
condition by nature, and gives it a view of Christ in his
ability and readiness to save; so the soul, in
consequence of this discovery, immediately flees from
the wrath to come; puts its trust in Christ as the only
Saviour, and embraces him in all his offices, and cleaves
to him in all his relations. Thus it is that we are brought
to acquiesce cordially in the gospel scheme of salvation,

and to accept of Christ as made of God unto us, wisdom, righteousness, sanctification, and redemption. Thus we receive him as all and in all to our souls: as our Prophet, to guide and instruct us; as our Priest, to atone for our guilt, and make intercession for us before God; and as our King, to sanctify our souls, and to rule and reign in our hearts. Then a vital union between Christ and the soul takes place, maintained on the part of Christ by his word and Spirit dwelling in the heart, and on the part of the believer by the constant actings of a lively faith, cleaving unto Christ, and holding him fast, even refusing to let him go. Thus it is that we come to realize, in our own happy experience, the truth of these remarkable words, "We are crucified with Christ: nevertheless we live; yet not we, but Christ liveth in us; and the lives which we now live in the flesh, we live by the faith of the Son of God."

The remark that regeneration is just a name for the work of the Spirit, in fitting and disposing the mind for faith in Christ, I conceive to be of some practical importance. To every subject, almost, to which we direct our thoughts, and in none more than theology, we are in great danger of substituting names for things, and flattering ourselves that we understand all that is necessary about a subject, when we have made ourselves acquainted with the language, and can fluently use the phrases by which our ideas should be expressed. The remoteness of spiritual matters from our usual trains of thought, the difficulty of forming distinct conceptions about them, an intellectual indolence, which wishes to be spared the fatigue of close thinking, and an aversion of heart to the things of the Spirit of God, in whatever form they are presented to us, all concur in aiding this delusion. Hence then; are some, I apprehend, who talk fluently of regeneration and being born again, without well understanding either what they say, or whereof they affirm. Now, to guard you against this delusion, and to assist you in conceiving distinctly of this important subject, the present remark appears to me of considerable importance. Regeneration is just another name for the work of the Holy Spirit, in disposing and enabling the mind to embrace the Lord Jesus Christ, by faith. Hence those who feel themselves at any loss in understanding distinctly what is meant by the question, Have *you* been born again? may aid their conceptions by proposing it in this other form, *have you* believed in Christ? These two things, if not exactly the same, always imply one another; and there is not a single circumstance that can be considered an evidence of faith, which is not also an evidence of regeneration. If, then, upon a candid examination, you find reason to conclude, that, you have been so convinced of the evil nature and dangerous consequences of sin, as to flee from it unto the Saviour, have been so persuaded of the insufficiency of your own righteousness, as to renounce all dependence upon it, and to build all your hopes upon the finished righteousness of Christ, if you are willing, in short, to receive Christ, as he is offered in the gospel, and to be indebted to his free grace for the whole of your salvation, you need entertain no doubt, that as you believe, so you have been born again. "He that believeth that Jesus is the Christ is born of God."

6. Regeneration is an all-important change. It connects with our deliverance from wrath and condemnation on account of sin, our introduction into the privileges of a justified state, and our enjoyment of eternal glory at last. This is a remark which flows very naturally from the text. "Verily I say unto thee, except a man be born again, he cannot see the kingdom of God." These words not only represent regeneration as an essential requisite to salvation, but as universally

preceding it. None who have not been born again, can ever enter into the kingdom of God; and all, on the contrary, who have been born again, shall, without fail, enter into it. In our last remark, we stated that regeneration is a change of heart, which has an inseparable connection with faith. Now faith is everywhere represented in scripture as the means of our introduction into a justified state, the medium of an interest in the Lord Jesus Christ, and inseparably connected with the salvation of the soul. All the blessings and privileges, therefore, which result from saving faith, may be also viewed as connected with regeneration. As without faith, so without regeneration, no man can be in a state of vital union to Christ, or have either part or lot in the blessings he bestows on his people; he remains, on the contrary, in a state of condemnation and death, a child of wrath, and an heir of hell. The moment, however, that the Holy Spirit works a saving change upon his heart, and he is born again, that moment he believes in Christ, passes from a state of condemnation and death, into one of justification and life, becomes a child of God and an heir of heaven. Thus it is, that he is "begotten again to a lively hope by the resurrection of Jesus Christ from the dead, to an inheritance incorruptible, and undefiled, and that fadeth not away."

In the language of scripture, there is a beautiful harmony between the expressions used to denote a saving change of heart, and those employed to describe the consequences of that change, which merits notice. That saving change which the Holy Spirit works upon the heart, is called regeneration, a being born again; and the relation to God, into which this change introduces us, is called a filial relation, a sonship. By being born again, we become the sons of God, and not only sons but heirs— "heirs of God, and joint-heirs with Christ."

These expressions are of frequent occurrence in scripture; and the consistent and harmonious allusion which they bear to the circumstances and customs of men ought not to be overlooked. When a child is born in a human family, he becomes a son in that family, and an heir of its inheritance. So in the family of God, when an individual is born again, he becomes a son of God, and an heir of his heavenly kingdom. Yes! every regenerated person, in consequence of his new birth, does claim God as his father, Christ as his elder brother, the whole household of faith as his brethren, and heaven itself as his inheritance. The new birth, my friends, is a holy, noble, and exalted birth. To be the son of an earthly king, and the heir of a rich and flourishing kingdom, is reckoned a high honour among men. But what is this, compared with the dignity which is conferred upon the saints, when, by regeneration, they become the sons of God, and the heirs of his heavenly kingdom? Compared with the inheritance to which they are born, all the kingdoms and riches of the world joined into one, are but a trifle. In comparison with the honour and dignity which awaits them, as sons in the family of God, the splendor of an earthly palace, and the honour of a monarch's throne, are an empty nothing, a short-lived breath of air, a vain and a perishing name. "Beloved, now are we the sons of God; and it doth not yet appear what we shall be: but we know that, when he shall appear, we shall be like him, for we shall see him as he is." 1 John iii. 2.

7. Regeneration is a permanent change. Its effects upon the state and character are of an abiding nature, and can never be destroyed. "Whosoever is born of God," says the apostle John, "doth not commit sin; for his seed remaineth in him, and he cannot sin, because he is born of God." These words plainly represent it as a consequence of the new birth, that its

happy subjects are not only delivered from the reigning power of sin for the present, but that they can never again come under its dominion. "Their seed remaineth in them, and they cannot sin, because they are born of God." Regeneration effects a glorious change upon the state and character; and this change shall abide forever. "Whosoever," says Jesus himself, "drinketh of the water that I shall give him, shall never thirst: but the water that I shall give him, shall be in him a well of water, springing up unto everlasting life." It were a comparatively small privilege to be delivered at present from a state of condemnation, on account of sin, if we had no security against falling back into that state. It were a matter of comparatively little importance to be adopted into God's heaven-born family today, if we were in danger, on account of our sins, of being cast out of it tomorrow. Blessed be God, however, this is not the way in which he deals with his children. All whom he once adopts into his family, be keeps there, and will never cast them out. His gifts and callings in this respect are all without repentance. The mountains may depart, and the hills be removed, but his loving kindness will not depart from any of his people, neither shall the covenant of his peace be removed from them. Think, my friends, on this important property of the new birth, and let it raise its value in your esteem, and stir you up to redoubled diligence in seeking an interest in it. To be born the son of a rich man, and the heir of an extensive property, may be thought an important matter; but, alas! the sons of the highest of mankind may die before they reach their inheritance; and even though they should reach it, it is only a few short years that its splendor and wealth can yield them any consolation. Death, the gloomy monarch of the grave, is no respecter of persons: he enters alike the palace of the king and the cottage of the poor, and will soon summon all, both high and low, away from their earthly wealth and occupations, to appear before the tribunal of God. Those who are born again, however, are placed beyond the reach of death, and can never be deprived of their inheritance. Natural death will indeed overtake them; but, instead of separating them from their inheritance, it only takes them to it. It is their father's messenger sent to recall from a world of sorrow, where it was his will they should sojourn for a time, and to conduct them home to himself, and put them in full possession of their rich and glorious inheritance. Happy they who are thus born again. Through all the troubles of the present life they shall be safely preserved. Death itself is converted into a privilege to them; and a crown of immortal glory shall as surely shine through all eternity on their beads, as if they were already possessed of it. They are begotten again to an inheritance incorruptible, undefined, and that fadeth not away; and of this inheritance they cannot fall short, for they are kept to it, securely kept, kept as in a *garrison*, as the original word imports, by the power of God through faith unto salvation.

Reserving the proper application of the subject, till we have discussed the remainder of the doctrine, we shall conclude, in the mean time, with two short remarks.

1. It is no easy matter to be a real Christian, and we are in great danger of deceiving ourselves to our eternal ruin, by trusting in false refuges, and mistaking partial reformations of character, or such attainments in religion, as unrenewed men may reach, for a saving work of the Spirit of God. I have been endeavoring, my friends, to open up the nature of regeneration, by describing a few of its properties; and, after what has been said, you cannot refuse to admit that it must be no easy matter to enter into the kingdom of God. It is not

an external reformation of life—it is not the acquisition of virtuous habits, and the cultivation of amiable tempers in your dealings between man and man; but a deep and permanent change of heart, effected by the supernatural agency of Divine Grace, that Jesus requires before he will admit you into his heavenly kingdom. Great is the deceitfulness of the human heart—numerous are the false refuges in which we are ever ready to trust. External respectability of character; moral integrity; honesty in dealing between man and man; regularity of attendance, on the ordinances of religion; orthodoxy of sentiment, and membership in the visible church; partial reformations after some awakening of conscience in matters of religion; considerable warmth of feeling, occasionally experienced in religious duties: these are only some of the refuges of lies, in which Satan tempts the children of men to put their trust, while they remain entire strangers to a saving change of heart. O my friends, beware of deceiving yourselves in a matter of such vast importance as the eternal welfare of your immortal souls. Think what a great and important change regeneration is, and beware, of substituting any partial reformation or external privilege in its room. Let it be a matter of frequent and serious inquiry with you, whether or not you have been really born again. Be frequent and earnest in your prayers to God to discover unto you your real change, and to begin and carry on the good work of grace in your souls. It is no easy matter, you may depend upon it to help a real Christian. To be born again—to have your natures willfully regenerated, your old hearts taken away, and this new heart that is given to you, is a work which nothing less than the almighty power of God can accomplish. Yet be not discouraged; wait upon God, and pray unto him, and he will willingly charge upon you. The gate of mercy is strait indeed; but, blessed be God, it is not shut. "Strive, then, to enter in at the strait gate: for strait is the gate, and narrow is the way that leadeth unto life, and few there be that find it."

2. Let all those exhorted to make the things of eternity their study, and to have their attention chiefly directed to the one thing needful. Sinners, you need this exhortation, for your time and attention are wholly engrossed by the things of the world; and it is well if you an; not as unconcerned about the salvation of your souls, as if you had not a soul that needed to be saved. Saints, you also need to attend to this exhortation; for you are too much concerned about the things of this life, and too little about the things of God. It is strange what can induce rational creatures, living on the brink of eternity, and uncertain but they may be summoned, ere an hour elapses, to leave their earthly occupations, and appear before the tribunal of God, to live in such indifference about their spiritual interests, and to have their cares and affections so exclusively engrossed by the things of the world. A person about to emigrate to a distant continent, makes timely preparation for his voyage, ceases to be much concerned about the houses, farm, and country, which he is soon to leave, and becomes anxious, mainly, how he may best secure a comfortable subsistence in that country, where he is to spend the remainder of his days. Yet, thoughtless mortal man scarcely thinks about anything else than the present world; and is in general as little concerned about futurity, as he would be warranted to be, if he had no eternity before him. O my friends, shake off this dangerous delusion, and be impressed with the consideration, that life is short and uncertain, and that, your main business in this world is to make preparation for the next. As you love your own souls, O neglect not the one thing needful; for, verily, if death

finds you in an unregenerate state, ye shall be miserable forever. "Except ye are born again, ye cannot see the kingdom."

SERMON III:
On Regeneration

"Verily, verily, I say unto thee, unless a man is born again, he cannot see the kingdom of God."—John iii. 3.

THERE is no doctrine in theology that can be established by a greater mass of evidence, both from scripture and experience, than that respecting the depravity of human nature. If we may judge of the general character of our species, from a review of what passes within our own hearts, we must pronounce it to stand low in the scale of moral excellence indeed; for there is in us a strong indifference, and even aversion, to what is good and a powerful inclination to what is evil. In vain and carnal thoughts we readily indulge, while to engage in any serious exercise about God and eternity, we are mournfully backward. If, from observing our own character, we turn to the world around us, we cannot fail to discover, that in them too there is a powerful principle of depravity at work, leading them to the habitual violation of the Divine law, rendering them enemies to God in the secret workings and dispositions of their minds, and causing them to exhibit this enmity by the habitual perpetration of wicked works. The whole world may, with the greatest truth, be said to be lying in wickedness, and even to be up in arms in a state of rebellion against their Creator.

What is the history of mankind, from the fall of Adam to the present day, but the history of one scene of guilt rising up after another? What barbarous wars, what treachery, what perfidy, what calumny, what want of brotherly-affection, what horrid impiety, what debasing superstition start up to view, in the history of every age and nation to which we can direct our attention! The deplorable state of Heathen and Mahometan countries, with respect to religion and morality, is too well known to need description. Their very systems of religion are systems of impiety and cruelty; they abound with rites the most absurd, lascivious, and cruel, imaginable. Instead of raising the national character in knowledge and virtue, they tend powerfully to debase it. Instead of being an indication of the piety and virtue of their votaries, they are a decisive proof of their impiety and wickedness; and a melancholy confirmation of the doctrine of human depravity. From Heathen countries, if we turn our attention to those which have been enlightened with the gospel, the scene is indeed considerably improved; but, alas! depravity, in the most horrid forms, still stares us in the face. So far from embracing and professing Christianity in its Divine purity and native holiness, mankind, in a great majority of instances, have perverted its doctrines, and corrupted its institutions. Statesmen have seldom embraced it with any other intention, than to use it as an engine of state policy; and that very order of men who are appointed its guardians and teachers, have too often disgraced their sacred character, and exposed religion to contempt, by converting it into a system of priestcraft. Even in those countries where the light of the gospel is enjoyed in its greatest purity, how small is the number of those who may be truly said to "love the Lord their God with all their hearts?" What vast multitudes are there who criminally neglect the means of grace altogether, and allow themselves to remain in utter ignorance of God and the way of salvation? and what vast multitudes more, to whom the great salvation is proclaimed, but they despise it; before whom Jesus Christ is evidently set forth crucified, but they trample him under foot,

count his precious blood an unholy thing, and do
despite unto the Spirit of grace? Oh! how great must
the depravity of human nature be, when man not only
has been unmindful of the God that formed him, and
forgets the Rock that begat him, but treats with
contempt that Saviour who shed his blood to save him;
and, at, the risk of his own eternal salvation, hardens
himself in sin, and can neither be awed by the terrors of
the law, nor gained by the allurements of the gospel, to
lay down the weapons of his rebellion against God, and
to believe in him whom he hath sent? In the history of
every age and nation of mankind, then, and in our own
individual experience, we may read the doctrine of
human depravity; but, lest even all this should be
insufficient to convince us of its truth, I must also add,
we may read in, in the Holy Scriptures. It is the
testimony of God himself—of him who knows
perfectly what is in man, and cannot pronounce a false
judgment of his character, that the human heart is
"deceitful above all things, and desperately wicked,"
that "every imagination of the thoughts of man's heart
is only evil, and that continually," that "there is not a
just, man upon earth that doeth good and sinneth not,"
that all the children of men, without a single exception,
"are gone aside, are altogether become filthy, and that
there is none that doeth good, no, not one."

The evidence of the doctrine of human
depravity is complete and satisfactory, and he must be
at once a stranger to the state of his own heart—a blind
observer of the world around him, and an unbeliever in
the-scriptures themselves, who either doubts or denies
it. It is of great importance that the hearers of the
gospel be well established in the belief of this doctrine,
and have their minds suitably impressed with its truth,
for it is closely connected with correct views of the
gospel. The gospel is a scheme of salvation, in all its

parts, predicated on human depravity, and if man is not a depraved, yea, a deeply depraved creature, this scheme of salvation, is not suited to his circumstances. We would readily accuse of foolish and improper conduct, the physician who should prescribe a powerful medicine to a patient who was only infected with a slight distemper. Can we then without impiously arraigning the infinite wisdom of God, suppose him to have provided a way of salvation for mankind through the blood of his own Son, and the sanctifying influences of the Holy Spirit, while yet human nature is only slightly, or scarcely at all, depraved. Man must be deeply depraved, because he needs to be born again. The necessity of the atoning blood, and meritorious righteousness of Christ, to expiate our guilt, and procure us acceptance in the sight of God, proves man to be naturally in a state of legal condemnation, from which he can do nothing to deliver himself. The necessity of the sanctifying influences of the Holy Spirit, in like manner, to regenerate his heart, and renew him after the moral image of God, proves him to be naturally under the dominion of a principle of depravity, which his own exertions are utterly insufficient to subdue. The doctrine of innate depravity is humbling to human pride, but let us not on this account refuse to admit it. Our nature is deeply diseased, but there is a remedy provided, and our being properly sensible of our disease is intimately connected with our reception of the remedy. "They that are whole need not the physician, but they that are sick." Except we believe and feel our depravity, how can we admit the necessity of regeneration? The hearts of mankind must be deeply depraved, because the faithful and true Witness has declared, that unless they are savingly renewed by the power of the Holy Spirit, they are totally unqualified for, and cannot be admitted into the enjoyments and felicity of heaven. Oh! how depraved must our hearts naturally be, when the old heart must be wholly taken away, and new hearts given to us, before we can meet with God in peace. Surely it is not without a reason, that Jesus so emphatically says to us, "Verily, verily, I say unto thee, except a man be born again he cannot see the kingdom of God."

II. In speaking from these words, I have already endeavored to open up the nature of regeneration, by stating, in a few observations, what kind of a change it is. And I now proceed to the second division of the subject, which was to explain why regeneration may be compared to a birth, or why the man who has his soul savingly renewed by the Holy Spirit, may be said to be born again.

In that revelation of his will, which he has given to man, God in gracious condescension to our slow understandings, and limited capacities, has generally employed figurative expressions in speaking of spiritual matters; and set before us the mysterious and heavenly truths of the gospel, in language borrowed from the affairs of common life, and bearing an allusion to the things of time and sense. There is not a single subject of a spiritual nature, in the whole compass of revelation, respecting which metaphorical language is not used. In speaking, for example, of himself, God very generally use figurative expressions. Thus we read of him as having eyes and hands, and other bodily members; of his being present at a particular place, or removing from it; of his being angry or displeased; of his being King among the nations, sitting on an exalted throne. All of these expressions, and thousands similar, which might have been mentioned, are obviously figurative; and provided we make a judicious use of them, and do not too literally interpret them, they are eminently conducive to our instruction, and better calculated to convey correct ideas to our minds than a strictly literal phraseology could have been. So in speaking of that spiritual and supernatural change of heart, which sinners must experience before they can enter into the kingdom of heaven, the Holy Spirit has used the figurative term, regeneration. The man who experiences this change, is said to be born again. Hence it becomes of importance to inquire what are the circumstances that have led to the selection of this metaphor—what points of similarity are there between natural birth, and that change of heart, usually designated regeneration, that the Holy Spirit has thought proper to express the one by language borrowed from the other. There must obviously be some points of resemblance between the natural and the spiritual birth; else the metaphor of the text is used without any propriety. To analyze this metaphor then, by stating some reasons why regeneration may be called a new or a second birth, is what is proposed in this division of the subject.

1. In illustration of the figure in the text, I remark, in the first place, that regeneration may be called a second birth, because it is the commencement of our spiritual existence. As by natural birth we are introduced into the natural world, and commence our natural lives; so by our spiritual birth, or by regeneration, we are introduced into the spiritual world, and begin to live a new and spiritual life.

The commencement of existence seems to be the principal idea which we attach to the period of our birth. When we turn our eye backwards through the years of youth and infancy, and fix our attention on the period of our introduction into the world, we overlook in a great measure the other circumstances that accompanied that event, and allow our whole thoughts to be engrossed with the idea, that then we began to live, when we entered upon that state of conscious existence, separated from which we cannot conceive of even the possibility of felicity. During the years that preceded our birth, where were we, or what were we? Sleeping in the dark and barren womb of non-existence, "the worm's inferiors, and in rank beneath the dust we tread on," we had no knowledge of any thing, yea, we ourselves were nothing, for the creating power of God had not yet called us into being. The material particles which now constitute our bodies, were not yet separated from the dust of the earth on which we tread, and our immortal spirits were not yet given us by the all-creating hand of God. No sooner, however, did the almighty power of Him who quickeneth the dead, and calleth those things that be not as though they were, quicken us into being, and separate us from our mother's womb, than we started from nothing into life, began to live, and move, and think, and act; and ever since, from that period to this, we have formed part of God's animated and rational creation, have drunk the pleasures of the golden day, and triumphed in the consciousness of existence. Such are the sentiments which pass through our minds, when we reflect on that immense change in our state, which took place at natural birth, and with feelings very similar to these, does the renewed man contemplate the period of his regeneration. Previous to that period he was lying sunk under the power of sin, encompassed with a worse than Egyptian darkness, and as totally destitute of spiritual existence as the child unborn. In a natural point of view, he was alive and active, but with respect to the spiritual life of faith, and love, and hope, and trust in God, and cordial obedience to his law, the pulse of his heart had not begun to beat. Motionless, and still at the silence of the tomb, dark as the chaos, "ere the infant sun had shed his beams athwart the gloom profound," his soul slumbered in spiritual death; not a single ray of the light of God's salvation had visited his understanding, nor a single, act of acceptable obedience to the will of God proceeded from his heart. A ruling and innate depravity kept all the faculties of his soul enslaved to the service of sin. As a creature supremely devoted to the glory of its Creator, and consecrating all its powers to his service, he was a blank in the creation of God, his heart was wholly set in him to do evil, and he possessed as little fitness for any actings of spiritual life as if it had had no existence. No sooner, however, did the happy day of regeneration arrive, and the Holy Spirit began the good work of grace in his heart, than these old things completely passed away, and all things became new. To use the emphatic language of scripture, he passed from death unto life, the enmity of his heart against God and his gospel was slain; his soul, quickened by the invincible energy of Divine grace, became spiritually alive, and he entered upon a new species of existence, as a child of God in a state of vital union to the Lord Jesus Christ, and manifesting the power of those principles of abiding holiness, which had been implanted in his heart, in a life of communion with God, and devotedness to his glory. The preceding part of his life, in which he wrought the will of the flesh, he regards as having been wholly lost, yea, worse than lost, misspent and abused. The day of regenerating grace he regards as the happiest that he ever saw, and second in importance only to that which shall, ere long, deliver him from the remaining power of sin, and introduce him into eternal glory. That new and spiritual life, into which he then entered, includes, in his esteem, everything that is desirable; without it, life itself, "this intellectual being, those thoughts that wander through eternity," would have been a curse rather than a blessing, a state of continued death rather than anything worthy of the name of life. In consequence of this new birth, however, he is become spiritually as well as naturally alive; he lives a life of faith on the Lord Jesus Christ; lives in the favour and the image of God, and will live through all eternity in his presence in heaven.

This commencement of a new and spiritual life, which takes place at regeneration, is perhaps the most, obvious, and, therefore, the best reason that can be mentioned why regeneration may be called a new or a second birth. It is, however, by no means the only one, and we proceed to remark, that,

2. Regeneration may be called a second birth, because it occupies the same place in the covenant of grace, that natural generation does in the covenant of works. As by being born, in a natural sense, we enter into the number of the seed of the first Adam, and become, involved in the guilt of his disobedience: so by being born again, we enter among the seed of the second Adam, and obtain an interest in the justification that is through his righteousness.

In both the covenants that God entered into for conveying happiness to the human race, he has acted upon the representative system. Our great progenitor, Adam, was immediately after his creation, constituted the federal representative of his posterity, and had both his own confirmation in a state of happiness, and that of his posterity, suspended on the condition of his perfect and persevering obedience. This condition of the covenant, however, he failed to fulfill, and his disobedience has entailed a sentence of condemnation and death on the whole of his natural offspring. "By one man's disobedience," says the Apostle, "many were made sinners. By the offence of one judgment has come upon all men to condemnation." As they come successively into existence, the curse of the broken covenant takes hold of them, subjecting them to guilt, and binding them over to punishment. No sooner is a man born than he becomes a child of the first Adam, and an heir of that guilt and condemnation which his disobedience entailed upon his posterity. Our introduction into the covenant of works is not delayed, till we have committed actual sin, or are grown up to years of maturity. We are born in a relation to it, and hence we are said to be by nature children of wrath, to be transgressors from the womb, and to be shapen in iniquity, and conceived in sin. Natural generation, then, according to the constitution of the covenant of works, is the appointed means of transmitting the blessing or the curse from the head to the members: had Adam fulfilled the condition of that covenant, we would all by natural birth have been introduced into a state of holiness and confirmed felicity, as we now are into one of a contrary character. Jesus Christ, the second Adam, is in like manner the federal representative of his spiritual seed. In their name he contracted to fulfill the condition of the covenant, of grace from everlasting; in their room he obeyed the law's precept, and endured its curse by his obedience unto the death in our nature, and for them he has wrought out a title to those blessings which they lost in the first Adam. Natural generation, however, is not the medium of introduction into the covenant of grace, and installment into its blessings, as it is with respect to the covenant of works. By being born, we are brought into a state, by condemnation through the disobedience of the first Adam, and we must be born again before we can obtain an interest in the justification that is through the righteousness of the second. It is by regeneration that our federal connection with the first Adam is dissolved, and a vital union to the Lord Jesus Christ commenced. By being born again, we become children in the family of God, members of Christ's mystical body, and heirs of eternal glory. Regeneration thus holds a similar place in the covenant of grace, that natural generation does in the covenant of works. As by being born, in a natural sense, we become the children of fallen Adam, and heirs of the curse of the broken covenant of works: so by being born again, we are made branches of that living vine, the Lord Jesus Christ, and obtain an interest in the blessings of the covenant of grace. By natural birth we are the seed of the first Adam; by regeneration, we are made the children of the second: by being born, we are the children of the god of this world, and heirs of eternal misery; by being born again, we become the sons of God, by faith in Christ Jesus, and heirs of his heavenly kingdom. The moment we are born in a natural sense, the curse of the covenant of works takes hold upon us, subjecting us to condemnation. But the moment we are born in a spiritual sense, the blessings of the covenant of grace become ours, and there is no more any condemnation, because we are in Christ Jesus. God then makes an everlasting covenant with us, ordered in all things and sure, and bestows upon us such rich blessings and exalted privileges, as that we may justly say concerning it, it is all our salvation, and all our desire.

3. A third reason why regeneration is called a second birth may perhaps be found in the completeness and comparative instantaneousness of the change. As by natural birth we are not brought partially, but wholly, into existence, possessed of all the members of body and powers of mind, that distinguish us at perfect manhood: so in regeneration, the new creature is completely formed, all the faculties of the soul are renewed, and all the graces of the Christian life

implanted. The holy scriptures give not the least countenance to the idea of a partial regeneration—*of the commencement in any instance of a work of grace, which is never brought to perfection.* As in a natural sense we have either been wholly born, or not at all; so in a spiritual sense there is no medium between a state of nature and a state of grace; between being converted and unconverted; between being a believer and an unbeliever; a child of God, and a child of the devil. As a new born infant possesses in miniature all the members of body and powers of mind of a full grown man, so the child of God that has been really born again possesses in his soul the seeds of all the graces and attainments of the most advanced Christian, though they be not yet so fully developed, nor have attained the same maturity and perfection in their exercise. As a child, too, however weak in infancy, gradually gathers strength till it attains the full vigor of manhood: so the principles of grace in the believer's heart are weak at first, but fed by the sincere milk of the word, he grows thereby, nourished by the greater than maternal care of the Redeemer. He increases in spiritual stature, till he comes unto a perfect man, unto the measure of the stature of the fullness of Christ. Hence, it is stated as the character of the righteous man, that is, of all who are truly born again, that he "shall flourish like the palm tree, and grow like the cedar in Lebanon; those that be planted in the house of the Lord, shall flourish in the courts of our God; they shall still bring forth fruit in old age; they shall be fat and flourishing." Yes, every real child of God is vitally united to the Lord Jesus Christ, and engrafted into him as a branch in the living vine, so that he cannot but grow and flourish. With occasional backsliding he may, indeed, be chargeable. At times his soul may be in a barren and withered state, but kept as he is by the power of God through faith unto salvation, he can never fall finally away, and his course shall in the main be progressive. "The righteous shall hold on his way, and he that hath clean hands shall wax stronger and stronger. The path of the just is as the shining light, which shineth more and more unto the perfect day."

4. Regeneration may be compared to a birth, because it is a change in which we are *wholly passive*. As the infant possesses no power, and exerts no efficiency to bring himself into existence; so the soul in regeneration is brought from a state of nature into a state of grace, not by its own power, but, by the supernatural agency of the Spirit of God. Fallen man is naturally in a state of spiritual death, all the powers of his soul are enslaved to sin, and he possesses neither disposition nor ability to deliver himself from that state. Except, then, Divine grace interpose to work deliverance for him, he must remain forever in the guilt and depravity of a natural state, and go on in the practice of sin, ripening himself more and more for destruction. As soon may the child unborn bring itself into its new state of existence, by an exertion of its own powers, as the unrenewed soul throw off the chains of its spiritual bondage, and commence in good earnest the practice of genuine holiness.

In mentioning this circumstance as a point of resemblance between natural birth and regeneration, it is proper to state that we consider it as an inference which may be fairly drawn from the metaphor in the text, rather than a reason which led to its selection. There are several other metaphors employed in scripture to express that change of heart visually denominated regeneration, which suggest the idea of our being passive in the production of this change, still more strongly, perhaps, then, the one before us. But a circumstance, it is obvious, which applies equally to several figures, cannot have given rise to the selection of one of these in preference to the rest. Still, however, the idea that regeneration is effected by a higher agency than our own, is so strongly and so obviously implied in the metaphor before us, that if the idea was not intended to be conveyed by it, the figure is incorrect and strongly calculated to mislead. The truth of this remark is much confirmed by the consideration, that there are several other figures used in scripture to express that saving change which the Holy Spirit works in the heart in the day of regeneration, which all harmonize with this one in teaching, that we are passive in the production of that change, and that there is not one which gives the least countenance to the opposite doctrine. Thus it is compared to the quickening of a dead body, or the raising of a dead man to life, to the opening of a blind man's eyes, to the stupendous and supernatural work of creation. It is called a taking away of the old heart, and giving a new one in its place. All these figures obviously suggest that regeneration is a change which we cannot accomplish by our own power; so that if this idea was not intended to be conveyed by them, it is altogether impossible to account, for so frequent a use of these figures. No impartial mind can attentively consider the uniform language of scripture on this subject, without being impressed with the idea that the Holy Spirit has purposely chosen such figures, and such alone, as imply the doctrine of our being passive in regeneration. Hence, this doctrine must be admitted as a part of the truth of the Divine word, and entitled to our cordial reception. This, then, is a striking point of resemblance between the natural and the spiritual birth, that they are both accomplished by a power superior to our own, and that we are ourselves passive in their production.

It were easy to mention several other

circumstances in which there is some kind of resemblance between natural birth and regeneration; but as we conceive it would be very improper to pursue a parallel of this kind too far, and as, in explaining metaphorical language, it is much better to fix upon a few of the leading ideas, than to trace points of fancied agreement, which often serve no other purpose than a display of ingenuity, those that have been mentioned shall suffice.

III. We proceed, then, to the last division of the subject, which was to mention some reasons why regeneration is absolutely necessary to salvation. Why is it that our Lord so emphatically declares, that no man, except he be born again, can ever see the kingdom of God?

By the kingdom of God in the text, some suppose the kingdom of grace to be meant, and accordingly understand our Lord as here stating to Nicodemus an essential requisite of admission into the gospel church; as if he had said, *No man who is not born again, by having his soul renewed by the power of the Holy Ghost, can be a true member of the gospel church, or have a real interest in the privileges of that spiritual kingdom which I am about to erect in the world.* By this expression, others suppose the kingdom of glory to be meant, and understand our Lord as here speaking to Nicodemus about the everlasting salvation of his soul: Except a man be born again, he can never get to heaven, or enjoy eternal happiness in the world to come. Were I under the necessity of adopting one of these opinions, to the exclusion of the other, I would unquestionably prefer the latter; for it is principally of the kingdom of eternal glory in heaven of which our Saviour speaks. The two views, however, are perfectly consistent with one another, and both may be considered as included. Without regeneration, we can neither be real members of Christ's spiritual kingdom upon earth, nor partakers of eternal glory in heaven. Unregenerated persons may indeed be members of the visible church, and have a name to live among the saints of God; but to the privileges connected with the invisible church, that spiritual kingdom which Christ erects in the hearts of his people, and which consists not in "meat and drink, but in righteousness, and peace, and joy in the Holy Ghost," they are entire strangers. Between an interest in Christ's kingdom of grace here, and an inheritance in the Kingdom of glory hereafter, there is an inseparable connection. None but those that obtain an interest in the kingdom of grace in this world, can inherit the kingdom of glory in the next; and all who are introduced into the kingdom of grace in this world, shall, without fail, be kept in it, and brought to the kingdom of glory in due time. By the kingdom of God, mentioned in the text, then, I understand primarily a state of grace and communion with God in this world, but ultimately and chiefly the enjoyment of eternal glory in the world to come. And:

1. I remark, in general, that without regeneration there is no true holiness, no acceptable worship of God, nor cordial obedience to his law. "Holiness," it is said, "becometh the house of the Lord forever." Holiness is the character of all the members of Christ's spiritual kingdom, and without holiness no man can see the Lord, either in a life of communion with him here, or in the full enjoyment of him hereafter. The very design of God in the work of redemption, was to deliver his people from the reigning power of sin, and to bring them back to the love and practice of true holiness. Hence, he is said to have "chosen them from the foundation of the world, that they might be holy." Hence, too, Christ is said to have given himself for them, that he might "redeem them from all iniquity, and purify unto himself a peculiar people, jealous of good

works." Man was originally created holy and happy, and possessed of both inclination and ability to glorify his Creator, by yielding obedience to his law, and paying him the homage of a spiritual and rational worship. By sin, however, man has cast off his allegiance to God, and disqualified himself for answering the great ends of his being. Now, the main design of the work of redemption by Christ, is to undo the effects of the fall, by bringing man back to the worship and the obedience of his Creator. But without regeneration, how can any of these ends be obtained? Man's carnal mind is naturally enmity against God, and is not subject to the law of God, neither indeed can be. The imaginations of the thoughts of his heart are only evil continually. His original apostasy has infected all the faculties of his soul with the taint of moral impurity, so that, his whole head is sick and his whole heart faint. His whole nature is defiled, and enslaved to the service of sin. His affections are alienated from the life of God, his understanding darkened, his conscience seared, his heart callous and unfeeling, yea deceitful above all things, and desperately wicked. While remaining in such a state it is impossible for a man to perform a single spiritually good action, far less to glorify his God and Saviour, by studying universal obedience to his law, and offering to him that homage and adoration which are his due. A fountain so poisoned as man's heart naturally is, can send forth nothing but polluted streams: a tree so corrupt can bear nothing but corrupt fruit. "Unto the pure," says the apostle Paul, "all things are pure; but unto them that are defiled and unbelieving, is nothing pure, but even their mind and conscience is defiled," Tit. i. 15. Nothing, then, can be more obvious, than that if ever man is to be brought back to a capacity for glorifying his Creator, by a life of obedience to his law, and the study and practice of true holiness, his nature must undergo a moral renovation: the leading inclinations of his soul must be changed, the old heart must be taken away, and a new heart given him, or, in other words, he must be born again. Unless he experience a change of this kind, he can never perform a single work characterized by true holiness, nor offer any acceptable worship unto God. The best work of unregenerated men accordingly are always spoken of in scripture as participating of the impurity of the polluted fountain from which they flow, and altogether unacceptable to God. "The sacrifice of the wicked," says Solomon, Prov. xv. 8, "is an abomination to the Lord, but the prayer of the upright is his delight." The common secular actions of unrenewed men may seem to us, if not characterized by extraordinary virtue, to be at least innocent and harmless, and free of vice. In the sight of God, however, who searches the heart, and sees the corrupt principle from which they flow, they appear in a very different light, for the very "plowing of the wicked is sin," Prov. xxi. 4. The Scribes and Pharisees of old were much distinguished for works of apparent piety and virtue: they fasted often, made long prayers, and were generally venerated by the great body of the people as men of extraordinary piety. Their hearts, however, had never been savingly changed, and their hollow pretences are accordingly exposed by our blessed Redeemer, and condemned in the severest, terms: "Woe unto you, Scribes and Pharisees, hypocrites! for ye are like unto whited sepulchers, which indeed appear beautiful outward, but are within full of dead men's bones, and of all uncleanness. Even so ye also outwardly appear righteous unto men, but within ye are full of hypocrisy and iniquity. Ye serpents, ye generation of vipers, how can ye escape the damnation of hell?" Mat. xxiii. 27, 28, 33. I wish these words, my friends, to be impressed on your minds, for they are as applicable to all in every age who assume the appearance of religion, while they do not feel its power in their hearts, as they were to the ancient Pharisees. It will be denied by none, that the sacrifices, and other rites of the ceremonial law, were of Divine institution; and that, when attended unto in the spirit of faith, and from a conscientious regard to the Divine authority that instituted them, they were acts of worship that were well pleasing to God: yea, as acceptable to him as the less pompous and more spiritual services of Christians under the gospel. Mark, however, in what strong language he declares his disapprobation of these ceremonies, when his professing people attended upon them from corrupt motives, and without proper principles of holiness in their hearts. "To what purpose," says he, in Isaiah i. 11-14, "is the multitude of your sacrifices unto me? saith the Lord: I am full of the burnt offerings of rams, and the fat of fed beasts; and I delight not in the blood of bullocks, or of lambs, or of he-goats. Bring no more vain oblations; incense is an abomination unto me; the new-moons and sabbath, the calling of assemblies, I cannot away with; it is iniquity, even the solemn meeting. Your new-moons and your appointed feasts my soul hateth: they are a trouble unto me; I am weary to hear them." In Amos v. 21-23, he speaks in similar and equally strong language, "I hate, I despise your feast-days, and I will not smell in your solemn assemblies. Though ye offer me burnt-offerings, and your meat-offerings, I will not accept them; neither will I regard the peace-offerings of your fat beasts. Take away from me the noise of thy songs: for I will not hear the melody of thy viols." Such, my friends, is the language in which God rejects our religious services, when we engage in them from unsanctified motives, or with a reigning love to sin in our hearts. Think on this circumstance, and learn the necessity of regeneration. Unless we are born again, our best works are an abomination in the sight of God: our prayers and praises, and religious worship, are the smoke of a strange fire in his nostrils; he cannot accept our persons, nor be pleased with our gifts. Our corrupt hearts within us are a poisoned fountain, continually bubbling up every vain and carnal thought—every impure and ungodly desire. The impurity of our hearts affects the works of our hands, and all that we do is polluted. Having purer eyes than to behold iniquity, God regards us with infinite abhorrence. Into his kingdom of grace upon earth he cannot admit us, for all the members of this spiritual society are holy persons, constantly employed in offering up spiritual sacrifices, holy and acceptable to God; and as little will he allow us to enter into his kingdom of glory in heaven. "I know you not whence ye are," shall be the dreadful language in which he shall address every unregenerated sinner at the day of judgment, "depart from me, all ye workers of iniquity."

2. Regeneration is indispensably necessary to salvation; because without it we can have no justifying righteousness—no interest in the atonement of Christ, the only means of deliverance from the wrath of God on account of sin, and the only medium of access to the Father.

It is the unequivocal and uniform doctrine of scripture, that it is only through means of the atoning blood and meritorious righteousness of the Lord Jesus Christ, that sinners can be delivered from that state of condemnation into which they have been brought by sin, and restored to the favour of God. Than Jesus, we are expressly told, there is none other name given, under heaven or among men, whereby we must be saved. Had he not pitied us in our low estate, and in the exercise of a love and condescension which fill heaven and earth with astonishment, undertaken to satisfy the demands of Divine justice in our room, the whole human race must have remained forever under the wrath of God, and been subjected through all eternity to that tremendous punishment which awaits impenitent transgressors in the world to come. The essential justice of the Divine nature which leads God as necessarily to punish sin as does his holiness to hate it, the general interests of his moral universe which forbade him to pardon guilty men in a way calculated to encourage his other creatures in the hope of sinning impunity, and the honour of his righteous law, which he had expressly sanctioned with the threatening of death for every transgression, all concurred to render it necessary for the Lord of glory to shed his precious blood, before an individual of our fallen race could be saved. In consequence of what he hath done and suffered, however, all these various claims have been satisfied, and a foundation has been laid for our being saved in a manner every way consistent with the glory of the Divine character. His blood is emphatically said to cleanse from all sin. It possesses sufficient merit, had God so appointed it, to have redeemed the whole human race from the effects of their transgression.

But since it is only a part of mankind that obtain salvation through the death of Christ, what, it will be asked, is the medium by which they come to obtain an interest in it? by what means are they made to differ from other men, and brought to participate the blessings of that salvation which Christ has wrought out? To this important question, we simply answer, it is by the exercise of a saving faith, and this faith flows from regeneration. Those who are born again, and embrace the Lord Jesus Christ by a saving faith, are clothed with his justifying righteousness, and obtain an interest in all the blessings of his salvation; while those who are not born again, remain in all the guilt and depravity of a natural state, and are as much the objects of Divine displeasure, as if Jesus had never died. The atoning efficacy of the Redeemer's blood, and the justifying merit of his righteousness, are imputed to none but those who have their natures changed, and the grace of faith implanted in their hearts, "he that believeth in the Son, hath everlasting life; and he that believeth not the Son, shall not see life: but the wrath of God abideth on him." The death of Christ has opened to guilty men, a sure and patent way into God's heavenly kingdom. Now, regeneration is the gate which stands at the head of this way, so that, if we do not enter by this gate, we can neither be found walking in the way of life, nor ever reach the happiness to which it leads. All those, therefore, who flatter themselves with the hope of entering into the kingdom of God without being born again, are in a sad delusion. If without an interest in Christ, then: can be no salvation; and if without regeneration, there can be no interest in Christ; then all who live and die in an unregenerated state, must be pronounced "without Christ, aliens from the commonwealth of Israel, strangers from the covenants of promise, having no hope, and without God in the world." Having no covering but the rags of their own righteousness to shelter them from the storms of God's vindictive justice, they must be found defenseless, and exposed in the day that God arises to judgment, and summons the world before him, that he may render to every man according to his works. Those that have been born again, and taken shelter under the cover of the Redeemer's blood, may meet God at the judgment seat without dismay; for though their own righteousness be as the filthy rags, in the Savior's righteousness they stand complete, and no evil can come nigh them. The unregenerated, however, having no interest in the Mediator's justifying righteousness, and appearing at the judgment seat in the naked deformity of their own character, shall assuredly be overtaken by the storms of Divine vengeance, and driven away in their wickedness into everlasting perdition. "Upon the wicked," says the Psalmist, xi. 6, "God shall rain snares, fire, and brimstone, and an horrible tempest: this shall be the portion of their cup."

3. Regeneration is indispensable to salvation, because the holiness of God necessarily excludes all unsanctified persons from his presence, and renders it impossible for any unclean thing to enter the new Jerusalem. In a former remark, we showed the necessity of regeneration to true holiness. Now, taking the connection between regeneration and holiness for granted, we proceed to show, more particularly, the necessity of holiness to salvation. "Without holiness," says the apostle, Heb. xi. 14, "no man shall see the Lord." God is himself a being of infinite holiness, and he requires his people to be holy as he is holy, before he allows them to enter his heavenly kingdom, or admit them to the enjoyment of himself. It is a necessary consequence of the essential holiness of his nature, that he is infinitely opposed to sin, and cannot but hold it in utter abhorrence. "O do not that abominable thing that I hate," is his own language concerning it. He is of purer eyes than to behold evil, and cannot look upon iniquity. "Thou art not a God that hast pleasure in wickedness," is the language in which the Psalmist describes his character; "neither shall evil dwell with thee. The foolish shall not stand in thy sight; thou hatest all the workers of iniquity; thou shalt destroy them that speak leasing; the Lord will abhor the bloody and deceitful man," Psalm v. 4-6. Now, if we consider that an unregenerated state is equivalent to one of deep moral

pollution and depravity, we must immediately perceive that it is altogether impossible for God to admit any who have not been born again, either into communion with himself here, or to the full enjoyment of him hereafter. Even though we could suppose the claims of his vindictive justice to be set aside, and his appointment of Christ as the only Saviour, and of regeneration as the means of an interest in him, to place no barrier in their way; still the very circumstance that he is holy, and they sinful, must keep them forever at an infinite distance, and debar them from the heavenly felicity. To unsanctified sinners, a holy God is necessarily a consuming fire. We cannot, my friends, enter into the kingdom of heaven in an unregenerated state, because the holiness of God forbids it. Shall he in whose eyes the heavens themselves are not clean, and who chargeth his angels with folly, admit into the enjoyment of himself a creature whose heart is filled with enmity against him, and whose whole character exhibits nothing but one unvaried mass of corruption? No, the new Jerusalem is the holy city into which there shall in no wise enter anything that defileth, or anything that worketh abomination, or maketh a lie. The tribes of the redeemed, that throng its golden streets, are all completely holy; it has been given to them all before they reached that blessed place, to be arrayed in fine linen, clean and white; they have all washed their robes, and made them white in the blood of the Lamb; their natures regenerated by his grace, while in this world, and freed at death from all remaining corruption, have become holy, as he is holy: hence he admits them into his immediate presence, and into that communion with himself, in which the chief happiness of heaven consists. To the eternal felicity of every unregenerated, unsanctified soul, then, that holiness which is as necessary to God as his existence, opposes an insuperable obstacle: either he must cease to be holy, or they cannot be happy in his presence.

4. Those who are not born again cannot see the kingdom of God, because they are altogether unqualified for entering into it: they could not be happy in heaven even though they were admitted there.

The exercises and enjoyments of heavenly beings all of a holy nature, must be altogether unsuited to the depraved propensities of an unrenewed mind. The blind, we know, can see no beauty in colors, nor the deaf derive any pleasure from the harmony of sounds: as little can the mind of man receive gratification from objects which are unsuited to its nature, and contrary to its dispositions. Regenerated persons, in consequence of the principles of the new nature within them, place their chief happiness in the enjoyment of communion with God, and the various holy exercises in which he requires them to engage. In heaven, therefore, where everything around them will be calculated to gratify their desires, they must enjoy the most consummate felicity. Unrenewed men, however, place their chief happiness in the pleasures of sin, and the enjoyments of the world, and have no desire nor relish for the more refined pleasures of communion with God, and the cultivation of holiness. Even though it were possible for them, therefore, to obtain admission into heaven, they would find nothing there to give them happiness. Like a fish of the sea removed from the waters, which nature has appointed for its habitation, and placed upon the dry land; or like a land animal taken from the vital air and sunk to the bottom of the sea; they would be out of their proper element, and could not therefore be happy. The scriptures plainly represent the chief part of the happiness of heaven, as consisting in the immediate enjoyment of God, and the contemplation of his glorious perfections. "Blessed are the pure in heart," says our Saviour himself, "for they shall see God," Mat. v. 8. "It doth not yet appear," says the apostle John, 1 John, iii. 2, "what we shall be; but we know that, when he shall appear, we shall be like him; for we shall see him as he is," but what pleasure, I ask, can such an exercise afford to them whose hearts are alienated from God, and then see nothing lovely in his character? The inhabitants of heaven are described as continually employed in the exalted exercise of praising God: "They rest not day and night, saying, Holy, holy, holy, Lord God Almighty, which was, and is, and is to come," Rev. iv. 8. But is there, I again ask, an unrenewed man in existence, who seriously thinks he could spend a happy eternity in this exercise? Is it possible for those who feel no pleasure in serving God upon earth, and cannot spend a single Sabbath in his service without weariness, to enjoy an exhaustless flow of the most refined pleasures, in praising him through eternity in heaven? No. In their ears, the blessed harmony that reigns among the celestial hosts must be grating discord; their triumphant acclamations of praise, the bursts of a senseless enthusiasm. Think not then, O ye who are destitute of a supreme love to God in your hearts, and strangers to the power of religion, that it is possible for you to spend a happy eternity with God in heaven. Blind and ignorant indeed you must be, if your own consciences do not convince you, that you are altogether unqualified for the enjoyments of that exalted state. "Verily, verily, I say unto you, except a man be born again, he cannot see the kingdom of God."

With a few remarks, by way of application, I shall now conclude this discourse.

1. Since regeneration is indispensably necessary to salvation, that numerous class of men who run on heedlessly in sin, without ever seriously inquiring

whether they have been born again, must be chargeable with indescribable folly. There are vast numbers in the world, even of those who frequently attend the means of grace, that have almost as little concern about their eternal welfare as the beasts that perish: the things of time and sense engross the whole of their attention; and provided they can enjoy the pleasures, or hoard up the wealth, of this world, they seem scarcely ever to spend a serious thought on what shall become of them in the next. The folly and danger of this conduct, there is no language sufficiently strong to describe. If there be any truth in the declaration of my text, or the numerous parallel ones in scripture, such individuals can have nothing before them but hell and everlasting destruction. Yet such is their infatuation, that they are no way alarmed by their danger, and never think of using the means of escape, which the gospel sets before them. Oh! my friends, it is an affecting thought; and in your case it seems to be verified, that the god of this world has blinded the minds of them that believe not, lest the light of the glorious gospel of Christ, who is the image of God, should shine into them. Surely there are no individuals in existence more chargeable with despising the offers of mercy, and neglecting the great salvation, than you are. How then can you escape? As you love your own souls, let me entreat you to continue no longer thoughtless and unconcerned about your salvation; and, for your encouragement, let me remind you, that aggravated as your guilt is, and hardened as your hearts have probably now become, there is still hope in Israel for you. There are indeed some persons of a very hopeless character in the world—some whose hearts are so hardened, through a lengthened course of sin, and a long continued and obstinate rejection of the gospel, that they may almost be said to have outlived their day of grace. All, however, are not of this description; and even to these the door of mercy is still open, and the glad tidings of salvation proclaimed. To every one of my hearers, then, without exception, let me recommend the unsearchable riches of Christ, and hold out that faithful saying, and worthy of all acceptation, that Christ Jesus came into the world to save sinners—the very chief not excepted. The blood of Emmanuel is of infinite value, and cleanseth from all sin. The influences of the Holy Spirit are infinitely powerful, and able to subdue the obduracy of the hardest heart, and to convert it into a heart of flesh. Oh! then, while the offers of mercy are still sounded in your ears, and death has not closed your eyes in everlasting darkness, take these things seriously into consideration, and secure an interest in the kingdom of God before it be too late. Under a deep impression of your danger, and the awful criminality of your past conduct, in turning so long a deaf ear to the offers of the gospel, repair to the throne of grace, and earnestly supplicate God to work a saving change upon your hearts, and to magnify the riches of his free grace, in plucking you as brands out of the burning. You have, indeed, nothing in yourselves to entitle you to so great a blessing, but plead upon the footing of his own gracious promise, when he says, "If ye, being evil, know how to give good gifts unto your children, how much more shall your heavenly Father give the Holy Spirit to them that ask him." Delay not to set about this work in good earnest. The longer you delay, the more will your hearts be hardened, and the more difficult will it become to have them changed. You know not how soon death may overtake you. And even though you should live to an old age, there is no small danger that your long and willful obstinacy under the means of grace, may provoke God to withdraw his Spirit altogether, and give you up to judicial hardness. The severest denunciations of the word of God, let me remind you, are directed against those who have the gospel preached to them, but despise it; who know the truth, but improve it not. You may think that because your present situation is safe and happy, and you see no appearance of immediate danger, that matters will always continue as they are, and that the evil day will never arrive: but, as sure as God is in the heavens, and the scriptures are his infallible word, there is a day coming, when "the Lord Jesus Christ shall be revealed from heaven with his mighty angels, in flaming fire, taking vengeance on them that know not God, and that obey not the gospel of our Lord Jesus Christ." Who are they, think you, that obey not the gospel of Christ? Those, unquestionably, are principally intended, who misimprove the day of grace, and reject the gospel offers of salvation. Well, all who are found guilty of this, "shall be punished with everlasting destruction from the presence of the Lord and the glory of his power, when he shall come to be glorified in his saints, and admired in all them that believe," 2 Thes. i. 7-10. "For those who sin willfully after they have received the knowledge of the truth," it is expressly said, "there remaineth no more sacrifice for sin, but a certain fearful looking for of judgment and fiery indignation, which shall devour the adversaries," Heb. x. 26, 27. Awful, then, beyond description, will be the fate of gospel despisers in the future world: the lot of the idolatrous heathen, who never heard of the gospel, shall be more tolerable than theirs. Beware, then, of living any longer unmindful of the one thing needful. O! be persuaded to attend to the things that belong to your everlasting peace, before they are forever hid from your eyes.

9. Since regeneration is indispensably necessary to salvation, all who flatter themselves with the hope of getting to heaven, while they have not experienced this

saving change, must be in a sad delusion, In my last remark, I addressed that class of men who are sleeping in carnal security, and giving themselves little or no concern about salvation at all. Now I am to address another, and perhaps a still more numerous class, those who profess some attention to eternal salvation, but seek to work it out in a wrong way, founding their hopes of being happy hereafter on false grounds. It is impossible for the intelligent observer of the prevailing religious sentiments of the present day, not to perceive that the greater proportion of mankind build their hopes of salvation upon a different foundation from that revealed in the gospel. Because they lead quiet and inoffensive lives in the sight of men, are useful and respectable members of society, attend generally upon the ordinances of religion, are chargeable with no flagrant immoralities of character, and are esteemed decent and sober people by their fellow creatures, many, very many, seem to think that they cannot but be the favorites of God, and that all must be well with them in the end. To all who hold sentiments of this kind; to all who build their hopes of salvation upon the decency and respectability of their character, or anything short of that sure foundation which God has laid in Zion, I would repeat the words of my text, and earnestly beg them to ponder their meaning: "Verily, verily, I say unto thee, Except a man be born again, he cannot see the kingdom of God." Is it not the plain import of these words, that a thorough and supernatural change of heart is necessary to salvation, and that, therefore, an externally decent character is not sufficient? Be assured then, my friends, that your characters may be highly respectable, and your conduct free from all flagrant vices, and still you may be strangers to the power of true religion, and in danger of everlasting condemnation. To convince you that this is no rash nor ill founded assertion, I propose a single question. Is it not expressly said, that "if any man love not the Lord Jesus Christ, let him be *anathema maranatha?*" and is it not the first and great commandment, that we "love the Lord our God with all our heart, with all our soul, and with all our mind." Now, is the love of God and Christ the supreme and ruling affection of your souls? do you delight to think upon God and Christ? do your hearts warm with love and admiration when you contemplate the inconceivable glory and moral excellence of God's nature, as he is in himself? and do your souls swell with gratitude? and do you call upon all that is within you to bless his holy name, when you think of his great and untainted goodness to you? Does the impression that God, being your creator and preserver, has a sovereign right to your highest esteem and continual obedience; that his all-seeing eye is constantly upon you; and that your present witness will ere long be your righteous Judge; that his great goodness to you in preserving you in life, and supplying your returning wants, and particularly in giving up his only Son to an ignominious death for your salvation, lays you under the strongest obligations to love him in return, and to make his glory the great end of all your actions, does the impression of these things, I say, rest at all times upon your minds, keep your hearts fixed in love to God, and make it your habitual study to obey him in all things? If you can answer these questions in the affirmative, I may address you in words of peace. If, however, your own consciences bear you witness that God is seldom in your thoughts: that you love the world in its pleasures and profits, more than God: that you seldom pray to Him in private, or do so only in a cold and formal manner: then I must tell you that, whatever be your external characters, you want that holiness without which no man shall see the Lord, that you have not been born again; and cannot, therefore, in your present state, enter into the kingdom of God. Deceive not yourselves, then, in this matter of eternal importance. See that your foundation be well laid; and pray to God to keep you from self deception; and rest satisfied with nothing short of a well founded persuasion, that you have felt the power, as well as assumed the form of godliness; and that you have, indeed, experienced that saving change of heart, which connects with an entrance into the kingdom of God.

3. Should there be any in this assembly stirred up to some concern about salvation, but encompassed with darkness and perplexity about the way to obtain it, to them also, I must address a few words. It is a hopeful circumstance, my friends, when any are brought to see their need of salvation, and are stirred up to some concern about it. Satan keeps the generality of the world in such a stupid indifference concerning their spiritual interests, that the thought of a state of happiness or misery after death, seldom enters their minds; and though living in a total forgetfulness of God, and disregard of his law, they never once suspect themselves to be in any danger. Cherish then the good desire of salvation that has been awakened in your minds, and persevere in the use of all appointed means for the attainment of that salvation, after which you inquire. Beware, however, of stopping short too soon, or resting satisfied in anything that does not come up to that saving change of heart of which we have been speaking. Many, upon experiencing some awakenings of conscience under the preaching of the gospel, betake themselves to amendment of life, the regular discharge of religious duties, and greater watchfulness against the commission of sin; and with a partial reformation of this kind, they too often satisfy their consciences, and

deceive themselves, perhaps, to their eternal ruin. Be you on your guard against this ensnaring delusion, into which Satan will do his utmost to beguile you, and rest satisfied in nothing short of a saving change being wrought in your souls. It is true you cannot work this change in yourselves; and this you may be ready to think an insurmountable obstacle in your way: but for your encouragement, let me inform you, that if you persevere in the use of all appointed means, cherish an humble sense of your need of Divine grace to regenerate you, and pray fervently to God for the out pouring of his Holy Spirit, you have no reason to think that this blessing will be withheld. Can anything be plainer than his own gracious words? Think upon them my friends—reduce them to practice, and give not way to despair. "Ask, and you shall receive; seek, and you shall find; knock, and it shall be opened to you." I might suggest many counsels, particularly suitable to those in your circumstances, but shall merely hint the following. Labor diligently to increase your store of religious knowledge, and to make your acquaintance with the gospel way of salvation as correct as possible. For this purpose, read the scriptures in private; wait attentively upon the preaching of the word; and enter into conversation with religious persons, whom you may think worthy of this confidence. This will have the effect of at once enlightening you in the nature of your duty, and keeping the desire of salvation alive upon your minds. Cherish, in a particular manner, a deep sense of your own vileness and unworthiness in the sight of God, and of your total insufficiency to do any good of yourselves. Reflect often upon the number and aggravations of your sins, and how just a thing it would be in God to leave you to perish for over. This frame of mind is particularly pleasing to God, and to it many encouraging promises are directed. "Come unto me, all ye that labor and are heavy laden, and I will give you rest." "To this man will I look, even to him that is poor and of a contrite spirit, and that trembleth at my word." Beware of entertaining hard thoughts of God, or prying unwarrantably into his secret purposes. This is an error into which many fall. Instead of directing their attention to the warrant which the gospel offer gives to sinners in general to believe in Christ, many begin with inquiring into the secret purposes of God, with respect to them, and perplex themselves with doubts, that they are not among the number of the elect. It is beyond doubt, my friends, that the decrees of God are unchangeable, and that they had unalterably fixed not only the final destination, but every circumstance in the lot of every one of us, long before we were born. Still, with the secret purposes of God, as the rule of our conduct, we have nothing to do, and we tread upon forbidden ground if we are in the least discouraged in seeking salvation from the fear that God may have no design to save us. Secret things belong to the Lord; but those only which are revealed belong unto us. The husbandman sows his seed in the spring, without ever perplexing his mind with the thought, whether God may have purposed to give him a crop or not. Yet the decree of God has as unalterably fixed whether such a man's fields shall yield a crop in harvest or not, as it has whether such a man shall be saved or not. To all of you, then, I would say, go and do like the husbandman. Be diligent and persevering in using all the means of salvation, and leave the consequences to God. To every hearer of the gospel, an offer of salvation is made, and with this offer it is their incumbent duty, and ought to be their immediate study, to comply. "Believe in the Lord Jesus Christ, and thou shall be saved." Those who are concerned about salvation, and seek after it in good earnest, I would still farther exhort, to meditate much on the death of Christ, the infinite value of his sacrifice, and his all sufficiency, and willingness as a Saviour. These truths are the grand source of consolation to a returning sinner; and it is chiefly by the instrumentality of meditation upon them, that the Holy Spirit effects a saving change on the heart. And, in the last place, let serious inquirers after salvation be exhorted to be frequent and fervent in the exercise of secret prayer. Implore the exercise of God's pardoning mercy in your behalf; confess to him that ye are poor unworthy sinners, deserving nothing but to perish forever; plead the freeness and the fullness of his sovereign grace, and the great glory it will bring to his own great name, to save such poor and wicked creatures as ye are. In these and similar exercises, persevere in waiting at the footstool of mercy; and if ye do, ye have no reason to fear that God will send you away without a blessing. But O let me remind you, that if, after putting your hand to the plough, ye look back, the consequences may be awful. If, after your present awakenings and resolutions, ye betake yourselves to any other refuge than that set before you in the gospel; or if ye return to your former indifference and unconcern, your guilt will be dreadfully aggravated, and your danger of perishing forever greatly increased.

4. Since regeneration is indispensably necessary to salvation, it must be a matter of the last importance for us all, to ascertain whether we have in reality experienced this saving change or not. Even real saints must be in a very uncomfortable state of mind, if they have not some satisfactory evidence of their regeneration; and for those who are still in a natural state, it must be of the utmost importance that they be driven out of all their false refuges, and made to see what their real character is, that they may be impressed with a sense of their danger, and stirred up to flee from

the wrath to come. To assist all of you, then, in judging whether you have indeed been born again or not, I propose the following criteria, which are only a few out of many which might have been mentioned, and which you are requested to apply to yourselves with impartiality, remembering that your eternal all may depend upon a right solution of the question.

(1.) Do you feel a deep and growing sense of your need of salvation? And do you account the attainment of it the most important of all concerns, and of more value than the whole world? This, though not the only, is always a very hopeful mark of the character of all in whom it is found. The prevailing character of unrenewed men, is a spiritual torpor and listless indifference about salvation, from which neither promises nor threatenings can arouse them. They may experience occasional awakenings, but these, in general, soon subside; so that, though they may sometimes feel a real, and even a deep, they have seldom a permanent concern about salvation on their minds. To you, then, my friends, who see yourselves to be undone forever, without an interest in Christ, and who esteem the salvation of your souls to be the main business of your lives, and would gladly give the whole world, were it in your power, to attain it, I must address myself in words of comfort. Such feelings of mind, and particularly if they are of a growing nature, savor strongly of a gracious work of the Holy Spirit; and though you may at present be filled with doubts, these, it is to be hoped, will, in due time, be removed, and your way become light before you. Cherish, then, the good desire in your minds, despise not the doing of small things; pray fervently to God not to forsake the work of his own hands, and wait patiently in the use of all appointed means, for a full manifestation of his mercy, and confirmed tokens of his love. But again:

(2.) Are you resting all your hopes of salvation on the Lord Jesus Christ, and looking for mercy only in that way which is revealed in the gospel? It will be of little importance that we are earnest in seeking salvation, except we seek it in the way that God commands us in his word. However deep, then, be your concern, or vigorous your exertions, if you are trusting for salvation to your own good works, or anything done or possessed by yourselves, and not to the righteousness of our Divine Redeemer, you are only wearying yourselves in vain, and spending your strength for nought. If, however, you have seen all your own righteousness to be as filthy rags, and your best works to be but an abomination in the sight of a holy God: if you have seen yourselves to be undone forever without Christ, and are convinced, that as he is the only, so he is an all sufficient Saviour; and if you feel a cordial willingness to accept of Christ as your only Saviour, and to be eternal debtors to his free grace for every blessing that you need, then I may safely say to you, ye are not far from the kingdom of God. This is a mark of the new birth, in the application of which one might think there is little room for mistake. The individual who feels his need of salvation, and is seeking it only in that way which the gospel directs— who is convinced that it can be obtained only through the death and righteousness of the Lord Jesus Christ, and is resolved to cast himself into the arms of this Saviour, saying, "If I perish, I perish;" "though he slay me, yet will I trust in him," is one whom the preacher of the gospel is warranted to address in terms of peace. However great, then, my friends, be your doubts and fears about the state of your souls, if ye are directing an anxious eye to the mercy seat, convinced that salvation can come from no other quarter, and determined to wait for it there, be the event what it may, I hesitate not to hail you as the highly favored of the Lord. Those who come to Christ in that humble self denied frame of mind which ye so obviously exemplify, he has promised that he will in no wise cast out. Persevere, then, in seeking salvation through the Mediator's atoning blood, and in casting yourselves at his feet as unworthy sinners, begging an interest, for his own name's sake, in the mercy which he delights to exercise to the poor in spirit, and fear not that in due time he will extend his compassion to you. Wait, then, patiently on the Lord, and be of good comfort. "Weeping may endure for a night, but joy cometh in the morning."

(3.) What are your sentiments with respect to the World? Unrenewed men seek all their happiness in the pleasures of sin and the enjoyments of the world; and could they be assured of enjoying these forever, they would have everything that their hearts could wish. Such men would never have a single wish to go and enjoy God in heaven, could they be permitted to continue in the enjoyment of their sinful pleasures upon earth. It is merely because they know they cannot remain always here, and are afraid of going to hell, that they ever express a single wish to go to heaven. Those that are born again, have seen a vanity and emptiness in all worldly enjoyments, convincing them they are no proper portion for their souls. They look to God, and the eternal enjoyment of him in heaven, as the only source of true felicity; and were they only sure of obtaining this, they could cheerfully part with everything below, that they might go to God, even to God their exceedingly.

(4.) Are you zealous and persevering in the study of holiness, living in the indulgence of no known sin, and the neglect of no known duty? This is a mark of the new birth, for the want of which no other can compensate. Vain is that man's pretension to regeneration, who has still a secret hankering after sin in his heart, deliberately indulges in sinful practices in private, which he would be ashamed to avow in public, and is actuated in the profession which he makes of religion, more by a desire to sustain a good character in the sight of man, than by a disinterested regard to the glory of God. Examine yourselves, then, impartially by this rule, and if you see reason to conclude that you entertain a deep and genuine hatred of sin, a sincere and growing love of holiness, and a desire to be like God; if the workings of inward corruption are a burden to you, and ye are maintaining a perpetual struggle against them; if, even in your darkest seasons, ye cannot think of the commission of sin without horror, and are determined, be the consequences what they may, that ye will never return to the practice of sin, but persevere in keeping all the commandments of God, ye possess what I would consider the most satisfactory of all evidences of regeneration. "He that is born of God doth not commit sin: he cannot sin, because he is born of God."

By these and similar marks, of which you may easily put yourselves in possession, try how matters stand between God and your souls. Supplicate the Holy Spirit to assist you in the work, and to keep you from self deception, and thus endeavor to reduce to practice the apostle's exhortation: "Examine yourselves whether ye be in the faith." I am inclined to think, that some real saints entertain much more gloomy views of themselves than they ought to do, in consequence of confining their attention too much to the unfavorable parts of their character. Such, then, as are of a doubting and fearful disposition, I would particularly exhort to apply such marks of regeneration, as those we have mentioned, to their hearts; and if they find reason to think themselves possessed of them, to dismiss their doubts, and be no longer faithless but believing. God is their friend, though they know it not. Beware, then, my friends, of refusing to receive the testimony of the Holy Spirit, when, by the marks of a work of grace within you, he is bearing witness with your spirits, that ye are the children of God. Your doubts in such circumstances are nothing but the temptations of Satan, or the workings of an evil heart of unbelief, and ought therefore to be immediately dismissed. Lift up, then, the hands that hang down, strengthen the feeble knees, and encourage yourselves in the words of the Psalmist, "Why art thou cast down, O my soul? and why art thou disquieted within me? Hope in God; for I shall yet praise him, who is the health of my countenance, and my God," Psalm xliii. 5.

5. I shall now conclude the discourse with a few words of exhortation to those who have obtained satisfactory evidences of their regeneration. Your privileges, my friends, are inconceivably great, and ought to be frequently contemplated as a ground of encouragement, and as matter of thankfulness. Ye are born again, ye are the children of God, members of the mystical body of Christ, and heirs of the heavenly inheritance. O what unspeakable privileges are those! To sovereign grace, how immense your obligations! How loud your calls to gratitude and praise! Adoring gratitude, and continual praise ought, methinks, to form a part of all the exercises, and characterize the whole life of all confirmed Christians. Reflecting on the inconceivable gulf of misery from which they have been delivered; the high and endless glory to which they hope to be in due time exalted; and the costly price at which their redemption was purchased: they ought continually to be raising their hearts in fervent praise to God, who has so highly favored them, while he has left multitudes around them, by nature no worse than

themselves, to perish forever. Such language as that of the Psalmist, ought to be ever in their hearts, and often in their mouths. "I will praise thee, O Lord my God, with all my heart, and I will glorify thy name forevermore; for great is thy mercy toward me, and thou hast delivered my soul from the lowest hell." "Bless the Lord, O my soul, and all that is within me, bless his holy name. Bless the Lord, O my soul, and forget not all his benefits; who forgiveth all thine iniquities, who healeth all thy diseases, who redeemeth thy life from destruction, who crowneth thee with loving kindness and tender mercies." But your gratitude, my friends, must not evaporate in empty praises. Your new birth, let me remind you, not only entitles you to privileges; it also lays you under obligation to perform duties, and if these duties are neglected, all professions of gratitude will be unavailing. Being redeemed with the precious blood of the Son of God, you are to consider yourselves as no longer your own, but wholly God's, and are, therefore, to devote your time and talents, and all your influence, to the promotion of his glory in the world. Study by a holy deportment and every winning art, to recommend religion to those around you, and in your respective stations do everything in your power to raise up to the Redeemer a seed that shall do him service. Contend faithfully for the purity of his worship, and the interests of his church, and lift up a decided testimony against abounding error and immorality. Watch over the risings of corruption in your own hearts, and strive against them. Be much employed in fervent prayer to God for a blessing on yourselves, the church of Christ, and the generation at large. Thus adorn the doctrine of God your Saviour in all things.

SERMON IV:
On the Atonement

"Behold the Lamb of God which taketh away the sin of the world!"—John i. 29.

THE incarnation of the Son of God is, beyond question, the most wonderful event which this world ever beheld. Whether we consider the infinite dignity of the personage who then made his appearance, or the inconceivable importance of the work which he came to execute, we are led to regard this great event as the central point, towards which the light, reflected from all God's gracious dealings with men from the beginning of the world, directed its converging rays; and from which, again diverging, it will continue to illuminate the world till the end of time. Even before his expulsion from the garden of Eden, the scheme of grace was revealed to fallen man, and in that most comprehensive promise, "the seed of the woman shall bruise the serpent's head," he was directed, to the atonement, to be wrought out by the Son of God, in our nature, as the Divinely appointed medium through which all the blessings of salvation were to be communicated. In the leading promise of the Abrahamic covenant, "in thy seed shall all the families of the earth be blessed," the same person is not less eminently brought to view, and his incarnation represented as the great object of the church's faith and hope. The grand design of the sacrifices and other rites of the Levitical dispensation, was to direct the church's faith forward to the promised Messiah. Divest them of their typical import, and it will be difficult to prove that the pompous ceremonies, observed in the temple of Jerusalem, possessed any specific superiority to the superstitious rites performed by heathen nations, in honour of their imaginary deities. In the writings of all the Old Testament prophets, the person and work of the Messiah is the grand and favorite theme; and it is deserving of remark, that Malachi, the last of these prophets, closes his book with a prediction, that no more inspired messengers from God were to be expected, till that Great One whom all the prophets foretold, preceded by his harbinger, should make his appearance.

During the four thousand years that preceded the birth of Christ, everything had thus been calculated to keep up a constant expectation of his advent; and as the eventful period drew on, the dispensations of Providence thickened around it in interest and importance. Of the preparatory means that more immediately preceded his coming, none is more worthy of notice, than the appointment of John the Baptist to go before him as his forerunner, crying, "Prepare ye the way of the Lord, make straight in the desert a highway for our God." So illustrious was the character of this individual, that it is declared concerning him, by the faithful and true Witness himself, "Verily I say unto you, Among them that are born of women, there hath not arisen a greater than John the Baptist;" yet illustrious in character as he was, he regarded himself as nothing in comparison with Him, whose speedy advent he was sent to announce. "I indeed baptize you with water," was his reply to the multitudes eagerly inquiring who he was; "but there cometh one after me mightier than I, whose shoes' latchet I am not worthy to unloose." If it be a correct way of judging of the rank of a man to look to the dignity of his retinue, we must surely regard him as more than a man, of whom so illustrious a person as John the Baptist bore this testimony. Would we learn then who the extraordinary character is, of whom the prophets have said so much, and for whose appearance so mighty preparations had been made; and would we know what the important purpose was for which he came into the world, listen to the testimony of the Baptist in the words of the text: they contain an answer to both parts of the question. The person is the Lamb of God, and his work is to take away the sin of the world.

We do not at present enter into any discussion concerning the character of the person brought to view in the text, as we design to confine our attention almost entirely to his work. All that we remark, then, concerning the expression, "Behold the Lamb of God," is, that the person meant is unquestionably the Lord Jesus Christ in his mediatorial character, as God and man in one person, and that he receives this name principally in allusion to the sacrificial language of the Old Testament. Various circumstances might indeed be mentioned in which Christ may be said to bear some resemblance to a Lamb, and each of these assigned as a reason for the application of this name to him. But in explaining metaphorical language, it seems much better to confine our attention to the leading idea in the metaphor, than to trace points of fancied resemblance, which, as they are not peculiar to the figure under consideration, but common to it with many others, might be wholly out of the view of the inspired Speaker when he uttered it. Christ then, in our opinion, receives the designation of the Lamb of God, not exclusively nor chiefly, because like that animal, he was meek, and harmless, and gentle, but because he was the antitypical Lamb, or propitiatory victim provided by God to expiate the guilt of a ruined world. In the sacrifices of the Levitical dispensation, the lamb was more frequently offered than any other animal. Hence, its name has been appropriated to express the Messiah, whose death in blood was so often shed to typify. And though the victims under the Old Testament were offered in sacrifice by Divine appointment, they were still provided and offered by man, and might therefore, without impropriety, be called lambs of man. Jesus Christ, however, was a victim of a more valuable nature than could be procured by the hands of man; his eternal designation to his office in the counsel of peace; his being furnished with a human nature in the fullness of time; his consecration to his work, his support under it, and acceptance in it, were all immediately from God himself; so that in distinction from all typical victims, he is here, with great propriety, designated the Lamb of God.

The work ascribed to our Redeemer in the text then, "He taketh away the sin of the world," is to be the subject of our present consideration. Viewing this expression in its most extensive sense, it might be supposed to include both parts of that work which our Lord Jesus Christ performs with respect to sin, namely, the expiation of the guilt of sin by making an atonement for it by his death, and the removal of the pollution of sin or the subjugation of its reigning power in the heart by his word and Spirit. These two parts of the Mediator's work are quite distinct from one another. The one he performed only in his state of humiliation, and completed at his death: The other he has been carrying on in all ages of the church, and it will not be completed till the end of the world. The one he performed exclusively as a priest, when he made his soul an offering for sin, and by his obedience unto the death, finished transgression, made an end of sin, and brought in everlasting righteousness. The other he performs partly as a prophet, but principally as a king, when he pours out the influences of the Holy Spirit from on high, and sends the rod of his strength out of

Zion, making his people willing in the day of his power. Viewing the words of the text in their most extensive sense, I have said, they may be supposed to include both these parts of the Redeemer's work, for they may both be called a taking away of sin. I presume, however, that it is principally to the former of these that the words of the Baptist refer. The original expression, which may be literally read, "he lifteth up, or beareth away the sin of the world," is the same with that commonly used to denote the atoning efficacy that is ceremonially ascribed to the sacrifices of the Levitical dispensation. It seems indeed to contain a pretty strong allusion to the confessing the sins of the whole congregation of Israel over the head of the scapegoat on the great day of atonement, which sins he was said to bear upon him, and to carry away into the wilderness. Now, the typical reference of this rite unquestionably was to Christ's work of making atonement for the guilt of sin, and not so much, if at all, to his work with respect to its pollution, in subduing its reigning power in the heart. Besides, when Christ is introduced as the Lamb of God taking away the sin of the world, it is most natural to understand the work thus ascribed to him as connecting with the character in which he is brought to view, and performed by him in that character.

Now when he is called the Lamb of God, he is plainly introduced in his sacerdotal character, and there is an undoubted reference to his being provided and appointed by the Father as a sacrifice to make atonement for sin. Hence it is more natural to understand the taking away of sin here mentioned, as referring to that work of atonement which he performed as the Lamb of God, than to his other work of subduing the power of sin in the heart, and cleansing the soul from its pollution, which, though performed by

Him who is the Lamb of God, yet is not performed by
Him only as he is the Lamb, but also and rather as he is
King in Zion, and exalted to the Father's right hand to
be a Prince and a Saviour, to give repentance unto
Israel, and forgiveness of sins.

We propose then, in this discourse, to direct
your attention to that fundamental doctrine of the
Christian religion—the atonement; but before
proceeding more directly to the subject, I think it
necessary to explain, in a few words, what is meant by
Christ's making atonement for sin. When we say then,
that our Lord Jesus Christ has taken away the guilt of
sin, by making an atonement for it by his death, all that
can be meant is, that he has thus paid the price of our
redemption from the law and justice of God, or which
comes to the same thing, has removed the legal
obstructions which sin had raised between God and us,
preventing the egress of his pardoning mercy. No
sooner had man cast off his allegiance to God by
transgressing his law, than he became a criminal in the
eyes of Heaven, and deserving of punishment. Nor was
it a matter of indifference with God, whether or not
this punishment was inflicted; there were certain
reasons, on the contrary, arising from the perfections of
his nature, and the interests of his government, which
rendered it inconsistent and improper, and therefore
impossible for him not to inflict it. Had this not been
the case, his infinite benevolence would undoubtedly
have led him to shew mercy to fallen man, and to have
pardoned his sins without an atonement. It was not
then to incline God to exercise mercy to fallen man, but
to render this exercise of it consistent with the holiness
of his nature, and the honour of his law, that Christ
died upon the cross. This was all that it was necessary,
yea, all that was possible for him to do, by way of
making atonement for sin. Upon his removing the

obstructions that previously forbade its egress, pardoning mercy issues forth: upon his performing a work, which renders the punishment of sinners no longer a matter of necessity, God receives them into favour, and reinstates them in their forfeited privileges. What then, it will be asked, are those obstructions which sin had raised between God and man, that Jesus has removed? What, in other words, is that atonement by which the Lamb of God has taken away the sin of the world? To this we reply in the three following remarks.

1. It includes the satisfying of the claims of God's vindictive justice. The justice of God requiring that the sinner be no longer permitted to enjoy the happiness of an innocent creature, but be subjected to a suitable punishment, was the first reason that rendered our salvation without an atonement impossible. The satisfaction of this justice, accordingly, forms the first thing included in that atonement.

That vindictive justice is an essential attribute of the Divine nature, or, in other words, that it is necessary for God to punish sin, is a truth written on the natural conscience of man, and clearly taught in scripture. Of the attributes ascribed to him, by the inspired penmen, justice is mentioned with peculiar emphasis and frequency. In Deut. xxxii. 4, we have the following beautiful verse, "God is the Rock, his work is perfect; for all his ways are judgment: a God of truth, and without iniquity; just and right is he." In Psal. lxxxix. 14, "Justice and judgment" are said to be "the habitation of his throne." In Zeph. iii. 5, He is called "the just Lord in the midst of Jerusalem." In Job xxxvii. 23, He is said to be "excellent in power and in judgment, and in plenty of justice." In Isaiah xlv. 21, his own words are, "I the Lord am a just God, and a Saviour:" and in Rev. xv. 3, the redeemed hosts are represented as exclaiming, "Great and marvelous are thy works, Lord God Almighty just and true are thy ways, thou King of saints." Now, in order to ascertain the meaning of these expressions, we remark that the term *justice* seems to be used in three senses among men, in some of which it must be understood when applied to God. 1. We call that man just who never wrongs any one, nor transgresses the rules of strict justice by the commission of positive injury. This being a mere negative virtue, cannot, we think, be the justice ascribed to God in the above passages. The justice of God is something of a positive nature. Besides, it was altogether unnecessary for the inspired writers to be so often telling, that God never violates the laws which he himself has made, nor capriciously tramples upon the happiness of his creatures when they have given him no provocation. This were something like saying of a person, of whose character we wished to convey a very high idea, that he is no murderer nor adulterer, but one who abstains from all atrocious crimes; which to affirm of a person of established reputation and exemplary virtue, were obviously to disparage rather than to commend him. 2. We call that man just who conscientiously discharges every contracted obligation, and never receives a favour from any one without returning a suitable compensation. This is perhaps the most common meaning of the term justice, when applied to men. But it is easy to see that this cannot be the sense in which it is used with respect to God. For he is infinitely removed above the possibility of being profited by his creatures. So that he can never be called to distribute rewards from the claims of justice, nor to dispense favors, on the ground of benefits received. 3. It remains then, that the term justice, when applied to God, be understood in the third sense in which it is used among men, namely, to point out what is commonly called punitive justice; the justice exercised by the Judge when, without listening to the voice of mercy, he will be prevented by no consideration from awarding to the criminal a punishment suited to his deserts. God is said to be just, because he will not allow sin to pass unpunished, nor the impenitent transgressor of his law to escape with impunity. If God be not just in this sense of the term, I cannot conceive a reason why the inspired writers so frequently and emphatically represent justice as one of the essential attributes of the Divine character.

A number of collateral passages might be quoted to prove that this is indeed the principal thing included in that justice, which the scriptures everywhere ascribe to God. Heb. xii. 29, "Our God is a consuming fire." The design of the apostle, in introducing these words, is to stimulate the Hebrews to the duty of persevering in the faith of the gospel. Should they apostatize, he assured them, and so fall short of an interest in the blood of atonement, their everlasting destruction would be inevitable; for as it is the very nature of fire to consume and destroy all that comes in its way, so is it that of God to punish unbelieving sinners. "Our God is a consuming fire." It is his very nature to be such to every worker of iniquity. In chapter x. 31, of the same epistle, he says, "It is a fearful thing to fall into the hands of the living God." There is something exceedingly emphatic in these words. To fall into the hands of the living God, and to fall into the hands of a God who will not allow our sins to pass unpunished, are evidently represented as the same thing. To punish sin then, is as necessary to God as it is for him to live. Nah. i. 2, "God is jealous, and the Lord revengeth, and is furious; the Lord will take vengeance on his adversaries, and he reserveth wrath for his enemies." Though language of this kind is by no means to be understood as if God felt any turbulent emotions against wicked men; yet, as it is the very disposition of an angry man to seek to wreak his vengeance on the object of his resentment, so it is obviously implied, that it pertains to the nature of God to inflict punishment on impenitent sinners? Nor is the doctrine of God's vindictive justice taught only by abstract statement in the argumentative parts of scripture; it forms part of the prophet's song, and is set before us in the lofty language, and splendid imagery of poetry. "Lebanon," says the prophet Isaiah, chap. xl. 16, "is not sufficient to burn, nor the beasts thereof sufficient for a burnt offering." These expressions are uncommonly grand and strong, but to give a proper idea of their meaning, a short explanation is necessary. Lebanon was a lofty mountain, or rather a range of lofty mountains, on the northern side of the land of Canaan. The valleys among these mountains, and the fields along their sides, were uncommonly fertile, flowing with flocks and herds, and adorned with odoriferous shrubberies, and innumerable vineyards, producing the most delicious wines. Higher up on the mountains grew forests of mighty cedars, and other trees of uncommon size and beauty; so that altogether the stupendous size and extraordinary riches of Lebanon were quite proverbial, and formed one of the strongest images that could be presented to an inhabitant of the land of Canaan. Mark, then, the strength and grandeur of the prophet's words, when he declares, "Lebanon to be insufficient to burn, and the beasts thereof for a burnt offering." Though a sinner, we may understand him to say, wishing to appease the offended majesty of Heaven, and make atonement for his sins, should make choice not of a small artificial mound of stone or earth, but of towering Lebanon itself for his altar; should cut down all the forests that skirt its summits for the pile;

take all its shrubberies and odoriferious gums for incense; all the wine produced by its vineyards for a libation; and all the beasts that feed upon it for a propitiatory sacrifice, all would prove insufficient to turn away the displeasure of a holy God on account of sin, or even to expiate the guilt of a single transgression. The whole stupendous mass would consume to smoke in vain, and be regarded as nothing in the eye of infinite holiness. "Lebanon is not sufficient to burn, nor the beasts thereof for a burnt-offering." We mention only one passage more in proof of this doctrine, and it is one which alone might render all farther proof superfluous. Exod. xxxiv. 7, "The Lord will by no means clear the guilty." Jehovah is here proclaiming his name to Moses, and he dwells with particular fullness on his gracious character: "The Lord, the Lord God, merciful and gracious"—Lest, however, any should abuse this view of his character, as a ground to expect impunity, though living in sin, he assures us in this strong expression, that punitive justice is as essential as mercy to him, "that will by no means clear the guilty."

To place this subject in a still clearer light, and produce an additional argument in its support, let us briefly view sin in its relation to the holiness of God. Holiness, or the love of what is right, and the hatred of what is wrong, none will deny, is an essential attribute of the Divine nature. Wherever sin exists, then, it is the necessary object of God's infinite aversion. "O do not that abominable thing which I hate," is his own language concerning it. "He is of purer eyes than to behold evil, and cannot look upon iniquity." But if God necessarily hates sin, and cannot, without ceasing to be God, cease to hate it, he must also necessarily determine its punishment. His hatred of it cannot be a mere dormant inactive feeling in his mind. In his mind there are no vain inoperative desires. His love of holiness, it will not be denied, is not a mere internal feeling, but an active principle, which universally exerts itself towards its object, in protecting him from suffering, and securing to him the enjoyment of happiness. But if it be necessary for God to protect his innocent subjects, by preserving them in a state of happiness, it must be no less necessary for him to punish the guilty, and subject them to misery. To maintain the one of these positions without the other, appears to me as absurd and inconsistent with correct views of the Divine character, as it would be to say, that God's hatred of sin is less necessary or less intense than love of holiness.

1. From these remarks, we think ourselves warranted to conclude, that it follows, from the very nature of God, that between sin and suffering, between guilt and punishment, there is a necessary and inseparable connection. In the view of the holy mind of God, the infringement of this connection is as abhorrent to his nature as the commission of a sinful action. Some have spoken of the atonement, as if a sovereign act of the Divine will, or at most the honour of the Divine government, in the view of the moral universe, were the sole ground of its necessity. But that necessity has a higher origin. As God is holy, and cannot but hate sin, so he is just, and cannot but punish sin. So irrespective of the interests of the moral universe, in the first instance, is the impossibility of the pardon of sin without an atonement, that had God never brought into existence more creatures than one, and had that one creature sinned, he must either have been punished, or a mediator provided to make atonement for his guilt. When man, then, had cast off his allegiance to God, and wickedly raised the standard of rebellion against his authority, the first obstacle that

stood in the way of his being pardoned and restored to his former privileges, arose from the holy nature of God requiring him to be punished. The removal of this obstruction accordingly, the offering of a sacrifice to satisfy the justice of God or, in other words, the performance of a work, which might maintain the necessary moral connection between sin and punishment, and yet allow the sinner to escape, is the first thing included in that atonement by which the Lamb of God has taken away the sin of the world.

Sin being committed against a God of infinite excellence, and the violation of an infinite obligation, must involve an infinite guilt, and subject to an infinite punishment. Wherever sin is committed, then, God, in order to act a part consistent with the infinite holiness of his nature, must testify his infinite disapprobation of it, by inflicting, on its account, such a punishment as its infinite malignity deserves. If, however, this punishment be inflicted at all, it seems a matter of no essential difference, whether it be borne by the sinner in his own person, or by a surety placing himself in his room, and an undertaking to pay his debt. By the latter method, as well as the former, the justice of God receives satisfaction to the full amount of its claims; and the infinite purity of his character testifies its irreconcilable opposition to sin, as strongly as it could have done by the punishment of the sinner himself. Now this is precisely what has been accomplished, in behalf of our fallen world by the Lord Jesus Christ. *When the sword of Divine justice was unsheathed against us, and our immediate destruction appeared to be inevitable, this illustrious personage, in the riches of his unbounded love, graciously interposed, and warded off the stroke. Being both God and man in one person, he was every way qualified, as the Surety of an elect world, to endure that punishment, which the accumulated guilt of all their innumerable transgressions deserved. The infinite dignity of his person imparted to his mediatorial work an infinite value, and rendered his sufferings, though limited in respect of duration, infinitely efficacious as to merit. By the sufferings, both of body and mind, which he endured during the whole of his life, and particularly by those in the garden and on the cross, the justice of God has been satisfied, the honour of his holiness maintained, and a foundation laid for the salvation of guilty men, in a way perfectly consistent with the glory of all the Divine perfections.* [This is one of the best paragraphs I have ever read in any book on any topic of the atonement. CMM]

On this view of the atonement, as consisting primarily in a propitiatory sacrifice, offered up to the justice of God, we have dwelt the longer, because it is one against which the carnal mind has strong objections, and which there seems to be a considerable disposition in the present age to overlook. Here we have its necessity, in order to maintain the honour of the law and moral government of God in the view of his rational creatures, spoken of by some who keep the essential justice of God entirely out of view. Such a partial representation of this all important doctrine appears to us extremely exceptionable. In the fifth place, it gives an imperfect and distorted view of the perfections of the Divine character, and thus materially affects our conceptions of the Object of worship. It tends to lower our ideas of the infinite purity of his nature as opposed to sin, by exhibiting him as having no objection to dispense with its punishment, were it not for the sake of his creatures, who might thence be led to encourage themselves in sin, from the hope of impunity. And, in the second place, it is inconsistent with sound and scriptural views of the atonement itself. In scripture it is expressly stated, that "Christ gave himself for us, an offering and a sacrifice to God;" that "he reconciled us to God by his death;" and that

"God has by Christ; reconciled us to himself." But if the honour of the Divine law and government, in the view of the moral universe, was the only, or even the chief reason, that rendered the atonement necessary, it was not properly to God at all, but rather to the interests of his creatures, that the sacrifice upon the cross was offered, and that Christ reconciled us by his death. Even in human governments, the opinion that the punishment of criminals is merely for the good of society, is liable to insurmountable objections. There is something in the unalterable relations of right and wrong, as written even on the natural conscience, that connects punishment with crime, altogether irrespective of the interests of society. Should the murderer, for example, bury the blood which he had shed under the earth, then wash his hands, return to society, and never commit another crime, the interest of society, it is obvious, could suffer nothing by his escaping with impunity; but will any maintain, that he ought, on this account, to be exempted from punishment? No: The sacred law of justice, proclaimed by the authority of God, and written on the conscience of man, is, "Whosoever sheddeth man's blood, by man shall his blood be shed." In the Divine government, in like manner, that which is morally right is the primary consideration, and that, which is profitable or expedient is only a secondary one. Even though the interests of the universe, then, had suffered nothing from the gratuitous pardon of sin, still the justice of God would have rendered an atonement necessary. Besides, if the honour of his government, in the view of his creatures, was the only reason why God would not pardon sin without satisfaction, why did he require and provide an atonement of infinite value? he might surely have found some easier method of preventing his other subjects from abusing the exercise of mercy to fallen man as an encouragement to sin, than the giving up of his only Son to such tremendous sufferings as those which he endured. Is it, to say nothing more, a reasonable supposition, that so glorious a person as the eternal Son of God, should leave the realms of glory above, descend, in circumstances of the deepest humility, to our world, live a life of sorrow, and we endure the reproaches and persecutions of ungodly men, the most furious assaults of the powers of darkness, the pains of an ignominious death, and the wrath of God itself, all for no higher purpose than to inform the remaining subjects of Jehovah's empire that his laws were not to be violated with impunity? Surely the interest of the universe, which at most is but a finite end, could not in the eyes of infinite wisdom be a sufficient reason for shedding the infinitely precious blood of the Son of God. If punitive justice be an essential attribute of God's nature, which he can as little cease to exercise as cease to be God, not a drop of Christ's blood has been shed in vain: Infinitely precious as it is, our salvation could not be purchased at a lower price. But how it was worthy of God to demand and provide an infinite atonement, when a finite object was all that was to be accomplished, is a difficulty, we conceive, which all the ingenuity of man can never solve.

It cannot be denied, that this view of the atonement, as a satisfaction of the essential justice of God, is one on which there rests much mystery. What pleasure, our presumptuous minds are ready to ask, could God take in the blood of his own Son, that he should require it to be shed, before he would allow sin to be pardoned? What has the atonement done to God, that in view of it, he has declared his willingness to save fallen sinners, whom he would otherwise have consigned to endless perdition? These are questions, to which we profess not to return a direct answer. But to check the presumptuous spirit, that thinks every mystery attaching to a doctrine an objection against the doctrine itself, we remark, that the same questions may he asked, with equal plausibility, concerning the eternal punishment of the wicked. What pleasure can God take in the misery, the eternal misery, of this hopeless portion of his creatures?—what do their sufferings do to him, that he will by no means dispense with their infliction? To this we can only answer, that there is a moral connection between guilt and punishment, which cannot be dissolved. It is as much the nature of God to be just, as to be wise, holy, or merciful, and therefore sin must be punished. The eternal misery of the wicked can indeed add nothing to the happiness of God; neither has the utmost ingenuity been able to discover sufficient reasons for its necessity in the moral interests of the universe. The only satisfactory ground of its necessity, is the justice of God connecting guilt with punishment, by an unalterable law of moral rectitude. The sufferings of our Lord Jesus Christ, in like manner, though strictly speaking they could do nothing to God, were still necessary to satisfy the claims of his vindictive justice, and to maintain that necessary moral connection between sin and punishment, which, being founded on the moral nature of God, is as immutable as his immutable perfections. By pouring out his soul unto death, our Lord Jesus Christ has satisfied the claims of God's essential justice, and thus removed the first and the grand obstruction which stood in the way of our salvation. "Behold, then, the Lamb of God, which taketh away the sin of the world."

2. A second thing included in that atonement, by which the Lamb of God taketh away the sin of the world, is the vindication of the law and government of

God in the view of his intelligent creatures. In providing salvation for guilty men, God is not to be viewed merely as an absolute sovereign, raising up one and putting down another at pleasure; he bears the farther character of the Governor of the universe; the administration of a great empire is in his hand, and the duty which he owes to his subjects, (if I may use the expression,) unites with the rectitude of his nature in requiring that all his dispensations be founded on justice, and characterized by equity. The public good must in no instance be sacrificed to the interest of a few individuals. The disobedience and rebellion of the human family must not escape with impunity, lest the universal at large should be encouraged to repeat the crime.

It will be denied by none, that God maintains a moral government over his rational creatures. It would have been altogether inconsistent with his character as a Being of infinite wisdom, to have brought them into existence, without designing them for some important end; and no other end of such importance can be conceived, as that they should glorify their Creator, by obedience to his law. The best interests of the creatures themselves, are inseparably connected with their subjection to the will of God. It was impossible for God himself to make them happy any other way, than by placing them in a state of subordination to his authority, and requiring them to obey his law. It results necessarily, then, from the relation subsisting between God and his rational creatures, that they are the subjects of his government, and under obligation to yield obedience to his laws. While they continue to give that obedience, it is his part to reward them with his Fatherly protection and the continued enjoyment of happiness: but by a single act of disobedience, they at once forfeit their privileges as subjects under his protection, and expose themselves to the punishment of rebels—to wrath and everlasting condemnation. Nor is this latter appendage a less necessary part of the Divine government than the former. Among men, the punishment of offenders is absolutely necessary to the support of regular government. Without this, authority must soon degenerate into a mere name, and society exhibit nothing but lawless anarchy and wild confusion. But it is surely most inconsistent, to suppose that God has established that as a law among men, to which he himself pays no regard; or to impute that to the Governor of the universe as a virtue, which in a human magistrate we would reprobate as a crime. Had God, then, when mankind had wickedly transgressed his law and cast off their allegiance to his authority, gratuitously pardoned their offences, and restored them to their former felicity, without doing anything to testify his infinite detestation of their rebellious conduct, he would have violated the principles upon which his own, and every well regulated government is founded, and held up to his remaining subjects an example, calculated to encourage them in sin, with the hope of impunity. The moral interests of his empire would have been wounded in the tenderest part: Those who might at any time be tempted to rebellion, would have had but feeble motives to deter them; and all would have had their motives to watchfulness greatly diminished. Socinians have raised clamorous objections against the doctrine of the necessity of the atonement, as held by Calvinists, as altogether inconsistent with the infinite mercy of God; but it is easy to see, that mercy exercised, in the way for which they contend, to the guilty subjects of the Divine government, would have been an act of cruelty and injustice to the innocent.

The maintenance of the Divine government,

then, or, in other words, the very end for which God brought his creatures into existence, required to support the honour of his laws, by allowing no transgressor of them to escape unpunished; or, at least, without such a manifestation of displeasure at his offence, as might effectually deter others from repeating the crime. If, however, this object can be gained by any method, whether it require the personal punishment of the sinner or not, all that is necessary to the honour and stability of the Divine government is obtained, and the moral interests of the universe sufficiently guarded from injury. Now this, to the highest perfection, has been accomplished by the obedience and sufferings of our Lord Jesus Christ. The immutable obligation of the Divine law, in its penalty, as well as its precept, has been placed on the surest basis, and the honour of the Divine government advanced to the highest, when it is proclaimed, as by a voice from heaven, that no sinner can escape unpunished, except a mediator, of no less dignity than the Son of God himself, undertake his cause, and suffer unto the death in his room. The intelligent creation have thus been most impressively taught what an evil and bitter thing sin is, how opposite to the holy nature of God, and how terrible the punishment to which it exposes. Can any now presume to encourage themselves in sin, from the hope that God will again send his Son, or the Son again submit to suffer and die to redeem them? and pardon on easier terms than these they have thus been assured is utterly unattainable. Had God, in short, allowed the sentence of the law to take its natural course, and condemned the whole human race to eternal misery for their sins, he would not have done so much to inspire his creatures with reverence for his authority, or to maintain the honour and stability of his government, as he has thus done, in exacting the punishment of sin, in all its extent, from his own Son.

Perhaps it may be thought an objection against the consistency of the atonement, with a regular administration of government, that the very principle of it, namely, that of substitutionary punishment, is inadmissible among men. Human laws allow the transference of debt, but not of crime. A debtor, upon finding a surety to make payment of the sum which he owes to his creditor, has a just claim to be exempted from sill farther obligation. But the criminal, who has forfeited his life to the laws of his country, must bear his punishment in his own person; and the law would not accept the life of another in his stead, even though a substitute, willing to die for him, could be procured. But in reply to this objection, I remark, that the reasons which render substitutionary punishment inadmissible among men, are peculiar to men, and therefore form no objection against this measure in the Divine administration, of which we are speaking. In the first place, substitutionary punishment is inadmissible among men, because no man has the right to lay down his own life at pleasure, even though it were to deliver a fellow creature from death. Our Lord Jesus Christ, however, being God as well as man, had a sovereign power over his own life, to lay it down at his pleasure. Though no mere man ever could, he could truly say, "I have power to lay it down, and I have power to take it again: this commandment have I received of my Father." 2nd, Substitutionary punishment is not permitted among men, because it would deprive society of an innocent, and perhaps a useful member. But the society of the universe was not deprived of a member by the death of Christ; for he only laid down his life to resume it, after a very short period, with increased glory and usefulness. 3rd, Substitutionary punishment is inadmissible under human governments;

because it would furnish no sufficient antidote to the commission of crime. It would rescue the criminal from punishment, without giving any security to society for his not commencing his career of guilt afresh. But the death of Christ, in the room of his people, has not purchased for them an exemption from punishment, to allow them to continue in sin. On the contrary, it infallibly secures the sanctification, as well as the justification, of all whoever reap its benefits. Instead, then, of having a pernicious influence on the moral interests of the Divine government, the atonement has established and advanced them. It has been, and will be, the means of delivering a vast multitude of fallen creatures, not only from the guilt, but from the pollution of sin, and restoring them both to the character and privileges of obedient subjects of Jehovah's empire.

This view of the atonement, as removing the objections, to the arbitrary remission of human guilt from the general interests of the universe, is, no doubt, of inferior importance to the one last mentioned. At the same time, it is of sufficient consequence to be assigned a prominent place in a discourse on that sacrifice, by which the Lamb of God has taken away the sin of the world. Everywhere, in scripture, God appears solicitous to give no false views of his character to his rational creatures, and employs every means to prevent them from thinking him such a one as themselves. When the Israelites, in the wilderness, murmured at the report of the spies, and despised the promised land, the only reason by which he was prevented from inflicting on them an utter destruction, is represented as being, lest he should bring a reproach on his holy name, by giving the surrounding nations occasion to say, "Because the Lord was not able to bring this people unto the land which he gave unto them, therefore he hath killed them in the wilderness," Num. xiv. 16. Speaking, accordingly, of this event in the book of Ezekiel, chap. xx. 8, 9, he says, "When they rebelled against me, and would not hearken unto me, then I said, I will pour out my fury upon them, to accomplish my anger against them in the midst of the land of Egypt. But I wrought for my name's sake, that it should not be polluted before the heathen, among whom they were, in whose sight I made myself known unto them, in bringing them forth out of the land of Egypt." But if the fear of polluting his holy name in the sight of the heathen was a consideration which influenced the Divine mind in his dispensation towards his ancient people, much more may a regard to the honour of his character, in the sight of the surrounding universe, be supposed to be a circumstance which he kept always in view when providing redemption for his church. In Rom. iii. 25, 26, we read, "Whom, (Jesus Christ,) God hath set forth to be a propitiation through faith in his blood, to declare his righteousness for the remission of sins that are past, through the forbearance of God. To declare, I say, at this time his righteousness, that he might, be just, and the justifier of him who believeth in Jesus." In these words, the setting forth of Christ, to be a propitiation, is plainly represented as not only a thing right in itself, but as intended to declare God's righteousness, and to manifest to the intelligent creation that God is just at the same time that he justifies the ungodly. The only class of innocent intelligent creatures, that the scriptures bring to our knowledge, are the holy angels, and they are frequently represented as taking a deep interest in the work of redemption, and deriving a large portion, both of their knowledge and enjoyments, from the contemplation of its holy mysteries. The display of the Divine glory, furnished them by this astonishing work, a display far surpassing all that the wonders of ten thousand suns, and as many revolving systems, can afford, fills their minds with ineffable delight. Hence they sing with emotions of rapturous adoration, "Glory to God in the highest, and on earth peace, good will toward men." Here they behold mercy and truth meeting together, righteousness and peace kissing each other; and hence they unite with the redeemed hosts in glory in triumphant acclamations of praise to God and to the Lamb. "And I beheld," says the apostle John, "and I heard the voice of many angels round about the throne, and the beasts, and the elders; and the number of them was ten thousand times ten thousand, and thousands of thousands, saying, with a loud voice, Worthy is the Lamb that was slain to receive power, and riches, and wisdom, and strength, and honour, and glory, and blessing. And every creature which is in heaven, and on the earth, and under the earth, and such as are in the sea, and all that are in them, heard I saying, Blessing, and honour, and glory, and power, be unto him that sitteth upon the throne, and unto the Lamb, forever and ever," Rev. v. 11-13. In these words the whole universe is represented as uniting in one mighty chorus, to praise God for the wonderful work of redemption. The idea, then, that the work of the Lamb of God in taking away the sin of the world, besides its particular reference to the human family, had also a general design to display the Divine glory to the moral universe, is completely scriptural, and our remark that one of the obstructions to the salvation of the human family, removed by the death of Christ, was the honour of the Divine character and government in the view of the intelligent creation, is shewn to be no vain fancy, but a truth founded on, and taught by the infallible word of God.

3. A third thing included in that atonement, by which the Lamb of God has taken away the sin of the world, is the satisfying the penal sanction, and fulfilling

the condition of the covenant of works. Man, like all the other creatures of God, was, antecedently to any positive institution, subject to the moral law. In his case, however, this law, immediately after his creation, was given to him in the form of a covenant. Obedience to all moral precepts, together with the observation of a positive institution, was the condition on the fulfillment of which himself and all his posterity were to be confirmed in the enjoyment of eternal felicity. In case of disobedience, however, he was not only to forfeit the promised blessings, but to incur the awful penalty of eternal misery. That in the federal transaction between God and man in the garden of Eden, Adam acted as the representative of his posterity, as well as for himself, is a doctrine which I am aware is much controverted. In proof of it, we can only remark at present, that the moral relation subsisting necessarily between God and man, laid a sufficient foundation for such a constitution. The circumstance of Adam's being the natural root of his posterity, and the goodness of God, which may be supposed to have provided for the human family the readiest and speediest access to a confirmed state of felicity, render the actual formation of such a constitution probable; and positive evidence, both from scripture testimony and the present state of man, renders it certain. "By one man sin entered into the world." "By the offence of one judgment came upon all men to condemnation." "By one man's disobedience many were made sinners." These express scripture assertions, together with the universal prevalence of sufferings, and death, even over infants that never sinned, and the fact, of which there is such abundant evidence both from scripture and experience, that mankind come into the world in a state of moral estrangement from God, and with a ruling propensity to evil, which can only be accounted

for on the supposition of a judicial transmission of
Adam's guilt to his posterity, form irrefragable
arguments that in consequence of the breach of the
covenant of works, a sentence of condemnation has
passed upon the whole human family. Now, this was a
sentence of which the veracity of God, as well as his
justice, required the execution, he had sanctioned the
covenant with the express threatening, "In the day
thou eatest, thou shalt surely die." But had he set this
declaration at nought after man had sinned, instead of
manifesting himself to be the faithful and covenant
keeping God, he would have exhibited himself a
capricious tyrant, terrifying his creatures with empty
fulminations, and retracting on a change of
circumstances his own most solemn declarations. He
would at once have given the lie to his own words, and
left Satan ground to boast that he held the truth when
he tempted our first parents to sin, by saying to them,
"Ye shall not surely die," and thus rendered untrue
what our Saviour says of that arch-deceiver, "he is a liar
from the beginning."

The veracity of God, then, pledged in a solemn
declaration, and the justification of his procedure in
placing man under such a constitution at the first,
required that none of Adam's family be restored to
happiness in a manner inconsistent with the
obligations lying upon them, in consequence of the
breach of the covenant of works. The violation of the
covenant, it is obvious, had placed two obstructions in
the way of our enjoyment of eternal life, the condition
of happiness was left unfulfilled, and a penalty of death
incurred. Adam, by his disobedience, at once fell short
of that righteousness which the covenant required as
the condition of life, and subjected himself to the
threatened curse of eternal death. In order, then, to the
deliverance of fallen man, from the effects of his

transgression, both these claims of the broken covenant must be satisfied, and both of them, we proceed to state, have actually been satisfied by the Lamb of God, the second Adam, our Lord Jesus Christ. This illustrious deliverer of mankind, so far from setting aside the obligations of the first covenant as a preparatory step to the dispensation of the blessings of the second, took up the work of our advancement to happiness at the very place where Adam had left it, removed the obstructions which his disobedience had placed in the way of its completion, and accomplished what he left unfinished. By the perfect obedience which he gave to the Divine law, during his life, he wrought out that righteousness which the first covenant required as the condition of life; and by his sufferings unto the death, he endured its bitter curse, and thus procured his people a title to salvation on the very terms of that covenant. In consequence of their interest in him, who is the Lord their righteousness, believers can present a claim to eternal life on the same grounds that they could have done, had Adam, their former representative, fulfilled the condition of the first covenant in the room of his posterity.

This view of the atonement as a fulfillment of the obligations lying upon man, in consequence of the breach of the covenant of works, is one which is often brought to view in the Holy Scriptures. It is obviously suggested by all those passages which speak of Christ as made under the law, fulfilling its righteousness, and enduring its curse, for he is thus plainly represented as entering into our relation to the broken covenant, taking upon himself, and removing from us, the curse which it had denounced against our disobedience, and thus restoring us to the privileges which our violation of it had forfeited. In those passages, too, where Christ is introduced in the character of the second Adam, there is a plain intimation that his work, as the surety of his people, was designed, among other things, to deliver them from the effects of the breach of the first covenant. What the first Adam failed to do, the second Adam has accomplished; the breaches which the former made, the latter thus repaired; the blessings which the former forfeited and cast away, the latter has gathered up and recovered. Indeed, one of the most obvious grounds of the necessity of Christ's procuring his people a positive title to happiness, by the righteousness of his life, as well as purchasing them a legal right of exemption from punishment by his sufferings unto the death, may be found in the obligations descending from the covenant of works. The essential justice of God, and the honour of his law and government in the view of the moral universe, prove the indispensable necessity of an atoning sacrifice to expiate their guilt before any of the human family could be saved, but do not so directly discover the necessity of justifying righteousness to furnish them with a title to everlasting happiness. The obligations descending from the covenant of works, however, show the justifying merit of Christ's righteousness to be as necessary to our salvation as the atoning efficacy of his blood. That covenant, by an unalterable appointment in moral rectitude, had required the giving of perfect obedience to the Divine law during a limited period, as a condition of indispensable necessity, in order to the confirmation of the human family in a state of happiness. This condition, however, the first Adam failed to fulfill, and, of consequence, left his posterity debtors to do the whole law, in order to their inheriting the promise. Corrupted and debased by sin, this debt they were unable to pay, and since it became necessary for our Lord Jesus Christ in working out salvation for his people, to obey for them as well as to suffer for them, to procure them a positive title to happiness, by the righteousness of his life, as well as to purchase for them an exemption from punishment by the merits of his death. The former of these things we could as little accomplish for ourselves us the latter. Without paying the remaining debt of our undischarged obedience, as well as cancelling the contracted guilt of our disobedience, Jesus would not have been a complete Saviour, not being made perfect himself, as his people's surety, he could not have become the author of eternal salvation to them that obey him.

The harmony between the law and the gospel, with relation to the fulfillment of the covenant of works by the obedience and sufferings of Christ, affords a striking display of that infinite wisdom which characterizes the whole scheme of redemption, and cannot be contemplated by a serious observer of the works of God, without lively emotions of pleasure. The covenant of works, though it did make, and could make, no provision for the deliverance of fallen man from a state of guilt, was, at the same time, in the highest degree consistent with his being delivered by such a scheme as that revealed in the gospel. If it would have extended the blessings of a confirmed state of happiness to the whole human race on the fulfillment of a certain condition by their first parents, it could not be unfriendly to Christ's becoming a second Adam, assuming like the first a representative character, and fulfilling the conditions of salvation in the room of those whom he represented. By constituting Adam the federal head of his posterity, and devolving the whole work of fulfilling the condition of happiness on him alone; it distinctly recognized the principle on which the whole gospel scheme is founded; namely, the substitution of Christ for his people, and the imputation to them of a righteousness wrought out by him. If, while it annexed a punishment to the commission of sin, if, at the same time, held out a promise of happiness to perfect obedience; it could not refuse upon the hearing of that punishment, and the fulfillment of that condition, by our Divine surety, to restore fallen man to all the privileges which his disobedience had forfeited. Jesus, then, has magnified the law, and made it honorable. Instead of setting aside the obligations of the first covenant to prepare the way for dispensing the blessings of the second; he has at once confirmed and fulfilled them. "Do we then," the apostle triumphantly asks, "make void the law through faith? God forbid," he replies, "yea, we establish the law," Rom. iii. 31.

In illustration of that atonement, by which the Lamb of God has taken away the sins of the world, we have thus endeavored to show that it includes the satisfaction of the claims of God's vindictive justice; the vindication of the honour of his law and government in the view of his rational creatures; and the fulfillment of the obligations lying on man, through the breach of the covenant of works. To this list of the obstructions raised by sin in the way of man's salvation, which the death of Christ has removed, perhaps it may be thought that a fourth might be added, from the consideration of the depraved nature, and hardened impenitency of man himself. *With respect to the completion of our salvation in the full enjoyment of God in heaven, our own depravity is no doubt a most important obstacle, necessary to be removed; but instead of viewing this as a preparatory step to our salvation, it is more correct to call it a part of salvation itself.* The legal obstructions to our salvation, removed by the death of Christ, were not those which interposed between us and the enjoyment of God in heaven, so much as those which forbade our introduction into a state of grace on earth, where we might experience the sanctification of nature, necessary to qualify us for that enjoyment. The removal of the depravity of man's nature, then, or in other words his sanctification, is not one of the immediate effects of the atonement, effected by the sufferings and death of Christ, but rather the work to which that atonement was preparatory. That was the foundation to be laid, this the superstructure to be raised. *The purchase of his people's redemption, which laid the foundation stone of the spiritual temple, Christ completed on the cross, when by one offering, he perfected forever them that are sanctified.* The building up of that temple, in the application of the purchased redemption to the heart, is another part of that work which he has been carrying on in all ages, and which will not be completed till the end of the world. It was only the former of these parts of the Mediator's work that we proposed to consider; and we now, therefore, hasten to a conclusion, by deducing a few inferences from what has been said.

1. From this subject, we may see, in the first place, the infinite love of God in providing salvation for guilty man, notwithstanding all the obstructions that stood in its way. To say nothing of the continued impenitency, and hardened depravity of the sinner himself, which might have served, one would think, to repel the love of God rather than to attract it; there were other obstacles of no ordinary magnitude, standing in the way of our salvation. The essential justice of God, that justice which declares, "I will by no means clear the guilty" "The soul that sinneth it shall die," required our subjection to misery. The general interests of the Divine government demanded our punishment as a band of rebels, whom it was unsafe for society to permit to live, and the express threatening of the covenant of works, as irrevocable as the perfections of God are unchangeable, had already condemned us to

the awful penalty of eternal death. These were
obstacles, which, to a created mind, must have
appeared sufficient to have barred forever the degrees
of Divine mercy to fallen man, and to have shut him up
under the blackness of darkness forever. "But God's
thoughts," my hearers, "are not as our thoughts, nor his
ways as our ways. For as the heavens are higher than
the earth, so are his ways higher than our ways, and his
thoughts than our thoughts." From eternity's
unbeginning ages he had fixed his love on Adam's fallen
race, and designed to raise a part of them as eternal
monuments to the praise of his glorious grace; and this
love—O let our hearts thrill with gratitude when we
say it—was a love which no waters could quench,
which no floods could drown. The mighty difficulties
which stood in its way, difficulties which all the
powers of creation combined, could have done nothing
to remove, were counted as nothing before it. The
language in which it speaks, concerning them all is,
"Prepare ye the way of the Lord, make straight in the
desert a highway for our God. Every valley shall be
exalted, and every mountain and hill shall be made low,
and the crooked shall be made straight, and the rough
places plain, and the glory of the Lord shall be revealed,
and all flesh shall see it together; for the mouth of the
Lord hath spoken it," Isa. xl. 3-5. Prompted by this
unbounded love, infinite wisdom devised a scheme, and
Almighty power executed a work, which fills creation
with astonishment; and will, through all eternity, cause
the celestial mansions to ring with acclamations of
adoring joy. The Son of God himself, that glorious
personage who spoke creation into existence, and who
possesses all the perfections and glory of supreme
Divinity equally with the Father, descended in human
nature into our world, lived a life of sorrow and woe,
lay in a manger, expired on a cross, and slept in a tomb;

all to avert the stroke of Divine justice from the head of guilty man, and to ransom him from hell and destruction. Thanks be to God for his unspeakable gift! A greater gift than this men could not receive a greater gift than this Heaven itself had not to bestow! "Behold, then, what manner of love the Father Lath bestowed upon us, that we should be called the sons of God. Herein is love, not that we loved God, but that he loved us, and sent his Son to be the propitiation for our sins."

2. What an admirable scheme of salvation is that disclosed in the gospel, and how vastly superior to every false system that has been invented by the ingenuity of man. The reconciliation of God's moral and gracious attributes, in the pardon and salvation of guilty sinners, is a difficulty which has been felt in every age of the world. Natural conscience, notwithstanding all the arts that have been used to bias or silence its testimony, declares, with a voice too distinct to be misunderstood, and too loud to be neglected, that there is a moral connection between sin and punishment which cannot be dissolved; that it is the nature of God to be just as well as to be merciful; and that there must, therefore, be a sad reckoning for sinners in the world to come. In vain does the pagan, to remove this difficulty, stain the altar with the blood of innumerable victims, and subject himself to services, wearing the character of a rigorous severity. In vain does the papist multiply confessions, and masses, and penances, without number, and seek a foundation for his hopes to rest on, in almost everything in creation, but the blood of atonement. In vain do self-righteous persons of every name, hold up the merit of their own performances, as if by these they could avert the wrath, and secure the favour of an offended Deity. A costlier sacrifice than any of these must be provided, a better foundation for hope to rest upon must be found, if ever

guilty man is to obtain mercy in a way consistent with the moral attributes of God. This better sacrifice, this sure foundation, my friends, is set before us in the gospel. The atoning blood of Jesus has opened up a way for mercy, to receive all the gratification which her bleeding heart desires, without compromising in the least the superior claims of justice; has exhibited God to be just in the very act by which he justifies the ungodly, and has caused his gracious and moral attributes to mingle their ways in the work of our redemption. Here, then, is a sure foundation for our hopes to rest on; here the troubled conscience may lay aside its fears, and repose itself in peace. "The Lamb of God has taken away the sin of the world." What an encouraging thought to guilty sinners! In consequence of that great work which our Redeemer accomplished when he bare our sins in his own body on the tree; sinners, the most guilty and polluted, are invited to return unto the Lord, and aspired of a gracious reception. Can any words be plainer than those of Jesus himself. "Him that cometh unto me I will in no wise cast out." "Come unto me all ye that labor and are heavy laden, and I will give you rest." Thither then, ye weary and heavy laden souls, thither repair to be relieved of the burden of your guilt. All other refuges are but refuges of lies, and can at best but delude their votaries into a false hope. Here, however, is a refuge which will never disappoint you, here is laid a sure foundation stone, on which whosoever believeth shall never be confounded. The blood of Christ Jesus, alone, cleanseth from all sin; by his one offering he hath forever perfected them that are sanctified. Direct an eye of faith, then, to the Lamb of God, which taketh away the sin of the world, and your troubled consciences shall find peace; confess all your iniquities with the hand of faith laid upon our New Testament scapegoat, and they shall be carried away into a laud of forgetfulness, never more to be remembered in judgment against you.

3. Since it is the work of the Lamb of God alone to take away the sin of the world, all who despise him as a Saviour, or rest their hopes of salvation on any other object, must be in a state of the most imminent danger. It is impossible to take even a superficial survey of the prevailing religions sentiments of mankind, without observing a mournful want of evangelical views and feelings, with respect to the foundation on which their hopes for eternity are rested. Instead of trusting for the pardon of their sins, and the acceptance of their persons in the sight of God, to the blood and righteousness of an arisen Saviour, many seem to think that a righteousness wrought out by themselves will procure them all the pardon and justification of which they stand in need. If they abstain from gross and open violations of the Divine law, maintain quiet and peaceable lives in the sight of men, and attend with some measure of regularity on the ordinances of religion, they think they possess everything necessary for a happy entrance into eternity. Or if they feel any need of the righteousness of Christ at all, it is not that it may be the whole and only ground of their justification, but merely that it may supply a few deficiencies of their own. To all of this description— to all who rest their hopes for eternity on any other object, either in whole or in part, than the blood and righteousness of the Lord Jesus Christ, I must plainly say, that they make lies their refuge, and incur the greatest danger of perishing forever. To satisfy you that this is no rash nor ill founded assertion, I need only repeat I to you the words of my text, and entreat you to ponder their meaning. "Behold the Lamb of God, which taketh away the sin of the world." Do not numbers of similar passages in scripture, represent the taking away

or sin as the peculiar work of Christ? and do they not call us to withdraw our dependence from every other object, and to place it on him alone? A disposition to rest your hopes for eternity on any other foundation than his atoning blood, is radically inconsistent with correct views of the gospel, and dangerous in the extreme to the individuals that cherish it, Jesus Christ, my friends, is the only and the all sufficient Saviour, that, with his name, there is not another "under heaven, given among men, whereby we must be saved." His blood alone has satisfied the justice of God, and opened up to fallen sinners of Adam's family a way of access into his presence. Beware, then, as you love your own souls, of rejecting the glorious remedy which God has provided, by trusting for salvation to any other refuge. Since God has placed this sure foundation in Zion, you may be assured, that by setting it at nought, you will not only forfeit the blessings which trusting on it would confer, but expose yourselves to the severest effects of his terrible vengeance. "Whosoever shall fall on this stone, shall be broken; but on whomsoever it shall fall, it will grind him to powder." There is a passage in the book of Isaiah which represents the danger of trusting on any false refuge in such striking terms, that I cannot forbear to quote it on the present occasion. It exhibits God as at once making known a way of salvation to sinners, and preparing to inflict a terrible vengeance on all who trust in refuges of their own, to the neglect of this way. Isa. xxviii. 16-21. "Therefore, thus saith the Lord God, Behold, I lay in Zion for a foundation, a stone, a tried stone, a precious cornerstone, a sure foundation: he that believeth shall not make haste. Judgment also will I lay to the line, and righteousness to the plummet; and the hail shall sweep away the refuge of lies, and the waters shall overflow the hiding place. And your covenant with death shall be disannulled, and your agreement with hell shall not stand; (that is, every scheme of salvation which is of your own devising, shall come to nought;) when the overflowing scourge shall pass through, then ye shall be trodden down by it. From the time that it goeth forth it shall take you: for morning by morning shall it pass over, by day and by night; and it shall be a vexation only to understand the report. For the bed is shorter than that a man can stretch himself on it; and the covering narrower than that he can wrap himself in it. "For the Lord shall rise up as in mount Perazim, he shall be wroth as in the valley of Gibeon, that he may do his work, his Strange work; and bring to pass his act, his strange act." You see, then, the folly and the danger of trusting on any other refuge than the one God has provided. Be wise, then, before it be too late; renounce all dependence upon your own righteousness and every created object, and let the all meritorious sacrifice of the Lamb of God, that glorious foundation which God has laid for the salvation of guilty men, be the ground of all your hopes. Direct an eye of faith to the Mediator's atoning blood, flee for refuge under the cover of his all-meritorious righteousness, and thus shall ye be found building upon a foundation which shall never deceive you, a foundation which, even when the rains descend, the floods come, and the winds blow, and beat upon it, shall never give way, but sustain your souls in peace and safety through all eternity.

4. How happy, how inconceivably happy, are they who are savingly interested in the Lamb of God, and, that great salvation which he has wrought out. Believers, to you the joyful truth is proclaimed, that your almighty Saviour has borne the punishment of your sins, which can never, therefore, be charged against you. His blood, shed for the remission of the sins of many, has satisfied the claims of God's avenging

justice, and allowed you, the obnoxious delinquents, to escape, has answered the demands, and maintained the honour of his law, and delivered you, the condemned criminals, from its curse. "There is therefore now no condemnation to you who are in Christ Jesus." United by a living faith to the Divine Saviour, all the privileges connected with a justified state, the pardon of sin—the acceptance of your persons in the sight of God—and a sure title to the heavenly inheritance, have become yours. By your interest in the Lamb of God, and his peace speaking blood, you have at once obtained deliverance from all that is miserable, and an irreversible title to all that is blessed and glorious.

Such unspeakable blessings conferred upon you, who were formerly condemned rebels, and children of wrath even as others, ought unquestionably to be much in your thoughts, and to be ever raising your hearts in praise and thanksgiving, to this bountiful giver of every good and perfect gift. The love of a three-one God in devising and providing the glorious scheme of salvation, the love of the Father in sending his Son into our world, and subjecting him to an accursed death in our room, the love of the Son himself in assuming our nature, bearing our sins, and paying our debt; and the love of the Holy Spirit in applying the purchased redemption to our souls; this love, I say, ought to be often in your thoughts, and to be the favorite subject of your meditation in time, as it will be the burden of your song through eternity. An enlarged discovery of this love, is one of the highest attainments of the Christian—will contribute more than anything else to fill his mind with consolation, to keep his heart in a holy spiritual frame, and to strengthen him for the discharge of duty. An extensive knowledge of it, was an attainment for which the great apostle of the Gentiles prayed in behalf of the believing

Ephesians, in a glow of affectionate language, which sufficiently discovers the high idea he had of its importance. "For this cause," says he, "I bow my knees unto the Father of our Lord Jesus Christ, of whom the whole family in heaven and earth is named, that he would grant you, according to the riches of his glory, to be strengthened with might by his Spirit in the inner man; that Christ may dwell in your hearts by faith; that ye, being rooted and grounded in love, may be able to comprehend with all saints what is the breadth, and length, and depth, and height; and to know the love of Christ, which passeth knowledge, that ye might be filled with all the fullness of God," Eph. iii. 14-19. Desiring to drink into the spirit that dictated these words, let us, my friends, be frequently standing at the cross, contemplating that glorious work by which the Lamb of God paid the price of our redemption. To this be our faith directed, by this let our hopes be animated, and around this let our affections glow with a holy admiration. Here let our love of sin and the world be crucified, by this let our zeal be quickened, and hence let our resolutions to study universal holiness, be confirmed and strengthened. Thus, let the love of Christ dwell in us richly, and by its sweet and alluring influence, constrain us to live not to ourselves, but to him who died for us and who rose again.

5. I shall now conclude this discourse with briefly calling upon all to a believing improvement of the Lamb of God, and that great salvation which is through precious blood. Sinners, you have transgressed the Divine law, and wrath to the uttermost is ready to overtake you. Yielding the habitual homage of your heart to the service of sin and Satan, and living without God and without Christ in the world; no language is sufficiently strong to paint the danger of your situation. The state of the man under the law, who had slain his

neighbor unawares, was pursued by the avenger of blood, and had not yet got within the walls of a city of refuge, was perilous enough; but his danger was little, yea, nothing at all in comparison with yours. It was only the wrath of a fellow mortal from which he was in danger; but it is the Almighty God himself that is in arms against you, and depend upon it, you are not safe a single moment from the stroke of his terrible vengeance, until you are got within the walls of the gospel city of refuge, and have placed yourselves under the cover of Christ's atoning blood. To the blood of Jesus then, be it your immediate exercise to flee. Your danger is too urgent to admit of any delay. The glorious gospel is this day sounding the invitation in your ears, "Behold the Lamb of God which taketh away the sin of the world;" *and it is at your infinite peril, if you reject it.* When the Israelites in the wilderness were stung by the fiery serpents, would they not have acted a most foolish part, if they had neglected to look upon that brazen serpent which God had provided for their healing, that their deadly wounds might be cured? Infinitely greater still, is the folly of those who sit under the preaching of the gospel, but turn a deaf ear to its invitations, who have the Lamb of God exhibited to them for the saving of their souls, but never seriously think of embracing him as their Saviour, or applying to him to have their sins washed away, and their spiritual diseases healed. Be persuaded then, my friends, to live no longer strangers to Jesus; though you be the very chief of sinners, he is still offering himself to you as a Saviour, and inviting you to come unto him, that ye may have life. If his gracious offer is accepted, and you flee to his atoning blood as your refuge from the day of wrath, your eternal welfare is secure. If, however, his offers are despised, and his precious blood trampled underfoot, the time is coming, when he shall "laugh at your calamity, and mock when your fear cometh." He who now offers himself in the meek and endearing character of the Lamb of God, shall ere long appear in terrible majesty, as the Lion of the tribe of Judah, taking vengeance on his enemies, and dashing them to pieces with his iron rod. "Now then is the acceptable time, now is the day of salvation." "Behold the Lamb of God which taketh away the sin of the world."

SERMON V:
On the Sovereignty of Divine Grace in the Election and Salvation of Men

"It is not of him that willeth, nor of him that runneth, but of God that sheweth mercy." Rom. ix. 10.

THE epistle to the Romans is an invaluable compendium of Christian doctrine. It is not like some parts of the inspired volume, a collection of detached statements, or a series of practical exhortations, but a connected exposition of the leading doctrines of the Christian system, couched in a regular chain of reasoning. The design of the first eight chapters of this epistle, is to explain the great doctrine of a sinner's justification through faith in the righteousness of Christ, with the particular view of refuting the grossly erroneous notions of the self righteous Jews on that fundamental subject. A great part of the members of the Church at Rome being Jews, they in common with the rest of their countrymen, were filled with such elated ideas of their privileges, as the lineal descendants of Abraham, and their being the only nation under heaven to whom God had given a revelation of his will, and chosen to himself for a peculiar people, that they thought these privileges alone gave them a particular interest in his favour, and raised them to a great superiority above the uncircumcised Gentiles. To purge out the remaining leaven of these errors from the believing Romans, and to furnish the church in all ages with a correct exposition of the great doctrines of her faith, the apostle shows at large in this epistle, that mankind, both Jews and Gentiles, being equally the descendants of fallen Adam, and having all transgressed the law of God in their own persons, were all without exception in a state of condemnation and death, from which they could be delivered in no other way, than through the free grace of God as manifested in the righteousness of Christ. This method of salvation had long been unknown to any but the house of Israel; now, however, it was revealed to the Gentiles, as well as to the Jews; and both were equally welcomed to an interest in its blessings. "Is he the God of the Jews only? Is he not also of the Gentiles? Yes, of the Gentiles also. Seeing it is one God who will justify the circumcision by faith, and the uncircumcision through faith." This subject occupies the first five chapters of the epistle. In the 6th and 7th chapters, the apostle vindicates the doctrines of grace from the charge of being inimical to practical holiness; and in the 8th, he concludes this part of the epistle, with an exalted description of the privileges of those "who are in Christ Jesus, and walk not after the flesh, but after the Spirit." At the beginning of this 9th chapter, he enters upon a quite different subject, on which he continues to the end of the 11th, namely, the vindication of the Divine procedure in rejecting the Jews, and calling the Gentiles into the Christian church. From the continued and obstinate rejection of the gospel, by the great body of the Jewish nation, and certain predictions of our Saviour, implying that they would continue in unbelief and impenitence, till they brought upon themselves a terrible destruction, it must now have been generally understood in the church, that that nation, so long called *Ammi*, was now to become *Loammi*, and to be altogether cast out of the privileges of the visible church. To the Jews, who viewed the promises of God to their fathers, as securing their seed in the perpetual enjoyment of the privileges of God's covenant people, this was, no doubt, a very stumbling dispensation. Since God had promised to their fathers to be their God, and the God of their seed forever; yea, had expressly made an everlasting covenant with Abraham, to be a God to him, and his seed after him; how is it, they were ready to ask, that we, the lineal descendants of those who received such promises, can lose all interest in the blessings of Messiah's kingdom, and be cast wholly out of the church? To the consideration of this subject, the apostle introduces himself with great address. He begins with stating his deep and unfeigned sorrow for his unbelieving countrymen, and his readiness, if that could be the means of their salvation, to undergo almost any curse in their behalf. Their rejection from the church, however, he proceeds to show, did not make void the promises of God to their fathers; "For," says he, verses 6th and 7th, "they are not all Israel which are of Israel: neither, because they are the seed of Abraham, are they all children." These promises were made to Abraham, not so much in the name of his natural seed, the Jews, as of his spiritual seed, believers of all ages. God, then, does not violate his promises to the father of the faithful, by casting his natural offspring out of the church, provided he raised up a spiritual seed, from the tribes of the Gentiles, in their room. This I consider to be the scope of the apostle's reasoning, from verse 6th to 13th. From verse 14th and onwards, he proceeds to show, that in dispensing the blessings of his saving grace to some, and withholding them from others, in a way of pure sovereignty, God is chargeable with no unrighteousness, but only exercises that right, which even a man possesses, of doing what he wills with his own. "What shall we say then?" says he, "Is there unrighteousness with God? God forbid. For he saith to Moses, I will have mercy on whom I will have mercy, and I will have compassion on whom I will have compassion." The position that forms our text, is introduced as an inference from this quotation: "So then, it is not of him that willeth, nor of him that runneth, but of God that sheweth mercy."

In order to ascertain the meaning of the inspired apostle in these words, all that seems necessary, is to inquire what that is, concerning which he says, "It is not of him that willeth, but of God that sheweth mercy." Does he mean, that nations, or bodies of men, cannot, by their own wills, bring themselves to the enjoyment of the means of grace, if these are not conferred upon them by the kind providence of God? Or does he wish us to understand, that it is not of the will of individuals, even when they enjoy these means, to improve them to their salvation, except God, in rich mercy and condescension, is pleased to accompany them with his saving grace? That the former of these explanations, which is the one generally given by the enemies of the doctrine of the free and absolutely sovereign grace of God in the salvation of sinners, is not the true one, nay, I think, be satisfactorily established from the whole bearing of the context. It is admitted on all hands, that the apostle, in the passage, is speaking of that dispensation of Divine sovereignty, by which the great body of the Jewish nation were excluded from the Christian church. Now, comparing his reasoning with the state of matters in fact, let us see wherein God did exercise sovereignty in this dispensation. Were the Jews, in the dispensations of Divine Providence, externally favored with the means of grace, or were they not? Did their rejection from the church arise from a sovereign command of God, prohibiting the gospel to be preached to them, and thus giving them no opportunity of retaining their privileges as his chosen people? or did it proceed from their own wicked hearts misimproving the means of grace, and obstinately rejecting the gospel, even when it was preached to them? These questions are too plain to need an answer. In his instructions to the apostles about preaching the gospel, our Lord had expressly commanded them to begin at Jerusalem; and we find that they obeyed his mandate, not only by continuing to preach a considerable time at Jerusalem, before they went abroad among the Gentiles, but also by making the offers of salvation to the Jews first, in the various places to which they afterwards came, and only secondarily to the Gentiles. With respect to external privileges, then, the Jews, in the apostolical age, were at least as highly favored as the Gentiles; and it is not true, in fact, that they were excluded by God, as a nation, from the means of grace. The only way, then, in which he exercised any sovereignty in rejecting them from the church, must have been by withholding from them, as individuals, that saving grace, without which no external means will be of any avail.

The doctrine, then, which I conceive to be taught in the text—the doctrine which the natural meaning of the words suggests, and the whole context supports is, that it is not of man's own will to turn from sin unto God, and to improve the offers of grace which the gospel makes, to the saving of his soul. *When some individuals attain salvation under the means of grace, and others continue hardened and impenitent, the cause of difference is not in this one willing or that one running, but in the sovereign pleasure of God making a difference, and communicating saving grace to whom he pleases.* The words, I am aware, contain other doctrines; but this I conceive to be the loading idea, and to it, at present, I mean to confine my attention. The doctrine is one which has been much controverted, and against which the carnal mind is ever ready to start objections. It is, however, plainly and frequently taught in scripture, and an important part of that whole counsel of God, which the preacher of the gospel ought not to shun to declare unto his hearers.

All that is proposed in this discourse, is to mention a few arguments in proof of the doctrine which I conceive to be that of the text, and to answer some objections.

I. The doctrine that it is not of man's own will to turn from sin unto God, or to believe in Christ to the saving of his soul; that the salvation of some individuals under the means of grace, and not of others, is to be ascribed not to their willing or running, but entirely to the sovereign grace of God, may be proved, in the first place, from the depravity of human nature.

It is the plain and unvarying doctrine of scripture, that ever since the fall of Adam in the garden of Eden, all mankind, without exception, have been subject to the power of a reigning depravity, which totally unfits them for any spiritually good action, and inclines them only to the commission of sin. "The imaginations of the thoughts of man's heart," that is, of man, in general—of man in all ages, and in all circumstances, are expressly declared to be "only evil, and that continually," Gen. vi. 5. "The heart," it is no less emphatically said, in another place, "is deceitful above all things, and desperately wicked," Jer. xvii. 9. When God himself, whose judgment is always according to truth, and whose omniscient eye cannot be deceived, looks down from heaven upon the children of men, the account which he gives of them is, "They are corrupt; they have done abominable works; there is none that doeth good. They are all gone aside, they are altogether become filthy; there is none that doeth good, no, not one," Psal. xiv. 1, 3. What the Psalmist says concerning himself, is true of the whole human race: "Behold I was shapen in iniquity; and in sin did my mother conceive me," Psal. li. 5. "The wicked," he tells us in another Psalm, lviii. 3. "are estranged from the womb; they go astray as soon as they are born, speaking lies." Nor does this innate corruption of nature incline men only to sin seldom, or to sin occasionally; it leads them to sin greedily and habitually; yea, to do nothing else but sin. Hence they are described as "foolish, disobedient, deceived, serving divers lusts and pleasures, living in malice and envy, hateful, and hating one another," Tit. iii. 3. Hence, too, they are said to "have given themselves over to lasciviousness, to work all uncleanness with greediness," Eph. iv. 19. Yea, so intent are they on their sinful gratifications, that they are compared to a thirsty animal, greedily drinking up large quantities of water. "How abominable and filthy is man that drinketh iniquity like water!" This corruption of heart and nature may exert itself in various ways on different individuals. While it leads some to a life of open profaneness and immorality; it may, in others, be disguised under the fair show of an externally decent character. In all, however, it produces a thorough alienation of heart from God, and a total disinclination and unfitness for anything that is good. What less than this can be meant, when it is declared concerning the carnal mind, that is, the mind of man in its natural state, that it is enmity against God—is not "subject to the law of God, neither indeed can be," Rom. viii. 7. When men, in their natural state, are described as "dead in trespasses and sins," it is impossible, surely, to understand less by the expression, than that as a dead body exhibits none of the symptoms, and can perform none of the functions, of natural life, so every soul that has not been quickened by the power of the Holy Spirit, is dead to every feeling of genuine love or obedience to God, and is totally incapacitated for any act of true holiness.

From these quotations, (and many others to the same purpose might easily have been mentioned,) it appears, that mankind, without exception, are naturally under the power of a reigning depravity, which has estranged their hearts from the love of God, and inclined them only to the practice of sin. In this state it is altogether impossible that the sanctification of their natures, or their conversion from sin to holiness, can proceed from their own wills. An unholy cause cannot produce a holy effect. If mankind are the slaves of sin, and naturally inclined to seek the gratification of their carnal lusts, it just requires some cause, distinct from their own wills, to change these inclinations, and to convert them to the love of holiness. To maintain that man's own will, whose only and unvarying tendency is to love sin and hate holiness, may change its natural inclinations so far, as to bring itself to hate what it formerly loved, and to love what it formerly hated, is to suppose the possibility of an effect, not only when there is no cause to produce it, but oven when there is a powerful cause operating to prevent its production. An animal, we know, cannot change the color of its skin, nor alter the natural shape and appearance of its body; as little can the unrenewed man change the natural dispositions of his heart. For, says the Lord, by his prophet Jeremiah, "Can the Ethiopian change his skin, or the leopard his spots? then may ye also do good, that are accustomed to do evil," chap. xiii. 23. If mankind are naturally in a state of spiritual death, their own wills must be utterly insufficient to deliver them from that state. For nothing is more certain, than that it is altogether out of the power of a dead body to recall the departed spirit, and restore itself to life; as little, it is obviously implied in this expressive comparison, can the spiritually dead soul subdue its sinful lusts, and renew itself to the love of holiness.

From what the scriptures testify of the depravity of human nature, the two following conclusions may be fairly deduced. 1. In no one instance can a true conversion of heart proceed from the sinner's own will; and, 2. In all the instances in which such conversion takes place, the sovereign grace of God must be the only cause. The extent of our depravity establishes the first of these positions; and its universality, the second. Since its extent is so great, that it has infected all the faculties of the soul, and enslaved the whole man to the service of sin, no one individual can deliver himself from its power; and since it is universal, being essentially the same in all mankind, that precise number of individuals shall be saved, and no more, to whom God communicates his saving grace. Truly then, it is not of him that willeth. The human race, in the sight of God, are like so many carcasses, all destitute of life, and loathsome through corruption. If he resolve to exert his Almighty power, in restoring them all to life, they shall all be saved; if he resolve this of only a part of them, that part shall be saved and no more; but if he resolve this of none of them, they must inevitably perish. Like a lump of unfashioned clay in the hands of the potter, are the whole fallen race of men before God. If the potter applies his powerful hand, the clay, or certain parts of it, may be formed into honorable and useful vessels. If, however, this is not done, it must all retain, forever, its rude unfashioned shape.

To evade the force of this argument, some deny that the will of man is inclined only to evil, and maintain that though his nature be in some degree depraved, yet this depravity is not so great, that he has no power to embrace the gospel. He may, say they, comply with the offers and invitations of grace which the gospel sets before him, in the same way that he complies with any good and wholesome advice. The gospel presents such strong and persuasive motives to his mind, that these are sufficient, by the force of moral suasion, to convert his soul from sin to holiness, notwithstanding any depravity that attaches to him. In refutation of this opinion, we do not at present insist on its irreconcilable inconsistency with the whole tenor of scripture doctrine, which represents the truths and alluring motives of the gospel as totally insufficient to convert the soul, except they be accompanied with the supernatural working of the Holy Spirit. This idea will occur under another argument. But we oppose to it two other objections that are altogether insurmountable. 1. It is inconsistent with the fact, that numbers who sit under the preaching of the gospel, and are speculatively acquainted with its doctrines, continue, nevertheless, entire strangers to its sanctifying power. Were there no depravity in the will but what moral suasion might remove; surely, such strong and overpowering motives, as the hope of eternal happiness, and the fear of everlasting misery, the wrath of an offended God, and the love of a dying Saviour, must cause the offers of the gospel to be immediately embraced by every individual to whom they are made known. Since, however, experience daily testifies, that motives so strong, so tender, yea, in a rational point of view, so irresistible as these, are proposed to, and even earnestly inculcated on, the mind of man in vain; the conclusion is amply warranted, that his will is under the dominion of a depravity too strong for any rational argument to remove. 2. It is contradicted by the express testimony of scripture, which represents it as one of the unvarying effects of man's depravity, that he naturally rejects the gospel even when it is proposed to him, and continues to pursue his sinful courses, notwithstanding all the

motives to forsake them which it sets before him. 1 Cor.
ii. 14, "The natural man receiveth not the things of the
Spirit of God: for they are foolishness unto him; neither
can he know them, because they are spiritually
discerned." 2 Cor. iv. 3-4, "If our gospel be hid, it is hid
to them that are lost: in whom the god of this world
hath blinded the minds of them that believe not, lest
the light of the glorious gospel of Christ, who is the
image of God, should shine into them." That in both
these passages, the apostle is speaking of sinners in
general, and not of such only as have gone great lengths
in sin is evident; for in the former text, the natural man
is opposed, in the following verse, to the spiritual man,
that is, the man whose mind has been supernaturally
enlightened by the Holy Spirit; and in the latter, he
speaks of all without exception, "who are lost"—of all
"who believe not." Now, when the natural character of
sinners is said to be, that they receive not the things of
the Spirit of God, account them foolishness, and cannot
know them, and that their minds are so blinded by the
god of this world, that the light of the glorious gospel
cannot shine into them, we are certainly given to
understand, that even when the gospel is set before
them, their wills are under a moral inability to make
any saving improvement. We have another striking
testimony to the same truth in the words of our Saviour
himself: John viii. 4, 5, "Because I tell you the truth, ye
believe me not." What our Saviour testifies of sinners in
these words, is, that they believe him not; and the
reason he gives for this, is the very singular one, that he
tells them the truth. Were his doctrines a system of
lying vanities, suited to their depraved inclinations,
they would embrace them without hesitation; but
because he tells them the truth—testifies to them the
true state of matters between God and their souls, and
the true way of salvation, his doctrines are so unsavory

to their lusts and carnal minds, that they reject them with contempt. "Because I tell you the truth, ye believe me not." In chap. vi. 40 of the same book, he speaks in terms equally decisive to our present purpose: "Ye will not come unto me, that ye might have life." The plain meaning of these words is, that though Jesus offers himself to sinners, in all his fullness and sufficiency as a Saviour, still they will not come unto him; and the reason, we learn from his own words in another place, is, that "no man can come unto him, except the Father draw him," chap. vi. 44.

Since, then, it is one of the effects of man's natural depravity, that he universally rejects that salvation which the gospel reveals, even when it is offered to him, it follows that something more than moral suasion is necessary to bring him to the enjoyment of it, and that his own will is totally insufficient to accomplish the work. In bringing the sinner to the Saviour, as well as in providing the Saviour for him, the sovereign grace of God must be all in all. Leave either of these parts of the work of salvation to the same himself, and it must remain forever unaccomplished. "It, is not of him that willeth, but of God that sheweth mercy."

The doctrine that the salvation of some individuals, under the means of grace, rather than others, is not owing to themselves willing or running, but entirely to God in adorable sovereignty, shewing mercy to whom he pleaseth, may be proved from direct scripture testimony. In dispensing the blessings of his grace among men, God is everywhere represented as exercising an absolutely free and unconditional sovereignty.

The enemies of the doctrine of free grace, do not deny that God exercises some sovereignty in man's salvation. They professedly admit that it was an act of sovereign grace in God to provide a way of salvation for guilty man, when his sins had rendered him deserving of nothing but punishment. After this salvation is provided, however, they generally say, it is left to our own wills, whether we improve it or not. God, they say, has offered a Saviour in the gospel: If we choose to embrace him by faith, he will save us; but if we reject him through unbelief, he will leave us to perish. Others, who do not carry these opinions quite so far, allow that some Divine assistance is necessary to enable us to embrace the Saviour; but instead of ascribing the whole work of conversion to the Holy Spirit, they divide it between him and the sinner himself, maintaining that when God perceives in certain individuals a sincere desire after salvation, or foresees that after their conversion they will be remarkably zealous in his service, he, in consideration of these things, communicates to them such assistance as is necessary to crown their own exertions with success. Now, to all doctrines of this kind, to every opinion which makes any superior goodness of theirs, either possessed or foreseen, the reason why some individuals obtain salvation rather than others, we oppose the plain and unequivocal testimony of scripture, assorting that God communicates his saving grace to some, and withholds it from others, altogether irrespective of anything in them, and *for no other reason but because it is his own sovereign pleasure.* Of passages to this purpose, we quote, in the first place, the one of which our text is a part: Rom. ix. 14-21. We have already remarked, that though in this passage the apostle is speaking of the rejection of the Jews from the Christian church, he speaks of them not as a nation excluded from the means of grace, but as individuals, from whom grace itself was withheld. For since it is not true, in fact, that they were deprived of the gospel as a nation, the only way in which God exercised any sovereignty in their rejection, must have been by withholding from them, as individuals, that saving grace, which is necessary to make the gospel effectual. The passage itself, we proceed to state, contains decisive infernal evidence, that this is its meaning. When the apostle speaks, verses 22 and 23, of "vessels of wrath fitted to destruction," and of "vessels of mercy prepared afore unto glory;" he cannot surely refer to nations deprived of, or favored with, the means of salvation. The ordinary use of common, not to say scripture language, will not warrant such an explanation. Vessels of wrath, fitted to destruction, are unquestionably individuals, left to perish in eternal misery for their sins; and vessels of mercy, prepared unto glory, are as unquestionably other individuals, chosen of God to everlasting felicity. So in verses 30 and 31, when the apostle speaks of the Gentiles as having attained to righteousness, even the righteousness which is of faith, and of the Jews as not having attained to righteousness, because they sought it not by faith, no criticism can consistently interpret these expressions of external privileges. The whole passage, then, we conclude, refers primarily to individuals; and plainer or stronger language, in support of the doctrine before us, than what it thus contains, it is impossible to conceive. Let us attend to a few of the expressions; Verses 15, 16, "For he saith to Moses, I will have mercy on whom I will have mercy, and I will have compassion on whom I will have compassion." "So, then, it is not of him that willeth, nor of him that runneth, but of God that sheweth mercy." These words are so plain and luminous in themselves, that I am afraid any comment I could make on them, would only darken their meaning and weaken their force. In selecting the objects of his redeeming love, God disclaims all regard to the will of the creature, or any other consideration, than his own sovereign pleasure. "I will have mercy on whom I will have mercy;" "So then, it is not of him that willeth, but of God that sheweth mercy." Language more definite or expressive was never used on any subject. So long as these expressions remain in the Bible, so long may the Calvinist maintain the absolutely free and unconditional sovereignty of Divine grace in the election and salvation of men, notwithstanding all the cavils that are raided against it. In verse 17, the apostle illustrates his doctrine by a reference to the case of Pharaoh. As God raised up this individual in the exercise of his uncontrolled sovereignty, to make him a monument of his mighty power, and an instrument for declaring his glory throughout the earth, so does he in every age, select individuals to be the objects of his pardoning mercy, or give them up to their own hearts lusts, to be ripened for destruction, just as he pleaseth. "Therefore hath he mercy on whom he will have mercy, and whom he will he hardeneth." In verse 19, he anticipates an objection, which he saw would be urged against this doctrine: "Thou wilt say then unto me, why doth he yet find fault? for who hath resisted his will?" If God bestows on us his saving grace, to change and sanctify our hearts, or gives us up to our own hearts lusts, to be ripened for destruction, he cannot justly condemn us, for we do not resist his will, and it is not our fault that we are not saved. To this specious, and common objection, the five following verses contain a reply, which ought to silence every cavil, and put every objector to the doctrines of sovereign grace to the blush: "Nay but, O man, who art thou that repliest against God? Shall the thing formed say to him that formed it, why hast thou made me thus? Hath not the potter power over the clay, of the same lump to make one vessel unto honour, and another unto dishonour?

What if God, willing to show his wrath, and to make his power known, endured with much long suffering the vessels of wrath fitted to destruction; and that he might make known the riches of his glory to the vessels of mercy, whom he had afore prepared unto glory, even us, whom he hath called, not of the Jews only, but also of the Gentiles?" If these verses do not establish the doctrine of the absolute unconditional sovereignty of Divine grace in the salvation of men, it is impossible for any language to do it. As the potter takes up a lump of clay, and makes some parts of it into vessels of honour, and others into vessels of dishonour, so does God, out of the same corrupt mass of Adam's fallen family, select individuals to be vessels of mercy, or leave them to perish as vessels of wrath, from his own sovereign pleasure.

We have dwelt the longer on this passage, because we conceive it to be the strongest scripture testimony to the truth of the doctrine before us. It is not, however, the only one. A number of others might be produced, but we can only mention a few without illustration. 2 Tim. i. 9, "Who hath saved us, and called us with an holy calling, not according to our works, but according to his own purpose and grace, which was given us in Christ Jesus before the world began." Eph. i. 4, 5, "According as he hath chosen us in him before the foundation of the world, that we should be holy and without blame before him in love. Having predestinated us to the adoption of children by Jesus Christ to himself, according to the good pleasure of his will." Mat. xi. 25, 26, "I thank thee, O Father, Lord of heaven and earth, because thou hast hid these things from the wise and prudent, and hast revealed them unto babes. Even so, Father, for so it seemed good in thy sight." Rom. xi. 5-7, "Even so then, at this present time also, there is a remnant according to the election of grace. And if by grace, then is it no more of works; otherwise grace is no more grace. But if it be of works, then is it no more grace; otherwise work is no more work. What then? Israel hath not obtained that which he seeketh for; but the election hath obtained it, and the rest were blinded." 2 Thess. ii. 13, 14, "But we are bound to give thanks always to God for you, brethren, beloved of the Lord, because God hath from the beginning chosen you to salvation through sanctification of the Spirit, and belief of the truth. Whereunto he called you by our gospel, to the obtaining of the glory of our Lord Jesus Christ." It were easy to make a few explanatory remarks on each of these passages, exposing the erroneous glosses that have been put upon them, and pointing out their application to our present argument. But this is unnecessary. The plain unsophisticated meaning of the words, without any comment, must satisfy every candid mind, that God's own sovereign pleasure, and free eternal purpose, is the only reason why he bestows the blessings of his saving grace upon some, and withholds them from others. Nothing in the character of man, then, either possessed or foreseen, has any influence in recommending him to the love of God, or procuring the exercise of his pardoning mercy. Free grace is altogether sovereign in the communication of its blessings, and the selection of its objects. It is not of him that willeth.

3. The salvation of some individuals, rather than others, can be owing to nothing in themselves, but must proceed solely from the sovereignty of Divine grace, because the scriptures everywhere represent the scheme of salvation as having been purposely so constituted as to hide pride from man, and leave him no ground of boasting. The language of the gospel is, "that the lofty looks of man must be humbled, and the

haughtiness of man bowed down, and the Lord alone exalted." It is an expression which occurs oftener than once in scripture, "He that glorieth, let him glory in the Lord." "Where is boasting then?" says the apostle to the Romans, "it is excluded. By what law? of works? Nay; but by the law of faith." "You see your calling, brethren," says the same apostle in another epistle, "how that not many wise men after the flesh, not many noble are called, but God hath chosen the foolish things of the world to confound the wise;" and his design in all this is, that no flesh should glory in his presence. Eph. ii. 8, 9, "By grace are ye saved through faith, and that not of yourselves; it is the gift of God: Not of works, lest any man should boast." 1 Cor. iv. 7, "Who maketh thee to differ from another? and what hast thou that thou didst not receive? Now, if thou didst receive it, why dost thou glory, as if thou hadst not received it?" These quotations seem sufficient to establish the position, that one of the leading and characteristic features of the gospel is, that it leaves man no ground of boasting, but saves him in such a way as secures all the praise to Divine grace. Now, this is a consideration which is diametrically opposed to every system of doctrine that suspends salvation either more or less upon man's own will. Granting that it was an act of sovereign grace in God to provide a way of salvation for guilty man, still if it is of his own will to improve that salvation when it is provided, he has in that circumstance whereof to glory, and boasting is not wholly excluded. If the reason why some individuals attain salvation under the means of grace, while others do not, be that the former, by their own wills, improve these means, while the latter, though they possess equal powers of doing so, neglect to improve them; or even if it be in consideration of some better dispositions, which God observes in some more than others, that he communicates his saving grace to the former, while he withholds it from the latter, on either supposition, the individuals who are saved have some ground of boasting over those who are not, they have something in themselves whereof to glory, they cause themselves to differ from others, and possess something which they did not receive: all which is in direct contradiction to the express testimony of scripture. Since sinners, then, are saved in such a way as leaves them no ground of boasting, their own wills can have no share in the work. In the application of salvation to particular individuals, as well as in providing in the gospel that it may be offered to sinners in general, the saving grace of God must have all the praise.

4. Another argument for the doctrine that salvation is wholly a work of free grace, and in no respect suspended on the will of man, may be deduced from all those passages of scripture which represent the regeneration and sanctification of the heart, as a supernatural work of the Spirit of God. If it be true, in fact, that sinners have a share in the work of sanctifying and regenerating their hearts, their salvation is so far of their own wills, and all further reasoning on the subject is superseded. If, however, it be the doctrine of scripture that no man can repent and believe of himself, that before we can see the kingdom of God we must undergo a change of heart, which nothing less than the almighty power of God can accomplish; the conclusion will obviously follow, that we must be wholly indebted to Divine grace for our salvation, and that nothing done or possessed by us contributes anything to our becoming partakers of the new birth, and heirs of God's heavenly kingdom.

That the change of heart by which a sinner is delivered from the dominion of sin, and becomes an heir of the kingdom of God, is not, as some represent it, the gradual acquisition of virtuous habits by our own exertions, but a supernatural work of the Holy Spirit upon the soul, is a truth taught with the greatest plainness and frequency in scripture. The nature of the figures employed to express it, is a clear proof of this. Thus, it is called a new birth, John iii. 3, "Except a man be born again he cannot see the kingdom of God." It is called a new creation, Eph. ii. 10, "We are his workmanship, created in Christ Jesus unto good works." 2 Cor. v. 17, "If any man be in Christ he is a new creature." It is called a resurrection from the dead, or the restoring of that which is dead to life. Eph. ii. 1, "You hath he quickened, who were dead in trespasses and sins." Col. ii. 18, "And you being dead in your sins and the uncircumcision of your flesh, hath he quickened together with Christ." Now, in these figures, nothing is more obviously implied, than that the change which they are used to express, requires a supernatural exercise of Divine power for its production. No man, it is undeniable, can affect his own natural birth. No creature can create itself, or be the cause of its own existence. No dead body can recall the departed spirit, and restore itself to life. As little, we are assured from these expressions, can the unrenewed soul deliver itself from the dominion of its sinful lusts, and convert itself to the love and practice of true holiness.

In other passages, the regeneration of a sinner's heart is ascribed, in such express terms, to the immediate agency of God, that his own will is plainly excluded from having any share in its production. John i. 13, "Who were born not of blood, nor of the will of the flesh, nor of the will of man, but of God." James i. 18, "Of his own will begat he us with the word of truth." John iii. 5, "Except a man be born of the Spirit, he cannot enter into the kingdom of God." Chap. vi. 63, "It is the

Spirit that quickeneth; the flesh profiteth nothing." Ezek. xxxvi. 25, 26, "Then will I sprinkle clean water upon you, and ye shall be clean: from all your filthiness, and from all your idols, will I cleanse you. A new heart also will I give you, and a new spirit will I put within you; and I will take away the stony heart out of your flesh, and will give you an heart of flesh." In all of these, and many similar passages, God claims the renovation of a sinner's heart to himself, as his own peculiar work; a circumstance altogether inconsistent with the idea, that the sinner's own will produces it, or has even a share in its production.

The regeneration of the heart is immediately followed by the exercise of faith. Between these two things, indeed, there is such a close connection, that to regenerate an individual's heart, and to enable him to believe, are little else than expressions of the same thing. Now, faith is never described in scripture as an act originating in the sinner's own will, but is everywhere represented as a supernatural grace, wrought in the soul by the Holy Spirit. Eph. ii. 8, "By grace are ye saved through faith; and that not of yourselves; it is the gift of God." Col. ii. 12, "Buried with him in baptism, wherein also ye are risen with him, through the faith of the operation of God." Phil. i. 29, "Unto you it is given, in the behalf of Christ, not only to believe in him, but also to suffer for his sake." So far, indeed, is faith from being an act originating in the sinner's own will, that the strongest expressions which language affords, are employed to describe that operation of Divine power, which is necessary to its production. Eph. i. 18, 19, "That ye may know what is the exceeding greatness of his power to usward who believe, according to the working of his mighty power, which he wrought in Christ, when he raised him from the dead, and set him at his own right hand in the heavenly places." The strength of these expressions has scarcely a parallel in scripture. The exceeding greatness of Divine power, the working of that mighty power which was displayed in the resurrection and exaltation of Christ, is expressly declared to be necessary to implant and preserve the grace of faith in the sinner's heart.

These are only a few of the passages which might have been quoted, to prove that the change of heart by which a sinner is delivered from the reigning power of sin, and enabled to embrace the Lord Jesus Christ by faith, is a work which nothing less than the almighty power of God can accomplish. The doctrine, either explicitly stated, or indubitably implied, pervades every page of scripture; and the denial of it may, without exaggeration, be pronounced a complete infringement of the beautiful harmony of the Christian system. In the economy of redemption, the regeneration and sanctification of the heart belong to the Holy Spirit as his peculiar work. To maintain, then, that he had no such work to perform, or to represent it as consisting merely in suggesting certain truths, or presenting motives to the mind, which is no more than a created angel may do, is to cast a vile reproach upon the blessed Spirit, whose person and work ought never to be spoken of but with the deepest reverence. So necessary, indeed, is a work of the Holy Spirit to true holiness, that believers themselves can do nothing truly good without his supernatural influence. Deprive the church of the quickening and sanctifying influences of the Holy Spirit, and the consequences would be like removing the sun from the natural world; all her beautiful verdure and fertility would immediately disappear, and a scene of universal barrenness and desolation succeed.

Admit the necessity of a supernatural work of

the Holy Spirit, in order to true holiness, and all that we contend for, concerning the sovereignty of Divine grace in man's salvation, follows as a necessary consequence. In electing the objects of his redeeming love from eternity, God could not choose such as he foresaw would believe. As none can believe of themselves, his election of them must have included a purpose to bestow faith upon them, else their salvation could never have taken place. In calling them effectually by his saving grace in time, he must, in like manner, take the whole work into his own hands. Since a supernatural change of heart is necessary, nothing is more obvious than that, if it were left to their own wills, such a change could never take place. Since, too, no sinner can possess any good dispositions, or any sincere desires after salvation, till God himself bestows them; these cannot be the reason why God imparts the saving influences of his Spirit to some, while he withholds them from others.

5. Another argument for the doctrine that it is not their own wills, but the sovereign grace of God, that makes men to differ, causing some individuals to be saved, while others are not, may be deduced from what scripture and experience declare to be the way in which sinners have in every age been saved.

There can be no reasonable doubt that God's way of saving sinners is the same in all ages. If he works a saving change in the hearts of some, in a way of absolute sovereignty, we have sufficient reason to think that he does the same in all. Now, may not the apostle Paul himself furnish a remarkable instance of that manner of conversion, as wholly of free grace, for which we are contending? There was surely nothing about his character to recommend him to the mercy of God more than others, when he was breathing out threatenings and slaughter against the disciples of the Lord, and was on his journey to Damascus for the very purpose of gratifying his diabolical rage against the followers of Christ. In this instance, nothing is more evident than that God did not wait till he began to repent of his former conduct, and shew some better dispositions of heart than he had previously manifested. No! He arrested him in the very midst of his career of wickedness, and wrought a saving change upon his heart at the very time that his infuriated rage against the name of Jesus had reached its highest pitch. This apostle, then, certainly uttered nothing but what his own experience declared to be true, when he said, "It is not of him that willeth, nor of him that runneth, but of God that sheweth mercy." Should it be objected that Paul's conversion being of a miraculous nature cannot be adduced as a fair specimen of God's usual way of dealing with the souls of men; in reply to this we remark, that it was miraculous only with respect to external circumstances. Instead of speaking to him by the ordinary ministrations of the gospel, God addressed him by a voice and a vision from heaven. Still, with respect to the internal working of grace in the heart, the manner of his conversion was precisely the same with that of believers in every age. His own words in 1 Tim. i. 10, are a proof that he himself viewed it in this light, "For this cause," says he, "I obtained mercy, that in me first Jesus Christ might shew forth all long suffering for a pattern to them that should hereafter believe on him to life everlasting."

Other instances, though of a less striking nature, of the same sovereign method of conversion, might easily be produced from scripture, but on these we cannot insist. The experience of believers in every age, confirms the same truth. None of the sincere and humble disciples of Jesus, have ever yet claimed to their own wills any share in that work which brought them to a knowledge of the Saviour. No! Their harmonious testimony is, that in their natural state, their hearts were estranged from God, and they had neither disposition nor ability to return to him. On the contrary, they were only going farther and farther astray, and hardening themselves in their sinful courses more, till the Lord arrested them by his preventing mercy, and gathered them to himself. Thus his own word, by the prophet Isaiah, are fulfilled in the experience of all who are brought to know the grace of God in truth: "I am sought of them that asked not for me; I am found of them that sought me not." But this is not the only way in which the experience of believers confirms the doctrine of the text. Having had their minds illuminated by the Holy Spirit, they obtain such a discovery of the desperate wickedness of their hearts, and of the deep and universal depravity of their nature, as convinces them better than a thousand rational arguments, that no good thing ever did, or ever could arise from their own wills. Even in their renewed state, they find the workings of corruption so strong within them, that they are constrained to say with the apostle, "In me, that is in my flesh, there was found no good thing;" they are not sufficient so much as to think a good thought of themselves; and daily experience assures them, that if they wore not constantly supported and upheld by the power of Divine grace, they must soon fall a prey to their spiritual enemies. Feeling, then, this absolute dependence upon Divine grace, for the preservation of the good work in their hearts, even after it is begun, is it possible for them to believe, that it was by their own wills that it was commenced at the first? No. The language of the apostle is an exact expression of their sentiments on this subject: "By the grace of God, I am what I am." "I live, yet not I, but Christ liveth in me." Hence they are always represented in scripture as ascribing all the glory of their salvation to Divine grace, and claiming no part of it to themselves: "Not unto us, O Lord, not unto us, but unto thy name be the glory." "Not by works of righteousness which we have done, but according to his mercy he saved us, by the washing of regeneration, and the renewing of the Holy Ghost." "Unto him that loved us, and washed us from our sin in his own blood, and hath made us kings and priests unto God, and his Father, to him be glory and dominion, forever and over, Amen." Suppose for a moment, that the doctrine for which we are contending were not true, and that the salvation of some of Adam's fallen family, rather than others, is owing, either in whole or in part, to their own wills, would not these songs which saints in heaven and saints on earth unite in raising to redeeming love, be empty compliments, asserting a good deal more than the truth? And might not the redeemed hosts, with the greatest justice, keep back part of the praise of their salvation from Divine grace, and ascribe it to themselves, and thus mar the harmony of the celestial songs by their jarring and discordant notes? The absurdity of such a thing is so glaring, that none, I hope, will maintain it to be possible. Every doctrine, then, from which such a consequence can be fairly deduced, must be false and unscriptural. Man owes his salvation wholly to Divine grace. It is on account of nothing done or possessed by them, that some individuals are saved, while others are left to perish forever. "It is not of him that willeth, nor of him that runneth, but of God that sheweth mercy."

II. We proceed to vindicate the doctrine, which we have been endeavoring to establish, from some leading objections.

1. The doctrine that it is not their own wills, but God's sovereign grace, that causes some individuals to

be saved rather than others, cannot be true, because it is inconsistent with man's free agency. If we cannot repent and believe of ourselves, our not doing so is a thing which we cannot help, and for which, therefore, we are not to blame.

In reply to this objection, I briefly remark, that it is founded on a gross mistake as to the nature of that freedom, which a rational creature must possess, in order to make him a moral agent. The principle upon which it is founded, and from which it derives all its plausibility, is, that in addition to the power of doing that, and being obliged to do nothing but that, to which his own will inclines him, he must possess a further power of determining his volitions as he pleases, in order to render his conduct virtuous or vicious. This is a principle, which it were easy to show is both false in itself, and absurd in its consequences. It is not a freedom of the will, in directing its volitions and inclinations as it pleases, but a freedom of the man, in acting according to his inclination, which scripture and sound reason declare to be necessary to moral agency. Nothing is more obvious, than that if a man be, compelled by physical force to perform an action, in its own nature sinful, contrary to his own will, he, in that instance, possesses no freedom, and of consequence deserves no blame; and the converse of this is equally true, that whenever a man commits a sinful action with his own consent, let the manner in which he wished to give that consent be what it may, he, in that instance, acts both criminally and freely. The very existence of a depraved inclination in the will is sinful; and if that depravity be so inveterate as to be by human exertions incurable, the criminality, so far from being removed, is fearfully increased. A few examples will still more clearly show the correctness of these remarks.

We shall begin with God himself, to whom,

unquestionably, belongs the most perfect moral freedom, and whose freedom, all must admit, does not consist in a power over the inclinations of his will, to turn them to virtue or vice, to sin or holiness, as he pleases. To ascribe such a power to God, were to impute mutability and imperfection to the Holy One of Israel. That in which his freedom consists and surely no creature can pretend to a higher specie of freedom than its Creator, is that he is at full liberty to do all that, and is obliged to do nothing but that, to which his own holy will inclines him. His will is indeed necessarily inclined to hate sin and love holiness; but so far is this necessity from being inconsistent with true freedom, that it constitutes its chief excellence and highest glory. Holy angels and glorified saints are also both free and virtuous agents; yet their freedom does not include a power of altering the inclinations of their wills, so as to turn them to sin or holiness as they please from such a dangerous freedom, the confirming grace of God has forever delivered them. Their freedom, and a blessed freedom it is, consists solely in this: That they have a power of doing all that, and are obliged to do nothing but that, to which their own wills incline them. Fallen angels, to take an example of an opposite description, are also free agents; that is, they do nothing in consequence of external compulsion, but in everything follow the bent of their own wills. Yet this is no way inconsistent with their being so much under the influence of a principle of enmity against God, and a hatred of everything good, that their wills are exclusively and necessarily inclined to evil.

These remarks seem sufficient to establish our position, that that freedom, which is necessary to moral agency, does not include a power of turning the inclinations of the will this way or that way at pleasure, but consists solely in a liberty of acting according to these inclinations. The application of this principle, furnishes a ready and satisfactory refutation of the objection before us. Were fallen man prevented from changing his heart from sin to holiness, and embracing the Saviour as he is uttered in the gospel, by any physical impediment, extrinsical to his own will; were he, for instance, disqualified for this work, by the want of those natural powers and capacities of mind, which, as a rational creature, he in fact possesses, his inability would be of such a description as to free him from criminality. The fact, however, is, that his inability is purely of a moral nature; he cannot because he will not. His heart is filled with a strong and deep-rooted aversion to everything truly good, and a ruling propensity to evil, hence he cannot, or rather he will not, embrace the gospel, whose holy requirements be in diametrical opposition to these inclinations. To attempt to vindicate men from criminality in rejecting the gospel, on the plea of an inability of this description, is obviously to plead that as their excuse, which constitutes the very essence of their guilt. The very same species of inability which renders it impossible for God to sin, disqualifies them for making a saving improvement of the gospel; and it were just as reasonable to maintain, that God does not act freely and virtuously in hating sin and loving holiness, because the necessary moral rectitude of his nature renders it impossible for him to act otherwise, as to contend that sinners are free from guilt in rejecting the gospel, because the natural depravity of their hearts disqualifies them for a different line of conduct. Their own consciences, if they are not obscured with spiritual blindness, or hardened with a long course of sinning, must, we think, convince impenitent gospel hearers, that in remaining unimpressed and unsanctified under the dispensation of the gospel, they act both freely and criminally. When the offers of the gospel are proclaimed to them, they do not even make a sincere attempt to comply. On the contrary, their carnal lusts are so dear to their hearts, that they cannot bear the thought of cutting off a right hand, or plucking out a right eye, that they may enter into the kingdom. They deliberately, therefore, continue to indulge themselves in their lusts, and willfully put the calls of the gospel away from them, addressing them, if not in the contemptuous language of Pharaoh, "Who is the Lord, that I should obey his voice?" At least in the procrastinating spirit of Felix, "Go thy way for this time; and when I have a convenient season, I will send for thee." If conduct of this kind is not both free and criminal, I know not what criminality is. Instead, then, of thinking to excuse themselves for their unbelief, by saying it is a thing which they cannot help, let sinners rather shut their mouths in the presence of God, and take all the blame to themselves—that the inability to believe, under which they think to shelter themselves, constitutes a principal part of their guilt. Under a deep conviction of this, and feeling that salvation is utterly hopeless if it proceed from themselves, let them commit the whole work into the hands of God, and earnestly implore the influence of his Holy Spirit to subdue the depravity of their natures, to remove the enmity of their wills, and to fulfill in them all the good pleasure of his goodness, and the work of faith with power.

2. Another objection that is often made to this doctrine, is, that it is inconsistent with the goodness of God, and makes him a respecter of persons. To suppose, it has been said, that God elects and calls men to salvation in a way of pure sovereignty, without any regard to their relative worthiness, is to ascribe to him a conduct of such a grossly partial nature, as is quite inconsistent with the character of one who is good to

all, and "whose tender mercies are over all his works."

In reply to this objection, I need say the less, as it is about the very same with the one which the apostle states and answers a few verses after our text. "Thou wilt say then to me, Why doth he yet find fault? For who hath resisted his will? Nay but who art thou, O man, that repliest against God? Shall the thing formed say to him that formed it, Why hast thou made me thus? Hath not the potter power over the clay, to make of the same lump, one vessel unto honour, and another unto dishonour?" It is surely most inconsistent, yea, impious, to deny to God a right which even man claims to himself; namely, that of doing what he wills with his own. When the whole human family were lying sunk in sin, and subject to the curse of the broken law, none of them possessed any claim whatever to entitle them to Divine mercy, and God was at perfect liberty to save all of them, or none of them, or part of them, just as he pleased. In extending his sovereign clemency to a part of them, therefore, he did no injury to the rest, he left them just as he found them; and their eye surely need not be evil, because he is good. The criminal who deserves to die, deserves not his punishment the less, because another criminal equally guilty with himself is pardoned. Should it be insisted, that though in this sovereign Providence of God there be nothing unjust in the strict sense of the word, still there is a partiality in it, which we would not expect to find in a God of infinite benevolence. To this it is sufficient to reply, that such is the case in fact, and that it is gross presumption in man to charge God with folly, who worketh all things after the counsel of his own will, and giveth not account of any of his matters. But the whole of the works of God, whether in creation or providence, we may remark, discover a similar sovereignty in their Divine author. If it be partiality, or undue respecting of persons, in God to bestow eternal life on some men rather than others; it must be partiality also, to send the means of salvation to some nations, and not to others; it must be partiality and respecting of persons, to bestow greater natural talents on some men than others; it must have been partiality that provided a way of salvation for fallen men, and not for fallen angels; nay, it must have been partiality that made some orders of creatures superior to others; men, for instance, superior to brutes, angels to men, and archangels to angels. These are consequences which flow from the spirit of the objection before us; and since the consequences are of such a nature that none will admit them, the objection itself must be false in its principle, and can therefore militate nothing against the doctrine which it is intended to overthrow.

3. The only other objection to the doctrine of this discourse, of which we shall take notice, arises from its supposed inconsistency with the use of means. If God, it has been said, saves sinners in a way of pure sovereignty, and their own wills have no influence in bringing them to the enjoyment of his saving grace, then we may give ourselves up to a total inactivity and indifference about our salvation. If God has purposed to save us, we must be saved whether we use any means or not. But if he has purposed not to save us, no diligence nor activity of ours can put us in possession of that which he has purposed not to give.

In replying to a former objection, we remarked that man's inability to accept the gospel offer of salvation, being entirely of a moral nature, neither destroys his free agency, nor acquits him from criminality, in not accepting it. Now, if this be true of the actual acceptance of the gospel offer by faith, it must be equally true concerning all the means which God has appointed for bringing the mind to give that acceptance. Our inability to make a saving improvement of these means no more frees us from obligation to use them, than it does to seek the end for which they are appointed. With this remark, we might fairly dismiss the objection. God himself has expressly commanded sinners to make a diligent use of all the means of salvation which he has appointed, and their inability to yield a proper obedience to this command being entirely their own fault, can neither set aside his claims upon their obedience, nor free them from a deep and aggravated criminality, if that obedience is withheld.

Should it be said, that though sinners are under a moral obligation to make a diligent use of the means of grace, still if our doctrine be true, they have no encouragement to do so, because success, after all, does not depend on their diligence, but solely on the sovereign pleasure of God. To this I reply, that such a supposition is founded on grossly erroneous views of the nature of the gospel, and indeed of the nature of all those dispensations of Providence, in which means are employed in order to accomplish an end. In the purposes of God from eternity, as well as in the actual execution of these purposes in time, means and ends are inseparably included; so that in every instance where God has purposed to accomplish an end with respect to an individual, he has purposed also to make him use all the means that are necessary to that end. It is not, then, independently of the means of his own institution, but in the use of them, that God renews the heart. Every individual, therefore, who lives in the deliberate neglect of these means, willfully casts himself out of the way of converting grace; and if such grace is ever exercised to him, its first effect upon him must be to impress him with proper sentiments concerning these means, and to rouse him up to diligence in the use of them. Suppose such a mode of reasoning, as that used in this objection, were applied to the common affairs of life, to what indescribable absurdities would it lead? Were a husbandman, for example, to separate the end from the means in his view of the Divine decrees, and to say, "If God has purposed next harvest to cover my fields with an abundant crop, he must do so, whether I cultivate my lands and sow my seed or not. If, however, he has purposed to send me nothing but famine, no exertions that I can make will prevent this from taking place. I need not, therefore, be at the trouble and expense of cultivating and sowing my lands, as the decree of God must be executed, let me do as I may." Such reasoning, it is obvious, is equally plausible, and equally correct with that of the objection before us. In this instance, however, its absurdity is so obvious, that were any man to go so far as to reduce it to practice, he would, in all probability, be thought destitute of reason. Why it is not accounted equally absurd in the vastly more important concerns of salvation, is a circumstance which can be accounted for only by the inconceivable darkness with which the mind of man is naturally filled, concerning the things of the Spirit of God. In this, as well as in many other ways, we may observe a remarkable fulfillment of our Savior's words: "The children of this world are, in their generation, wiser than the children of light.".

I shall now conclude this discourse with a few remarks, by way of application.

1. From this subject, I would guard my hearers against the idea that the decrees of God are any discouragement to diligence in the use of means, or that the doctrine of sovereign grace places any obstruction in the way of the returning sinner. This is an abuse of these precious doctrines of scripture, into which the

carnal mind, through the ensnaring artifices of Satan, is ever ready to fall. Many continue, from year to year, in a state of listless indifference about their spiritual interests, without ever setting about, in good earnest, the great work of their salvation, from the delusive idea, that if God has a design to save them, his grace will, some time or other, find them out, and arouse them to activity, whether they bestir themselves or not; but that if he has no design to save them, it is vain for them to make any exertions to put themselves in possession of that which God has purposed they shall never obtain. Others, whose consciences have been awakened under the dispensation of the gospel, so that they can no longer allow themselves to sleep in carnal security, find the doctrines of sovereign grace a stumbling block in their way, which they know not how to get over. They feel the importance of salvation, and would cheerfully make any sacrifice, that could secure their eternal welfare; but the decree of God, consigning some to irretrievable misery, and predestinating others to everlasting happiness, appears to them an insurmountable barrier thrown across their path, fills them with perplexity how they are to proceed, and paralyzes their vigor in the diligent use of means, from the apprehension that they may not be amongst the number of the elect, and therefore all their prayers and endeavors prove ultimately in vain. Now all who act upon this principle, or feel themselves embarrassed by these difficulties, I would earnestly entreat to remember, that secret things belong to the Lord, and that it is only the things that are revealed that belong unto us. It is an unquestionable fact, that God has unalterably foreordained whatsoever comes to pass, and that he bestows the blessings of his saving grace on some rather than others, for no other reason but that such is his own sovereign pleasure. At, the same time, it is as unquestionable, that the individuals whom he has purposed so highly to favour, are totally unknown to us until the event of their becoming actual partakers of his saving grace hath declared it; and that we tread on forbidden ground, nay, impiously pry into hidden things, with which we have nothing to do, when we allow a thought about the secret purposes of God to have any influence on our conduct. Were man to act on such a principle as this in the affairs of common life, consequences the most absurd in themselves, and absolutely ruinous to society, would necessarily follow. The agriculturist would no more cultivate his fields and sow his seed, because, says he, God may have purposed to withhold those genial rains and that summer sun which are necessary to cause my seed to spring up and repay my labors with a crop; the merchant would no longer send out vessels, to enrich his native country with the produce of foreign lands, lest God should command the storms and the waves to rise against them, and sink his wealth to the bottom of the sea. The student of theology, or medicine, would no longer spend the early part of his life in the pursuit of knowledge, lest God should have purposed to deprive him of his faculties, or call him away by death, before he reached the years of maturity, or derived any advantage from his labors. The absurdity and impropriety of perplexing ourselves with discouraging thoughts about the secret purposes of God, in any of these instances, is abundantly obvious, and will be universally admitted. Why then, my friends, do you act upon a different principle, in matters connected with your eternal interests? As the husbandman cultivates his fields and sows his seed, without anxiously inquiring whether God has purposed to give him a crop, so be ye diligent and persevering in the use of the appointed means, and work out your salvation with fear and trembling, without once perplexing your mind with the inquiry whether you are elected or not. This is one of those secret things which are known only to the Lord, and with which we have nothing to do whatever. Without delay, then, I call upon every one of my hearers, to set about the work of their salvation in good earnest; be diligent and persevering in the use of all appointed means; labor to impress your minds with a sense of the evil nature of sin, and the awful danger to which you are exposed by remaining in an ungenerated state; wait attentively on the ordinances of religion; read the scriptures in private, and meditate seriously on their meaning; study the gospel scheme of salvation, and endeavor to bring your minds to a cordial acquiescence in it; pray fervently to God for the gift of his Holy Spirit, and entreat him, for his own name's sake, and for the glory of his own free grace, to have mercy upon you, and save your perishing souls. In these and like exercises, engage with earnestness, and persevere with unwearied diligence, and despair not of success. The scriptures, as clearly as they reveal salvation itself, promise that none who feel their need of salvation, and persevere in seeking it in the way of God's own appointment, shall be finally sent away by him without a blessing. Those that come unto the Saviour, he will never cast out. "Ask, and ye shall receive," is his own gracious language; "seek, and ye shall find; knock, and it shall be opened unto you. For every one that asketh, receiveth; and he that seeketh, findeth; and to him that knocketh, it shall be opened."

Before leaving this subject, I cannot help remarking, that the individuals who have least reason to discourage themselves with thoughts about the decrees of God, and the sovereignty of Divine grace, are the very persons who are most ready to perplex themselves with discouraging thoughts on these subjects. The individuals who have most reason to be alarmed at thoughts of the decrees of God, and his purposes with respect to them, are those who are still living in the habitual practice of sin, have little concern about their spiritual interests, and obstinately resist all the offers and invitations which the gospel makes to them. Would such individuals seriously consider their situation, they might find considerable reason to fear, that for their obstinate unbelief, and willful rejection of the gospel, God had ceased to strive with them, and given them up to judicial blindness, though even in these thoughts they would by no means be warranted to go so far as to question the efficacy of the Savior's blood, or doubt his willingness to save them. Instead, however, of feeling any alarm from such a consideration, they are generally presumptuous and confident in their own strength. They flatter themselves with the hope, that they can break off their sins, and commence a religious life, whenever they please, and seldom entertain a doubt of doing so in reality before they die. Those who are most ready to perplex themselves with discouraging thoughts about the decrees of God, are a very different class of persons. They are those who have been awakened to a sense of their lost and ruined state by nature, have seen their utter unworthiness in the sight of God, and are crying out with trembling anxiety, "What shall we do to be saved." Such persons, in the multitude of the fears with which they are encompassed, are peculiarly liable to give way to perplexing thoughts about the decrees of God, and to fear that they may have no interest in his purposes of election, and can never, therefore, be saved. Now, to such individuals I would not only repeat the remark, that secret things belong unto the Lord, and that it is not the secret will of God's purpose, but the revealed will of his word, that is the rule of our conduct, but would suggest the idea, that in their circumstances there seem to be favourable symptoms of a begun work of grace, and probable evidences that God has designs of mercy with respect to them. Who was it, my friends that aroused you from the slumbers of your former indifference and security, and put the good desire of salvation into your hearts? It was not yourselves, I am sure you will readily acknowledge, but God, by the instrumentality of his word and Spirit. Now what could be his design in causing you to differ from others, who are still living in indifference and unconcern, and bringing you forward to at least an entrance upon that course, by which he usually gathers home his elect to himself? We dare not give a definite! answer to this question; but this we may safely say, that it is not God's usual method to put desires into the heart, which he has no design to satisfy. Those, whom he once arouses to a sense of their need of salvation, and fills with hungering and thirsting desires after himself, he usually, in his own time and way, enriches with all the blessings of the everlasting covenant, and conducts to joy and peace in believing. Dismiss, then, your sinfully intruding thoughts about the secret purposes of God, and make it your solo concern to follow on to know the Lord in the path of commanded duty. Turn not aside to the right hand nor to the left. The darkness with which you are at present surrounded is only, we may hope, that increased thickening of the shades of night, which usually precedes the morning dawn.

2. This subject conveys important practical instructions to those who are asking the way to salvation, saying, "What must we do to be saved?" It tells them, in particular, that since it is not of man that willeth, but of God that sheweth mercy—since Divine grace is altogether sovereign in its exercise, and it is no

worthiness of theirs, that causes some individuals to be saved rather than others, it is their immediate duty to renounce all dependence upon their own exertions, and to come to the Saviour just as they are, with all their guilt and depravity about them, that he may save them. There is no error into which an awakened individual is more ready to fall, than to suppose that he has something to do, some duties to perform, and certain good qualities to acquire, in order to render him a proper subject for the saving grace of God. He may not, he thinks, in his present state of universal depravity and impenitence, venture to come to Christ for salvation, but must first qualify himself for this, by amending his life, mortifying his lusts, repenting of his sins, and becoming at least sincere and earnest in matters of religion. All ideas of this kind, while they are dangerous in the extreme to the individual that holds them, having a strong tendency to make him rest in his own good works and attempted reformations, and so not only to procrastinate the great duty of coming to Christ, but to neglect it altogether, are, at the same time, diametrically opposed to that important gospel doctrine which we have been endeavoring to defend. Since God dispenses the blessings of his grace among men in a way of absolute sovereignty, nothing done by us can have any influence in bringing us to the enjoyment of them. Since it is not of man that willeth, but of God that sheweth mercy, it must be presumption in us to think to will, in order that he may have mercy upon us. Our first and highest duty is to believe in Christ; and no attempts to repent or reform our ways, previous to this, can be accepted by God, or be of any advantage to ourselves. In pointing out the way of salvation to inquiring souls, they cannot be too strongly warned against this dangerous error, nor too plainly told, that one of the distinguishing properties of the gospel is, that it offers salvation to sinners as such, that it requires no previous performance of duties, inculcates no preparatory work of reformation, or amendment to qualify them for receiving its blessings, but call upon them, just as they are, with all their guilt, all their pollution, and all their depravity about them, to come to the Saviour for salvation; and that if they do not come to him in this character, they have no warrant, to come in any other. This is, no doubt, humbling doctrine to the proud and self righteous dispositions of fallen man. To be told that he cannot of himself wash away the guilt of a single sin, that he cannot mortify a single one of the numerous lusts that rage in his wicked heart, that he cannot so much as think a good thought, or bring the least good quality or virtuous disposition along with him, to recommend him to the mercy of God, but that he must humbly cast himself at the Savior's feet, as a poor perishing sinner, acknowledging his utter unworthiness of the least mercy, and asking salvation solely as a gift of free and sovereign grace, is a doctrine strongly opposed to the natural pride of the human heart; but humbling as it may be to human pride, and offensive to carnal reason, it is a doctrine which is inseparably connected with correct views of the gospel system; and we must either submit to it, and humbly acquiesce in it, or be content to perish forever. In compliance, then, with our Savior's requisition, let us strive to enter in at this strait gate; for strait indeed is the gate, and narrow is the way that leadeth unto life, and few there be that find it.

From this subject, I would call upon all the hearers of the gospel, to acknowledge the sovereignty of free grace, and to yield an unreserved submission of heart to the whole will of God, with respect to their salvation. The doctrines of salvation by free grace, have a strange and mysterious appearance to the unrenewed mind. That the fairest acts of human virtue should have no influence whatever in procuring us an interest in the love of God; that the profligate harlot, or bloated debauchee, should stand on the same level, in the view of Divine grace, with the most virtuous and amiable of mankind; that God, in dispensing the blessings of salvation among men, should pay no regard to virtuousness of character, refinement of manners, amiableness of temper, usefulness in the church or in the world, or any of those distinctions on account of which men generally think themselves superior to their neighbors; but should select as readily, and favour as highly, the most vicious as the most virtuous, the most licentious and abandoned, as the man of untainted honour and strict integrity, are doctrines highly offensive to carnal reason, and which the human mind is brought with the greatest difficulty to admit. But however offensive, my friends, those doctrines may appear, I must plainly tell you, that that pride of heart, which would lead you to oppose them, must be cast down, and you must be brought to a cordial submission to the terms of sovereign grace, else you can never be saved. "Verily I say unto you, whosoever shall not humble himself, and receive the kingdom of God as a little child, shall in no wise enter therein." Until you are brought to see your utter unworthiness in the sight of God, and to cast your guilty souls at the Savior's feet, acknowledging that you have no merit to plead, that it would be a righteous thing in him to condemn you, and that it will be a most signal display of unmerited grace if ever you are saved; but entreating, at the same time, that the riches of free grace may be magnified in your salvation, and cordially consenting to receive the blessings of eternal life from the Saviour, on whatever terms he may be pleased to give them, except, I say, your souls are thus humbled under the mighty hand of

God, and made cordially willing to be an eternal debtor to free grace for the whole of your salvation, the enmity of your hearts has not been subdued—ye are still strangers to the Lord Jesus Christ, and without an interest in that scheme of salvation, in which grace reigns through righteousness unto eternal life. The gospel is designed to stain the pride of human glory, to humble the lofty looks of man, to prostrate his towering imaginations in the dust and to exalt the Lord alone. "It is not of him that willeth, nor of him that runneth, but of God that showeth mercy." Before the carnal mind is brought to submit to this scheme of salvation, a mighty struggle ordinarily takes place. The strong man aimed keepeth his goods, and it is not till his stoutest opposition proves unavailing, that the longer that he succeeds in binding him, and taking away his armor wherein he trusted. Upon being first awakened to a sense of his need of salvation, the sinner generally flees to amendment of life, attempted repentance for his former sins, and the performance of religions duties; and under these false refuges he would deceive himself to his eternal ruin, did not sovereign grace prevent. It is but till the Holy Spirit has driven him from every other refuge, and shown him that he can be safe nowhere else, that he, at last thinks of betaking to the Saviour, and seeking protection to his guilty soul under the cover of his blood. Oh! how obstinate must the enmity of the human heart be, when it is so difficult to be subdued; how presumptuous must be its pride, how determined its rebellious disposition, when it holds out to the last, and will not, submit to the terms of sovereign grace, so long as it sees the most distant hope of safety from any other quarter! When reflecting on this subject, interesting emotions pass through the minds of the children of God. God's ways of gathering his people home to himself are not always the same, nor do they all remember them with equal distinctness; yet there are considerable numbers, I believe, who can attest from their own experience, that their submission to the terms of free grace was their last resource, and that it was not till they had been driven from every other refuge that they were induced to place an exclusive reliance on the Savior's merits. When aroused their need of salvation, they prayed and repented, and strived, and endeavored, and were made to see their prayers, and repentings, and strivings, and endeavors, to be nothing, before they would come to the Saviour, on the exclusive ground of the gospel offer, and consent to be indebted to free grace alone for the whole of their salvation. O my friends, let not the pride and enmity of your hearts any longer prevent you from acquiescing in the gospel scheme of salvation. Go no longer about to establish your own righteousness, but submit, without delay, to the righteousness of God. Bow to the sovereign authority of the exalted Saviour, acknowledge your utter unworthiness of the least favour, and cast your guilty and perishing souls into the arms of his mercy. Sovereign as he is in the dispensation of his blessings, he never rejects any who come to him with an humble sense of their own unworthiness, and an earnest desire after those blessings which he has it in his power to bestow. The hungry he filleth with good things; it is only the rich, the proud, and the self sufficient, that he sends away empty. Hearken, then, to his entreating voice, he counsels thou to buy of him "gold tried in the fire that thou mayest be rich, and white raiment that thou mayest be clothed, and eye salve to anoint thine eyes that thou mayest see." And what is the price at which he offers these inestimable blessings? Listen to the words of the Holy Ghost in another part of scripture—"Ho! every one that thirsteth, come ye to the waters, and he that hath no money: come ye, buy and eat; yea, come, buy wine and milk without money, and without price."

4. To believers who have already experienced a work of saving grace upon their souls, the doctrine of this discourse is also full of practical instruction. It loudly inculcates on them, in the first place, the duty of a life of humility, and fervent gratitude to God, for his distinguishing goodness. Since it was on account of no worthiness of theirs, but solely in consequence of his own sovereign pleasure, that he fixed his love on them rather than on thousands of their fellow creatures, whom he has left to perish forever; how humble and self denied ought they to be! How carefully should they ascribe all the praise of their salvation to free grace, and claim no part of it to themselves! What the apostle says to the Gentile Christians, as a body, may be addressed with propriety to every individual believer. "They were broken off by unbelief, and thou standest by faith; be not high minded, but fear." But, secondly, this doctrine no less loudly inculcates on Christians, the duty of continuing to place their dependence, for bringing the work of their salvation to perfection, upon that same sovereign grace by which it was begun. As it was not by their own wills that the work of grace was commenced, as little is it of themselves to carry it forward, and bring it to perfection. In all your religious exercises, in every step of your earthly pilgrimage, Christians, carry this principle along with you. "It is not you that live, but Christ that liveth in you." It is not in yourselves to direct your steps, to mortify your lusts, and to subdue your enemies. Learn then to live denied to your own wisdom and strength, and to go forth, through the wilderness, leaning on your Beloved. If you are not in some measure acquainted with this exercise, you know nothing yet as you ought to know. To know

that we can do nothing of ourselves, is the first lesson in the school of Christ, and a lesson which his most advanced disciple need to be always learning. No eminence of religions attainments, no usefulness in the church or in society, no regularity in the performance of duties, no diligence in the use of means, can furnish even the Christian with the least claim upon God, for the renewed communications of his grace. Even though he has done his utmost, then, in all these respects, he is still to acknowledge himself an unprofitable servant, to live denied to himself and all that he has done, and to approach God in no other character than that of a sinner asking nothing by way of merit, but depending upon free grace alone for every blessing of which he stands in need. Renouncing, in this manner, all dependence upon ourselves, and placing our sole reliance upon the free grace of the everlasting covenant, and the' strength of an all sufficient Saviour, let us go forward by the paths of commanded duty in our journey to the land of promise. And may God himself, who brought again from the dead our Lord Jesus Christ, that great Shepherd of the sheep, through the blood of the everlasting covenant, make us perfect in every good work to do his will, working in us that which is well pleasing in his sight, through Jesus Christ, to whom be glory forever and ever. Amen.

SERMON VI:
The Perseverance of The Saints

"The righteous shall hold on his way." Job xvii. 9.

IN estimating the value of a possession, two things must be taken into consideration, in order to come at a correct judgment:—1st, The intrinsic value of the possession itself, and—2dly, The security given for the permanent enjoyment of it. Put a trifling article into a man's hand, and tell him it is his own, never to be taken from him, he will consider himself little enriched by such a present; for though you set, no limits to the time of his possessing it, the article is of little value, and can never be of much advantage to him. Or suppose, on the other hand, you put him in possession of an article of the greatest value today, but tell him you expect that he will return it you tomorrow, he is as little enriched as before; for though the article he has received be of very great value, he is not to have permanent possession of it. The lives of wicked men are a possession given them by God, which they shall enjoy forever; but because they do not employ them in promoting his glory, but spend them in the service of sin, they are of little value to them; nay, they will prove in the end a curse, and not a blessing. The possessions and pleasures of the world are viewed by many as matters of the greatest value, but very unjustly; for even though we should admit their intrinsic worth to be as great as they are pleased to call it, there is no security for a permanent enjoyment of them. At the very farthest, we cannot enjoy them longer than the few short years given to man as the period of his earthly existence. Nay, for anything we know, tomorrow, my next moment may separate us from them forever. Apply these two principles, which common sense teach every man to apply in the ordinary affairs of life, to the spiritual privileges conferred by Divine grace on the saints of God, and they will be found to be indeed a possession of incalculable value. They are at once infinitely important in respect of intrinsic worth, and there is infallible security given for a permanent, yea, an everlasting enjoyment of them. They are infinitely valuable in respect of intrinsic worth, for they consist of nothing less than deliverance from infinite evil, and advancement to infinite good. They include the full pardon of sins of infinite malignity and demerit, an interest in the justifying righteousness of our Lord Jesus Christ, and a title to that inheritance which is incorruptible, undented, and that fadeth not away. Nor are they less valuable in respect of permanence and duration, than of intrinsic worth. Being blessings not of a temporal but of a spiritual kind, they are in their nature capable of being enjoyed to eternity; and the same Almighty power and grace that provided them, and bestows them on any at the first, have given infallible security, that they shall be enjoyed to eternity, by all that once obtain an interest in them. God does not bestow the blessings of his saving grace on any, with a view to recall them. No; "the gifts and callings of God are without repentance." Whenever he once begins a good work in the heart, he has pledged himself to carry it on. "The righteous," as it is said in our text, "shall hold on his way; and he that hath clean hands shall be stronger and stronger."

This text, which is one of the expressions that dropped from the mouth of the inspired patriarch of the land of Uz, in the course of his conversation with his three uncharitable friends, is as plain a proof of the doctrine of the perseverance of the saints, as language can be easily conceived to make it. By the righteous, or just man here mentioned, we are unquestionably to understand a real saint of God, one who has been made legally righteous through the imputed righteousness of Christ, and practically righteous by the sanctifying influences of the Holy Spirit. This is not only the proper meaning of the word, (none but a person of this description being worthy of the name of a righteous man,) but it is also its most common signification in scripture. Thus, in such expressions as the following: "The righteous hath hope in his death." "The righteous is taken away from the evil to come." "The just," or the *righteous*, "shall live by faith." "The righteous shall shine forth as the sun in the kingdom of their Father." "Let me die the death of the righteous and let my last end be like his." The term *righteous* is obviously a designation of the real saints of God, in distinction, both from refined hypocrites, and openly wicked sinners. I do not say that the word has always this signification in scripture, for it is sometimes used to denote no more than innocence of a particular crime; and in a few passages, it is applied to persons who are righteous only in profession; yet the above is its proper and most common meaning; and whenever it occurs in a different acceptation, the context sufficiently discovers the sense in which it is to be understood. That it has this meaning in the text, may be still farther proved from the parallel expression in the following clause: "He that hath clean hands." This same expression in used in the 24th Psalm, in describing the character of the man who shall ascend into the hill of God, and stand in his holy place, where it is impossible that any but a real saint can be meant. Now, when it is said that "The righteous shall hold on his way; and he that is clean of hands shall be stronger and stronger," or as the original, with peculiar emphasis and simplicity expressed it, "The righteous one shall hold fast his way; and he that is clean of hands, shall add strength," we are certainly told in the plainest manner, that all real saints, he who once become truly righteous and are of clean hands, shall assuredly hold fast their attainments, and persevere to the end. The meaning of the expression cannot be, as some would represent it, "that the righteous may hold on his way;" or, that this is in the nature of things to be expected; or, that the righteous shall hold on his way so long as he continues righteous. The very tenor of the inspired writer's language, sufficiently refutes all such glosses. There is nothing conditional, nothing doubtful, nothing problematical here; but all is fixed and certain. "The righteous shall hold on his way." It is a matter of absolute certainty, that none who are once made truly righteous, and have become partakers of the grace of God in truth, shall ever totally fall away from that state, or finally apostatize.

When we maintain that all real saints shall, without fail, hold on in grace and holiness, and persevere to the end, it is by no means to be supposed, that the security for their doing so lies in themselves. No! Adam in innocence, with no inward corruption to lead him astray, was soon worsted by the artifices of Satan, and had not grace prevented, would have been ruined forever. Much more would believers, whose holiness in this world is so imperfect, and who have such a strong body of corruption cleaving unto them, soon fall a prey to the enemy of salvation, were they not upheld by the confirming grace of God. The question, then, at issue between Calvinists and Arminians on the doctrine of perseverance, is not what believers would do, did their continuance and final establishment in a state of grace depend on themselves, but what is the purpose of God and the constitution of the scheme of salvation on this subject. Is it the doctrine of scripture, that all who are once introduced into a justified state, and vitally united to the Lord Jesus Christ, are secured from total and final apostasy, by the confirming grace of God, being kept by his mighty power, through faith unto salvation? Or has God so suspended the salvation of his people, even after their justification, upon their own continued faith and obedience, that it is possible for them to forfeit their privileges, return to their former sinful courses, and fall at last into everlasting condemnation.

In this discourse we propose to prove, by a few arguments, that the former of these opinions is the doctrine of scripture, and to answer some objections.

1. That all true believers shall certainly hold fast their attainments and persevere to the end, is a truth which may be established, in the first place, from the scripture doctrine of election.

It is a doctrine taught with great plainness and frequency in scripture, that God, from all eternity, had special designs of mercy respecting a certain number of Adam's fallen posterity. Foreseeing from everlasting, the miserable condition into which the whole human race would be brought by sin, he purposed to glorify his grace and mercy in the salvation of a part of them, and this select and highly favored part he is represented in choosing or electing from among the rest, and purposing to make partakers of grace and holiness in time, and everlasting happiness in eternity. Eph. i. 4, 5. "According as he hath chosen us in him, before the foundation of the world, that we should be holy, and without blame, before him, in love; having predestinated us unto the adoption of children, by Jesus Christ, to himself, according to the good pleasure of his will." In this passage, the two following truths, among several others are clearly taught. 1. God, from eternity, did elect a part of mankind to be partakers of special privileges above the rest. "He hath chosen us before the foundation of the world, that we should be holy; having predestinated us to the adoption of children." The very word, to *choose*, implies a preference of some individuals to others; for if all are taken, there is plainly no choice; if some are elected, others necessarily remain not elected. 2. This eternal purpose or choice of God, is not an election of churches as such, or of bodies of men, to the means of salvation, but of individuals to salvation itself. This is sufficiently obvious from the connection of the passage with the preceding verse; "God, the Father, hath blessed us with all spiritual blessings in heavenly places in Christ, according as he hath chosen us in him." The spiritual blessings here mentioned, must surely mean the special mercies of grace and salvation, and not merely external privileges. To say, that all who enjoy the dispensation of the gospel, and have access to the means of grace, are blessed "with all spiritual blessings in heavenly places in Christ," is an explanation founded on such a gross perversion of language, that no time need be spent in refuting it. Now, the enjoyment of these spiritual blessings is plainly represented as the fruit of election; "He hath blessed us, according as he hath chosen us;" of consequence, the design of the purpose of election was to bestow these spiritual blessings, and not merely to call to external privileges. This view of the passage is still farther confirmed from the consideration, that in the whole context, the Apostle's language is exclusively directed to true believers. The persons to whom he is addressing himself, are the saints who are at Ephesus, the faithful in Christ Jesus; they are such as have "redemption through the blood of Christ, even the forgiveness of sins:" such as had trusted in Christ, believed in him, been sealed with the Holy Spirit, of promise, &c. all which characters, it is undeniable, are applicable to none but true believers. Of course, that election, of which the apostle speaks in verse 4, must also be confined to true believers, and cannot, therefore, be a general election of all who are within the visible church, to the means of salvation. Another passage, in which the same doctrine is taught with equal clearness, is 2 Thess. ii. 13, 14. "We are bound to give thanks alway to God for you, brethren, beloved of the Lord, because God hath, from the beginning, chosen you to salvation, through sanctification of the Spirit, and belief of the truth: Whereunto he called you by our gospel, to the obtaining of the glory of our Lord Jesus Christ." Here, again, God is plainly represented as electing certain individuals from eternity, and that this election was not of bodies of men to the means of salvation, but of individuals to salvation itself, is as evident as language can make it. "You, brethren, the beloved of the Lord, God hath from the beginning chosen (not to the means of salvation, but) to salvation he hath called you by our gospel (not to external privileges merely) to the obtaining of the glory of the Lord Jesus Christ." In 2 Tim. i. 9, we read, "Who hath saved us with a holy calling, not according to our works, but according to his own purpose and grace, which was given us in Christ Jesus, before the world began." In this passage the order of arrangement is different, but the doctrine taught is the very same with that of the two just quoted. In these, the apostle begins at election as the fountain, and from that descends to the streams; but here he begins at the streams, and ascends to the fountain. This, however, does not at all diminish its importance in our present argument. For if believers are saved and called, according to the eternal purpose of God, the design of that purpose must have been to bestow these blessing upon them. In 1 Pet. i. 2, believers are said to be "elected according to the foreknowledge of God the Father." In Acts xiii. 48, they are represented as "ordained to eternal life." In Jer. xxxi. 3, God is said to have "loved them with an everlasting love." In Rev. xiii. 8, and several other places, their names are said to be "written in the book of life" all which expressions plainly imply, that God had a fixed purpose of mercy with respect to a certain number of individuals, whose salvation, long ere time began its course, was unalterably fixed in the counsels of heaven. These passages, and they are only a few out of many that might have been quoted, seem sufficient to prove, that God from all eternity had a fixed design to bestow eternal life upon a select number of fallen sinners, commonly called in scripture the elect. Hence the question comes to be, is this design of God carried into execution? Does he actually save in time all whom he purposed to save from eternity? Or do circumstances prevent the accomplishment of his purpose with respect to some of them? The very statement of such a question is certainly sufficient to answer it. God is that Almighty Being who "doeth according to his will in the armies of heaven, and among the inhabitants of the earth. None can stay his hand, or say unto him, What doest thou?" It is impossible, therefore, that any of his designs can ever be defeated. All that he purposed, with respect to his elect, he will infallibly accomplish, for his counsel shall stand, and he will do all his pleasure.

It is in vain objected to this argument, that God's purpose to save the elect is conditional, and that it depends upon their own perseverance in faith and holiness, whether it shall take effect or not. The whole tenor of Scripture doctrine is directly opposed to such a supposition. When God is said to choose men to salvation, and to ordain them to eternal life, if language has any meaning, these expressions imply, that between the purpose of God, and the end of that purpose, namely, the salvation or eternal life of the elect, there is an inseparable connection. It is indeed one of the most absurd things Imaginable, to say that the immutable purposes of God are in any instance conditional, or suspended on the will of man for their execution. There is no doubt an order in the Divine purposes, and some things are decreed which imply the previous existence of other things before they can be brought to pass. But this by no means makes these previous things to be conditions; they are themselves determined events as infallibly fixed in the purpose of God, as those succeeding things to whose accomplishment they are preparatory. The means and the end, to use a common expression, are both included in the Divine decree. When God elects men to eternal life as the end, therefore, he must also be understood to elect them to faith and holiness, and to perseverance in these as the means. As without these means, the end could not be attained, his purpose must either have included both, or else it included neither;—it, wag not in fact an election to salvation at all.

The argument for the perseverance of the saints from the doctrine of election, will be placed in a still stronger light, if we consider the decree of election, not only as it lay hid in God's eternal counsels, but as it takes accomplishment in its objects in time. The scripture not only assures us that God had an eternal design to save the elect, (from this alone we might have inferred, with indubitable certainty, that all the elect will be saved,) but they also exhibit him as carrying this design into execution, and conferring salvation on the elect, in pursuance of his eternal purposes respecting them. Rom. viii. 29, 30, "Whom he did foreknow he also did predestinate to be conformed to the image of his Son, that he might be the first-born among many brethren. Moreover, whom he did predestinate, them he also called; and whom he called, them he also justified; and whom he justified, them he also glorified." It is impossible to desire a stronger argument for the doctrine before us, than what is furnished by these words. God not only had an eternal purpose to save a part of the human family, but this purpose he carries into complete execution, with respect to every one of its objects. All whom he foreknew and predestinated from eternity, he also calls, and justifies, and glorifies. Surely then, there can be no such thing as falling away from a state of grace. All the elect shall, without doubt, be brought into a gracious state; for whom he foreknew, those he called and justified: and not only this, but they shall be kept in it, and enabled to persevere to the end; for whom he called and justified, them he also glorified. Sophistry has in vain tried its powers to darken and pervert this passage. Its testimony is too luminous to be darkened, too pointed to be set aside. From the purpose of God, respecting his elect, from everlasting, to their final glorification in heaven, all the blessings of salvation are here connected together, as links of a golden chain, which can never be broken. Arminians tell us that perseverance is a condition of election, or that God elects such only to salvation as he foresees will persevere, but the scriptures teach a very different doctrine, for they speak of perseverance as one of the *fruits of election*, and represent it as a thing altogether impossible for any of the elect to fall finally away, for this very reason, because they are the elect. 2 Tim. ii. 10, "Nevertheless, the foundation of God standeth sure, having this seal, the Lord knoweth them that are his." Mat. xxiv. 24, "There shall arise false Christs and false prophets, and shall shew great signs and wonders, insomuch, that if it were possible, they shall deceive the very elect." Rev. xiii. 8, "And all that dwell upon the earth shall worship him, (the beast) whose names are

not written in the book of life." In each of these
passages, which we cannot stop to explain particularly,
final   perseverance   in   faith   and   holiness,
notwithstanding all the artifices of deceivers, is
represented as a certain consequence of election.
Others may be seduced from the paths of rectitude, and
have their faith overthrown; but all those whom the
Lord knoweth to be his own are sealed by Him to
himself, and on this foundation they stand sure. The
false miracles, and busy artifices of false Christs, and
false prophets, may deceive others, but the elect they
never can. All the rest of the world may wonder after
the beast, and have their souls ruined through his
delusions, but that select number whose names are
written in the Lamb's book of life, shall escape the
general contagion, and be preserved from perishing
with their generation. May we not, then, justly exclaim
with the apostle, "Who shall lay anything to the charge
of God's elect?" Their salvation was unalterably fixed in
the counsels of heaven before the world began. God
loved them with an everlasting love, and his purpose
and love, like himself, are immutable. "I am the Lord, I
change not," are his own comforting words to his
people, "therefore, ye sons of Jacob are not consumed."
None but the elect can ever be saved. "The election,"
saith the apostle, "hath obtained it, but the rest were
blinded." "Ye believe not," says Jesus himself, "because
ye are not of my sheep." With respect to the elect,
however, salvation is a matter of absolute certainty, for
God hath purposed, and who shall disannul it. Not all
the powers of earth and hell, nor even the corruption!
and backsliding of their own hearts can prevent the
accomplishment of God's eternal purpose, or cause a
single one of the objects of his electing love to perish.
Having loved his own, he loves them to the end. "My
Father who gave them me," says our Saviour,

concerning these very individuals, "is greater than all, and none is able to pluck them out of my Father's hand."

2. The doctrine of the perseverance of the saints may be proved from the design of Christ's mediation, and his all prevalent intercession before the throne of God. In God's eternal purpose to save the elect, he had always a respect to the mediatorial work of the Lord Jesus Christ. Hence, when we read of them as elected before the foundation of the world, they are said to be chosen in Christ, and when their names are represented as registered in the counsels of eternity, it is the slain Lamb's book of life in which they are written. In the counsels of peace, that were entered into by the Divine persons from everlasting, the elect are represented as given, or made over, by God the Father to God the Son, for the purpose of being redeemed by him, and made partakers of eternal life. John xvii. 2, "Thou hast given him power over all flesh, that he should give eternal life to as many as thou hast given him." These words plainly represent it as the very design of Christ's appointment to his mediatorial office, that he should confer eternal life on the elect. It is only the elect whom he is commissioned to save; and all of them, without a single exception, he must either rescue from the dominion of sin and Satan, and make partakers of eternal glory, or prove unfaithful to his trust. John vi. 39, "This is the will of the Father who sent me, that of all which he hath given me I should lose nothing, but should raise it up again at the last day." From those premises, it clearly follows, that the salvation of the whole elect world is committed to the charge of Christ, and that if he allows one of them to perish, he disappoints the design of his Father in appointing him to his mediatorial office, proves unfaithful in the charge with which he has been put in trust, and loses some of

those whom the Father sent him to save. But surely this is an insinuation which it were blasphemy to make against the faithful and good Shepherd, he possesses all the perfections of supreme Divinity, so that no enemy can wrest his sheep from him by superior skill or strength, and as his faithfulness and love are as unbounded as his power, none of those can ever be permitted to perish through his inattention or negligence. He himself, accordingly, speaks of it as a matter of absolute certainty, that all who were given him by the Father shall be kept by him through faith and holiness unto salvation, and not one of them left to perish. John vi. 37, "All that the Father giveth me shall come to me; and he that cometh to me, I will in no wise cast out." Chap. x. 27, 28, "My sheep hear my voice, and they follow me, and I give unto them eternal life, and they shall never perish, neither shall any pluck them out of my hand." It is scarcely possible to conceive language more definite than these words. Surely if it is a thing absolutely certain, that all whom the Father gave to Christ shall come to him, and that those who come to him, he will in no wise, or as the original expression bears, he will never at no time, cast out; that he gives eternal life to his sheep; that they shall never perish, nor any pluck them out of his hand: then it must be beyond all doubt, that all true believers shall, certainly, hold on in faith and holiness, and persevere to the end. Those who are saints only in profession, may fall away and perish forever; but Christ's sheep never can. To his charge they have been committed by his heavenly Father; and as he is at once a Son faithful over all his house, and a Saviour able to save unto the uttermost, he will, without doubt, watch over the lambs that have been entrusted to his care; gather them home to himself by his word and Spirit in their respective times; preserve them in faith and holiness when they are gathered; and present them all at last, in one vast assembly, before the throne of God. Not one of those who were given him to redeem shall be wanting at that great day, when he delivers up the kingdom to the Father, else how shall he be able to say, "Behold I and the children which thou hast given me! Those that thou gavest me I have kept, and none of them is lost."

But in order to perceive the argument for the perseverance of the saints, furnished by the design of Christ's office and work, in its full strength, we must view his undertaking in connection with its execution. In his everlasting engagements with the Father, he stipulated to lay down his life a sacrifice for sin; and as his reward for this, it was promised that he should see his seed, or have the salvation of the whole elect world given unto him. This arduous condition of the covenant he has now fulfilled, and he is of consequence ascended to the right hand of God, to claim possession of his reward. The intercession of Christ is something more than a prayer for the communication of grace and salvation to the elect: It is a prayer founded on the merit of his blood; a prayer for things which he has a full right to demand; it is, in short, not a prayer merely, but a claim. It's very language sufficiently proves this. John xvii. 24, "Father, I will that they also whom thou hast given me be with me where I am, that they may behold my glory." In these remarkable words, viewed in connection with the rest of the chapter, we have sufficient foundation on which to rest our faith of the doctrine of the perseverance of the saints, though there were not another passage of the kind in the Bible. Believers can never fall totally away from a state of grace, or perish in final apostasy, because they have a glorious intercessor at the right hand of God, who is continually pleading their cause, and whose suit on their behalf can never be rejected. Nothing can be more inconsistent, than to represent the above prayer as merely a supplication for support and success to the apostles, in the perilous labors on which they were soon to enter. Jesus himself, so far from limiting it to the eleven disciples, expressly extends it to all whom the Father had given him. Verses 20, 21, "Neither pray I for those alone," that is the eleven disciples, "but for them also that shall believe in me through their word; that they all may be one, as thou, Father, art in me, and I in thee." Equally inconsistent is it to say that this prayer is fulfilled in behalf of such believers as persevere, and that those who apostatize cast themselves out of an interest in it. Jesus expressly prays in behalf of all his people, that they may be enabled to persevere, so that if a single one of them should ever perish, even through their own willful apostasy, his prayer must be unanswered. "Holy Father, keep through thine own name those whom thou hast given me. I pray not that thou shouldest take them out of the world, but that thou shouldest keep them from the evil." Surely, then, believers, in committing the keeping of their souls to this glorious Saviour, may have strong consolation, and dismiss all apprehensions of his ever casting them off. To every true saint, as well as to his first disciples, his intercessory prayer extends; and in behalf of every one of them, it infallibly secures the communication of all spiritual blessings in time, and everlasting glory through eternity. Directing an eye of faith to their great high priest within the veil, they need not be afraid that their sins or backslidings cast them out of their interest in the love of God. "For if any man sin." says the apostle John, "we have an advocate with the Father, Jesus Christ the righteous." Numerous enemies from within and without may plot against them, and seek their destruction, but their glorious intercessor will repel all their accusations, and they shall never prevail against them. He is able to save unto the uttermost them that come unto God by him, seeing he ever liveth to make intercession for them. Satan himself, that great accuser of the brethren, may desire to have them, as he did Peter of old, that he may sift them as wheat, but vain is the impotent rage, and unsuccessful will be all his attempt; for Jesus has prayed for them, that their faith fail not.

      3. A third argument for the doctrine of the perseverance of the saints, may be derived from the constitution of the covenant of grace, and the unconditional nature of its promises. In the everlasting covenant, that was entered into by God the Father with God the Son, for the salvation of the elect, the whole work of fulfilling the condition of happiness was devolved upon Christ alone, and provision was made for dispensing all the blessings of salvation to the elect, in the way of a pure testament, and without suspending anything on their faith and holiness, or any condition to be fulfilled by them. Arminians, I am aware, deny this, for they maintain that the gospel covenant is made with believers at the first on the condition of faith and repentance; and that their continuing within the bond of the covenant, after they are brought into it, depends upon their own perseverance. Very different, however, is the doctrine of scripture. Faith and holiness, and perseverance in these, are everywhere spoken of in scripture, as blessings promised in the covenant, and cannot, therefore, be its conditions. Faith, holiness, and perseverance are, no doubt, indispensably necessary to salvation; but instead of enjoining these things on sinners, as the conditions which he requires them to fulfill before he will save them, God bestows them on his people as free gifts. Instead of waiting till they of their own accord believe, repent, and persevere, and

then saving them, he takes the whole work, from first to last, into his own hand, arrests them in the midst of their sinful career, implants faith in their hearts, sanctifies them by his word and Spirit, and keeps them by his mighty power through faith unto salvation. Indeed it were easy to show, that had the scheme of salvation been differently constituted—and God required of sinners faith, repentance, and perseverance, as the conditions of their salvation, these conditions would never have been fulfilled, and a single individual could never have been saved; the work of Christ, in assuming our nature, and dying in our room, must have proved altogether in vain; and the street of the heavenly Jerusalem, instead of being thronged with a multitude of redeemed men, which no man can number, must have been, through all eternity, without a single ransomed sinner to sing the praises of God and the Lamb. Admitting, then, that the covenant of grace, as dispensed to sinners, has no conditions, in the proper sense of that term, the doctrine of the perseverance of the saints follows as a necessary consequence. It is on account of no merit possessed, or condition fulfilled by them, that believers are brought into a state of grace at the first; a little can it be in consequence of anything done by them that they are afterwards kept in it. Free grace must have the whole of the praise of their salvation, and their own merit can have as little influence in carrying on the good work, as it had in beginning it. The very constitution of the gospel scheme of salvation, then, which bestows everything in a way of free grace, and suspends nothing on human merit, refutes the doctrine that the salvation of believers, even after their introduction into a justified state, depends on their own perseverance. Christ has wrought out a full title to happiness in the room of his people; and this title he either confers wholly as a gift of sovereign grace, or he does not confer it at all. He nowhere says to his people, if you persevere in faith and holiness, I will save you; but if you draw back and apostatize, I will cast you off. No; the tenor of the gospel covenant runs in every different strain. "This is the covenant which I will make with the house of Israel, after those days, saith the Lord. I will put my laws into their minds, and write them in their hearts; and I will be to them a God, and they shall be to me a people. I will make an everlasting covenant with them, that I will not turn away from them to do them good, but I will put my fear in their hearts, that they shall not depart from me."

In connection with the constitution of the covenant of grace, I mentioned the unconditional nature of its promises, as an argument for the perseverance of the saints. The most superficial reader of the Holy Scriptures must have observed, that they abound with exceeding great and precious promises. Like the stars which bestud the azure firmament, they sparkle in every page, and emit on every hand the luster of their cheering rays, to lighten the Christian's path in his darksome journey through this vale of tears. Abundant in their number, suitable in their nature, and rich beyond all calculation in the blessings which they bring to view, they are calculated to comfort the believer's heart in every diversity of circumstances, and to assure him of the unchanging love and gracious designs of his heavenly Father, even under the gloomiest dispensations. Nor, among the numerous blessings which the promises of the covenant exhibit to his faith, is there any mentioned with greater frequency, than confirming grace to establish him in the ways of holiness, and to preserve him from apostasy. God the Lord is exhibited as a sun and a shield; he will give grace and glory, and no good thing will he withhold from them that walk uprightly. His express language to every individual of his saints is, "I will never leave thee, nor forsake thee." "The mountains shall depart, and the hills be removed, but my kindness shall not depart from thee, neither shall the covenant of my peace be removed, saith the Lord, that hath mercy on thee." In seasons of desertion and spiritual embarrassment, they may be tempted to doubt their interest in the love of God, and to fear that he will cast them off. But let them dismiss their apprehension; the sun is not departed from the firmament, when his rays are intercepted by a cloud. Zion said, The Lord hath forsaken, and my Lord hath forgotten me. Can a woman forget her sucking child, that she should not have compassion on the son of her womb? Yea, says Jehovah, they may forget, yet will I not forget thee. Behold I have graven thee upon the palms of my hands; thy walls are continually before me." So far is God from casting off his people when they go astray, that he promises to heal their backslidings, and to love them freely. If his children forsake his law, and keep not his commandments, he has indeed said, that he will visit their transgressions with the rod, and their iniquity with stripes. "Nevertheless," he adds, "my loving-kindness will I not utterly take from him, nor suffer my faithfulness to fail." While promise of this kind remain in the Bible, do we go too far when we assert, that all true believers cither must be preserved from total apostasy, and enabled to persevere to the end, or God proves unfaithful to his promise? The latter insinuation, however, it were blasphemy to make. "God is not a man that he should lie, neither the son of man that he should repent: hath he said it, and shall he not do it? hath he spoken it, and shall he not make it good?" The above promises, I need hardly stop to remark, are altogether unconditional, that is, God does not promise such and such blessings to his people, provided they do such and such things. Had this been the tenor of them, they would have been of little importance in our present argument. Their very nature, however, sufficiently precludes such a supposition. Surely when God promises to his people, that he will never leave them nor forsake them; that he will not turn away from them to do them good; that he will put his fear in their hearts, that they shall not depart from him, he intimates, in the plainest manner, that he expects the fulfillment of no condition by them, to entitle them to have his promises accomplished in their behalf. His promises, in their very tenor, are absolute and unconditional; and in the faith of them, every believer has sufficient ground for saying, "The Lord will deliver me from every evil work, and preserve me unto his heavenly kingdom. The Lord will not cast off his people, nor forsake his inheritance. Thou wilt guide me with thy counsel, and afterward receive me to glory."

In connection with the constitution and promises of the covenant of grace, I may mention the oath of God which has been annexed to that covenant, securing not only the fulfillment of its stipulations to Christ, but also the dispensation of its blessings to his elect seed, as proving the doctrine of the perseverance of the saints. The oath of God is never introduced in scripture except on very solemn occasions, and seems intended to denote the absolute certainty and immutability of what he thus promises or threatens. The constitution of the Aaronical priesthood had no oath annexed to it, because it was to come to an end, and the whole dispensation, of which it was a part, to be changed. Christ's priesthood, however, has an oath annexed to it, because it is unchangeable, and is to endure forever. Psalm cx. 4, "The Lord hath sworn, and will not repent, Thou art a priest forever, after the order of Melchisedec." We nowhere read of an oath being annexed to the covenant of works, because one of its parties was a mutable creature, and the covenant itself, therefore, liable to be broken, and to fail of the end for which it was appointed. The covenant of grace, however, in all its parts, is a sure and unchangeable covenant, and has, therefore, the oath of God annexed to it. Nor does this oath, it is particularly to our present purpose to remark, respect only the fulfillment of the stipulations of the covenant to Christ, the covenant Head; it also secures the dispensation of its blessings to believers, the covenant children. Psalm lxxxix. 3, 5, 30, "Once have I sworn by my holiness, that I will not he unto David." But what is that which God has sworn unto David, and with respect to which he will not be unto him? It is that "his seed shall endure forever, and his throne as the sun before him." By the *seed* of Christ is commonly meant in scripture his elect seed, that is, the whole of those whom the Father gave him to save. In these words, then, God has plainly promised by oath, that the whole of that seed which he gave, to Christ shall be saved. Can we demand a stronger proof that no true saint shall ever be left to perish? The same thing seems to be intimated by what is said, Isaiah xlv. 23, "I have sworn by myself, the word is gone out of my month in righteousness, and shall not return, that unto me every knee shall bow, and every tongue shall swear." By every knee bowing, and every tongue swearing to the Redeemer, we cannot suppose the whole human race to be meant. The constrained obedience which wicked men shall be compelled to give to Christ at the last day, is never, that I am aware of, designated by such expressions. Besides, the following words plainly restrict them to that submission of heart which believers yield to the Redeemer in the day of regenerating grace. Verse 24, "Surely shall one say in the Lord have I righteousness and strength." Verse 25, "In the Lord shall all the seed of Israel be justified, and shall glory." By comparing the 23rd with the 25th verse, it appears that it is not the whole human race, but only the seed of Israel, that is, the spiritual Israel, or the elect of God, that is spoken of, when it is said, "To me every knee shall bow, and every tongue shall swear." Here then is another passage in which God interposes his oath that the whole elect seed of Christ shall assuredly be saved. That the oath of God as annexed to the covenant of grace is intended to assure believers of the immutability of the love of God, and the certainty of the salvation of all the elect, is put beyond all doubt by what the apostle says on the subject, in Heb. iv. 16-18, "For men verily swear by the greater; and an oath for confirmation is to them an end of all strife. Wherein God, willing more abundantly to show unto the heirs of promise the immutability of his counsel, confirmed it by an oath; that by two immutable things, in which it was impossible for God to be, we might have a strong consolation, who have fled for refuge to lay hold upon the hope set before us." The immutable things here mentioned, I need scarcely say, are the promise and the oath of God. Now, the design of annexing the oath along with the promise is expressly stated to be, to show more abundantly to the heirs of promise the immutability of God's counsel, and to give them a strong consolation. Can, then, there be a single doubt in our minds concerning the infallible perseverance of all true saints, when we have not only the promise, but the oath of God to assure us of it? The covenant of grace, that glorious channel through which all the blessings of salvation are conveyed and confirmed to Christ's elect seed, is not only dispensed to them without conditions, is not only full and sure in its promises, but is ratified by the oath of God itself.

Those who are once brought within this covenant, then, can never be cast out. With every believer, as well as with David, God hath made an everlasting covenant, ordered in all things and sure; of which, therefore, they may well unite with him in saying, "It is all my salvation, and all my desire."

4. The doctrine of the perseverance of the saints may be proved from the sure privileges and confirmed state of happiness into which sinners are represented as brought when they believe on the Lord Jesus Christ. So long; as sinners continue in their natural state, and have not accepted the gospel remedy by embracing the Saviour by faith, they are in a state of condemnation and spiritual death, and not only may perish but must perish, and that forever, if they die in that state. "He that believeth not is condemned already, because he hath not believed in the name of the only begotten Son of God." No sooner, however, does the Holy Spirit work a saving change in their hearts, and enable to embrace the Saviour by faith, than they pass from death unto life, obtain acceptance in the sight of God through the Mediator, and enter into a state of confirmed felicity. The scenes of life, through which they henceforth pass, may be of a checkered nature, their experiences and frames may undergo many alterations; but their state, as justified persons, in the sight of God, remains unaltered, and they can never forfeit their title to the heavenly inheritance. We might quote many texts in proof of this, but must content ourselves with a few. John v. 24, "Verily, verily, I say unto you, He that heareth my word, and believeth on him that sent me, hath everlasting life, and shall not come into condemnation, but is passed from death unto life." In these words, the change in the believer's state which takes place upon his believing in Christ, in not, only very great in respect of present importance, "he is

passed from death unto life;" but it is irreversible and eternal, "He hath everlasting life, and shall not come into condemnation." Language more definite was never used on any subject. The apostle Paul speaks to the same purpose, when he says, Rom. viii. 1, "There is now no condemnation to them who are in Christ Jesus, who walk not after the flesh, but after the Spirit." Nobody, unless he had a theory to support, would ever imagine the meaning of these words to be, that there is no condemnation for any, so long as they continue in Christ, and walk not after the flesh, but after the Spirit. The very scope of the apostle's language refutes such a supposition. "There is now no condemnation to them who are in Christ," that is, there is not only no condemnation for them at present, but there can never be any. The apostle is obviously stating a glorious privilege belonging to all believers, but it must surely be admitted to be only a comparatively small privilege to be delivered from condemnation at the present moment, if in the next we may bring ourselves under that terrible sentence anew. In John iv. 11, Our Saviour says to the woman of Samaria, "Whosoever drinketh of the water that I shall give him shall never thirst; but the water that I shall give him shall be in him a well of water springing up into everlasting life." These words certainly declare, as clearly as language can, that if saving grace is once communicated to the soul, the eternal salvation of that soul will be the infallible consequence. Whosoever drinks of that water of life which Christ gives his people, has not only his thirst quenched for the present, but it is expressly said he shall never thirst; what he has received shall be in him a well of water springing up into life everlasting.

In scripture, faith is everywhere represented as having an inseparable connection with salvation — a consideration which decisively proves that there can be no such thing as falling away from a state of grace. The word of Paul to the Philippian jailor, and which are generally received as a summary of the gospel message to sinners, are an instance of this, "Believe in the Lord Jesus Christ, and thou shalt be saved." It is a matter of absolute certainty, and there is nothing doubtful or conditional about it, that all who truly believe in Christ shall be saved. The very design of God, in sending his only begotten Son into the world, is said, John iii. 16, to be, "that whosoever believeth in him should not perish, but have everlasting life." Chap. vi. 47, Our Savior's own words are, "Verily, verily, I say unto you, He that believeth on me hath everlasting life." In 1 Pet. i. 9, "The end of faith" is expressly said to be "the salvation of the soul." All which expressions plainly imply, that wherever true faith once exists, the everlasting salvation of the soul will unquestionably be the consequence. In 1 Pet. i. 5, Believers are said to be "kept by the power of God through faith unto salvation;" an expression than which it is scarcely possible to conceive a stronger or more definite. As a specimen of the Arminian mode of interpreting those passages which are commonly quoted to prove the perseverance of the saints, we may mention Dr. Whitby's gloss upon these words, "Who are kept by the power of God through faith unto salvation," "that is," says he, "all who are preserved to salvation are kept by the power of God, but not that all believers are so kept." A more unnatural and distorted perversion of scripture language than this, Socinians themselves have seldom exhibited. 1. It is altogether inconsistent with the scope of the inspired apostle in the passage. In the context, he is obviously speaking of all who were true believers, of all who had been begotten again to a lively hope by the resurrection of Christ from the dead, who were possessed of a true love to Christ, and rejoiced in an unseen Saviour. Now, if it be of all true believers without exception, that the apostle says they are kept, securely kept, garrisoned, as the original word imports, by the power of God, through faith unto salvation, it is little less than giving the inspired writer the lie, to say that it is not to all believers, but only to a certain class of them that his words refer. 2. It is as self-contradictory, and inconsistent with the Arminians' own, as it is with the scope of the apostle in the passage, "Who are; kept by the power of God through faith unto salvation," "that is," says our opponent, "all who are preserved to salvation are kept by the power of God, but not that all believers are so kept." But why is it that all believers are not so kept? Not surely, on the Arminian's own doctrines, because the power of God fails to keep them, but because they do not keep themselves. The reason, according to these sentiments, why some believers persevere unto salvation, while others do not, is not that some are more kept by the power of God than others, but because, some succeed better in keeping themselves. By these views, then, it is not the power of God at all, but their own steadfastness and voluntary perseverance, that keeps any unto salvation; so that, according to this explanation, the meaning of the apostle's words comes to this, believers shall be kept by the power of God if they choose to keep themselves; or, which comes to the same thing, God will enable them to persevere, if they choose to persevere; which is such an obvious perversion of the language of the Holy Ghost, or rather such a depriving it of meaning altogether, that it needs no refutation.

Had our limits permitted a full illustration of the argument for the perseverance of the saints, from the scripture account of the privileges connected with a justified state, the following considerations might have been stated and illustrated at length: 1. The Holy Spirit is represented as dwelling in all believers, being in them an earnest of their future inheritance, and sealing them unto the day of redemption; which certainly implies that their present happy state is inseparably connected with eternal glory, and that there is no possibility of their falling finally away. 2. They are spoken of as already justified, fully delivered from the law as a covenant which has no longer any power either to justify or condemn them. Christ is become the end of the law for righteousness to them, and they are not under the law but under grace. 3. Their spiritual life, with all its blessings, is represented as flowing to them through the resurrection of Christ, and connecting with that glorious life, which he now lives at the right hand of God. "Because I live," is his own language to the meanest of his genuine disciple, "ye shall live also." "Ye are dead, and your life is hid with Christ in God." They are members of the body of Christ, yea, (so intimate and inseparable is their connection with him,) "of his flesh and of his bones." They are dead with Christ, have been crucified and buried with him, and are now quickened together with him, have been raised together with him, through the faith of the operation of God. And as Christ, being raised from the dead, dieth no more; death having no more dominion over him. So they are to reckon themselves dead indeed unto sin, but alive unto God through Jesus Christ. Of all which, with many similar expressions, I cannot conceive the meaning, except the spiritual life of all true believers is bound up in the bundle of life with their arisen Lord; and their everlasting salvation, in due time, as certain as that Christ their representative, has already taken possession of glory in their name. 4. Believers are represented as animated by a principle of hope, even of good hope, through grace, a hope which the Holy Spirit, has implanted, a hope which anticipates nothing less than eternal life, and a hope which maketh not ashamed. But, alas! how miserably indeed would it make them ashamed, should any of them, instead of a place on the right hand of the judgment seat, find themselves, on the great day, stationed on the left; and in place of everlasting happiness, obtain eternal misery as their final portion. 5. Believers are frequently introduced in scripture, as speaking with the greatest confidence to one another of their eternal welfare, and comforting each other's hearts with the glory that awaits them beyond death and the grave; a thing which would be altogether unwarrantable, were there not a perfect certainty, that all who are at present in a state of grace, shall be kept, and established in it, to the end. "I am confident of this very thing," says the apostle Paul to the Philippians, "that he who hath begun a good work in you, will perform it," carry it on, or finish it, as the original word means, "until the day of Jesus Christ." "God is faithful," he says to the believing Thessalonians, "who shall establish you and keep you from evil." "I thank my God always on your behalf," he says to the Corinthians, "for the grace which is given you by Jesus Christ; who shall also confirm you unto the end, that ye may be blameless in the day of our Lord Jesus Christ." "God is faithful by whom ye were called into the fellowship of his Son." Paul's epistles abound with passages of this kind; and indeed the whole volume of inspiration breathes the same spirit. The saints everywhere recognize themselves and one another, as the distinguished favorites of Heaven, the heirs of eternal glory, and the objects of God's peculiar delight and unchangeable love.

The scriptures contain satisfactory evidence, that assurance of salvation is attainable in this life, things which could never be obtained were there not an inseparable connection between a state of grace here, and a state of glory hereafter. Whence is it that the saints both in the Old and New Testaments, speak in such strong terms of the certainty of their salvation, and express so much assurance of their enjoying God forever in heaven? Is it from the confidence they have in their own strength, and a persuasion that their habits of holiness are now so confirmed, that they could set their spiritual enemies at defiance? Oh! no, they knew too well the deceitfulness and wickedness of their own hearts, to rest their hopes on any such ground. Besides, they knew, from inspired authority, that he that trusteth in his own heart is a fool. Whence then did their assurance arise? From no other source, certainly, than their faith in the riches of redeeming love, and in the precious promises of the covenant, assuring them, that God will never cast off his people, nor take his love from any whom he has once gathered to himself. The Holy Spirit within them, bore witness with their spirits, that they were the children of God; hence, they could not doubt, that he who had given grace, would, in due time, give glory; and preserve them safe to his heavenly kingdom. If this was the ground of their assurance, it was a sure foundation on which it rested. On the supposition, however, that their perseverance depended on themselves, their strong expressions of assurance can be no better than an empty boast, a foolish trusting on an arm of flesh, which was much more likely to disappoint, than realize their expectations. These are arguments on which it would have been easy to have dwelt more fully.

The doctrine of the perseverance of the saints may be proved from the consideration, that the scriptures expressly state, that when individuals fall away from a profession of religion, it is only the profession from which they fall, and that they were never in reality true believers. In I John iii. 6, there is a text so expressive to this purpose, that it must put the matter out of all doubt, in the view of every reasonable mind; "Whosoever abideth in him," that is, God, "sinneth not; but whosoever sinneth, hath not seen him, neither known him." The expression, to sin, in this text, and indeed throughout this epistle, does not mean the committing of some sin, but an habitual and allowed course of sinning, such as unrenewed men alone are chargeable with. When it is said, that "whosoever is born of God, doth not commit sin," the meaning obviously is, not that regenerated persons cease altogether from sinning, but only that they do not sin in the same allowed and habitual manner that they did in an unconverted state. "They cannot sin," it is immediately added, "because they are born of God;" that is, the principles and the bent of their renewed natures are opposed to sin, so that they cannot sin, that is, indulge themselves in sin, or sin with greediness and delight. Now, when it is said, that "whosoever sinneth, hath not seen God, neither known him," we are plainly informed, that all who indulge themselves in the habitual practice of sin, are not only not in a state of grace at present, but have never been in it. "They have not seen God, neither known him." Let a man's profession of religion have been as pure, and his life as exemplary as it may—let him even have been in the opinion of his fellow creatures, an eminent Christian, or, as Arminians would say, a real saint; still, if it turns out in the end that he falls away from his profession, and returns to the habitual practice of sin, these words authorize us to say of him, that he never had a saving knowledge of God, or a vital union to the Lord Jesus Christ. In chap, ii. 19, of the same epistle, there is another passage equally decisive to our present purpose: "They went out from us, but they were not of us; for if they had been of us, they would no doubt have continued with us; but they went out, that they might be made manifest that they were not all of us." The apostle is here speaking of some who had apostatized from the Christian faith, and made it evident by their practice, that they were strangers to the power of true religion. Now, concerning these persons, does he say, as Arminians would probably have done, that they had fallen from a state of grace? No; the very contrary. They were never true believers, else they would no doubt have continued such. "They went out from us, but they were not of us; for if they had been of us, they would no doubt have continued with us." The argument we have drawn from these two passages, appears to us extremely satisfactory. The language of both texts is so plain and pointed, that no ingenuity of criticism can evade it; and its express testimony is, that when any fall away from a profession of religion, it is the profession only from which they fall. Hence it follows, as clearly as one thing can follow from another, that all those who have once truly experienced the power of religion shall, without doubt, hold fast their attainments, and persevere to the end, "All who are truly righteous shall hold on their way; and they that have clean hands, shall be stronger and stronger."

II. We come now to answer some of the leading objections that have been urged against this doctrine. But before proceeding, it is proper to observe, that when a doctrine is once fairly proved, all objections against it come too late, and may be considered as already refuted. Two opposite doctrines cannot be both true; so that if we have already shown it to be a doctrine of scripture, that all true saints shall persevere, we are entitled to hold fast this position, whether we answer objections or not, till our arguments have been refuted. On this principle, we might fairly pass over this branch of the subject altogether. The doctrine is already proved, and all objections, of course, fall to the ground. As objections, however, are sometimes a source of perplexity to the mind, even when it is satisfied they must be false; and as the certainty of a doctrine may appear from the weakness of the opposition that is made to it, as well as the strength of the arguments by which it is supported, we shall very briefly consider a few of them.

1. The doctrine of the perseverance of the saints has been objected to, as inconsistent with facts. There are instances in scripture, it is said, of persons who fell, some totally, and others finally, from a state of grace. David and Peter, among others, have been mentioned, as instances of the former kind; and Solomon and Judas, of the latter.

This objection is easily answered. With respect to those who are said to have fallen totally, though not finally, from a state of grace, we remark, that there is not the least foundation in scripture for such an opinion. Believers, it is readily admitted, may fall into very gross sins; but this by no means implies, that the principles of grace are, for the time, totally withdrawn from their hearts. The apostle John speaks of it as the character of all who are born again, that "their seed abideth in. them," an expression which seems to point out, that the principles of grace, when once implanted in the heart, can never totally depart, though they may for a time be dormant and inactive. David and Peter both fell into very gross and aggravated sins; but that neither of them was total, any more than a final, apostate, is evident from the consideration, that our Saviour had prayed for Peter that his faith might not fail; which prayer may have been unanswered, if his faith was totally destroyed, even when it yielded to the temptation: And that David, after he was brought to a proper sense of his sin, prayed that the Holy Spirit might not be taken from him; an expression which plainly implies, that this had not yet taken place. With respect to Solomon whom to me, with a presumption that is altogether unwarrantable, have pronounced a final, as well as a total, apostate; we remark, that great as his fall was, there in sufficient reason to think that he lived to see the evil of his doings, and became a true penitent. The book of Ecclesiastes, and part of that of Proverbs, we have every reason to believe were written in his old age, after he had seen the evil of his former courses; and they bear ample testimony to the depth and sincerity of his repentance, and see reality of his saintship, after all the falls he had been guilty of. With respect to Judas, the importance of the objection depends principally upon a text of scripture, which has been supposed to imply, that he was once a true believer. John xvii. 12, "I have kept," says Jesus to his Father, "those that thou hast given me, and none of them is lost, but the son of perdition; that the scripture might be fulfilled." Concerning this passage, however, I remark, that in the Greek language, the exceptive particles (Εἰ μη), here translated *but*, do not mean, that the person or thing excepted belongs to, or is one of, those from which it is excepted, but only that it is excluded from them. Thus, in Luke iv. 27, where the same particles are used: "And many lepers were in Israel in the time of Eliseus the prophet; and none of them was cleansed, saving (until, but, or except) Naaman the Syrian." From these words we are not to suppose that Naaman was one of the lepers of Israel, and the only one of them that was cleansed; for Naaman was a Syrian, and not an Israelite at all. The meaning of the words, then, must be this: There were many lepers in Israel in the time of Eliseus, and none of them whatever was cleansed; but, or only, Naaman the Syrian was cleansed. Now, giving the particles the same signification in the verse before us, its meaning will be as follows: I have kept, through thy name, the men that thou hast given me, and none of them is lost; but, or only, the son of perdition is lost. This is only the statement of a circumstance by the way. The expression does not imply that Judas was one whom the Father had given to Christ, any more than the verse just quoted, implies that Naaman the Syrian was one of the lepers of Israel. Were this the proper place for a discussion of this kind, it were easy to prove that this criticism completely removes the objection; but that even the English reader may be satisfied on the subject, we have another consideration to propose, which alone is sufficient to put the matter out of all doubt. There is ample evidence in scripture, that Judas never was a true believer; of consequence, the above passage must be explained in a way consistent with this: And it is altogether vain to adduce his fall as an instance of apostasy from a state of grace. By the evangelist John, Judas is represented as having been a mere hypocrite from the beginning. Thus, in chap, vi. 70, at a time when neither his external character, nor even, as we have reason to think, his preaching and miracles were at all inferior to those of the other apostle, our Saviour says, with respect to him, "Have not I chosen you twelve, and one of you is a devil?" He does not say, that, he would afterwards become a devil, but that he is one at present. Even then, that diabolical spirit, which was afterwards to manifest itself in betraying his Master was lurking within him, and though invisible to the eyes of men, it was well known to the omniscient Jesus. Hence, then, Judas is pointed out as having never been a true believer, his fall, which all allow to be final, in obviously no objection to the doctrine of the perseverance of the saints.

2. A second class of objections to this doctrine

has been deduced from texts of scripture, which are supposed to imply that it is quite possible for real saints to fall from a state of grace, and to perish forever. Of passages of this kind, few have been more insisted on, than Heb. x. 38. "The just shall live by faith, but if any man draw back," or, as Arminians strenuously maintain the words should be read, "but if he draw back, the soul shall have no pleasure in him." Concerning this passage, I remark, 1st, That, though the words, any man, in our version, are a supplement, they are a supplement which the connection requires, and the original sufficiently warrants. The Greek words[4] are most literally translated in an impersonal form, thus, "If there be a drawing back," without saying by whom. Besides, in comparing this verse with the one immediately following, it is plain that the apostle is speaking of two classes of men in the Church; the one drawing back unto perdition, the other believing unto the saving of the soul. These two classes, he plainly represents as altogether distinct; and the very scope of his language seems to preclude the possibility of any passing from the one class, and taking their standing with the other. "We are not of them who draw back unto perdition, but of them who believe unto the saving of the soul." Admit the Arminian gloss of the verse under consideration, however, to be correct, and the propriety of this distinction is destroyed. The apostle, in short, is just made to assert in one verse, what he denies in the next. To show still more clearly the futility of this objection, I remark, 2ndly, that even though we should admit the correctness of the reading, "The just shall live by faith; and if he draw back," &c. the words are still insufficient to support the argument

---

[4] Εαν υποστελητασ. Now viewing the verb impersonally, it obviously requires to have an indefinite nominative, such as τισ, (*any man*,) supplied to express fully its proper meaning.

that is drawn from them. Read in this way, the clause, "if he draw back," and it expresses only a supposition. A supposition, however, by no means implies the possibility of the thing supposed. Thus, when the apostle says, Gal. i. 8, "But though we, or an angel from heaven, preach any other gospel unto you than that which we have preached unto you, let him be accursed;" he evidently makes a supposition for the sake of argument, which never can be realized. "Though an angel from heaven were to preach another gospel," will any infer from this, that it is possible for a holy angel to descend from heaven, and preach erroneous doctrines to mankind? No; the thing is absurd. So, in this passage, the supposition of a just man drawing back, may be made merely for the sake of argument, and the thing supposed be altogether impossible. Certain passages in the book of Ezekiel, which speak of a righteous man turning away from his righteousness, and perishing in his iniquity, have also been advanced as objections to this doctrine, that concerning these, it is sufficient to remark, that the prophet may be only making a supposition for the sake of argument, or, which seems to be a true account of the matter, it is mere professional righteousness of which he is speaking. As no sinner, who truly repents, and amends his ways, shall be excluded from salvation, on account of his former wickedness. So no man that bears the character of a righteous person for a time, but afterwards falls away, and lives and dies in the practice of sin, shall escape condemnation on account of his former righteousness. The righteousness of the early part of his life, so far from compensating for his later wickedness, will thus be proved to have been a mere external form, without proper internal principle, and will, therefore, avail him nothing in the day of judgment. Another objection to this doctrine, has been drawn from the words of Paul to the Galatian church, v. 4. "Christ is become of no effect unto you; whosoever of you are justified by the law, ye are fallen from grace." But from the general scope of the apostle, it is easy to see that it is the doctrine of grace, and not a state of grace from which the apostle here says the Galatians had fallen. In other places of the chapter, he tells them he stood in doubt of them, and was afraid he had bestowed his labor upon them in vain. If, however, he had been sure that they were fallen from a state of grace, he could have been in no doubt about them whatever, but must have been certain, that his labor in preaching the gospel to them had been altogether in vain. With respect to the doctrine of grace, however, the fall of the Galatians was abundantly manifest; and in regard to this, the apostle had sufficient grounds for saying to them, without any hesitation, "ye are fallen from grace." Many other texts of scripture have been urged as objections to this doctrine, on which our limits forbid us to enter. It is sufficient to remark, in general, that they admit of similar explanations with those which have been quoted; and that they have been satisfactorily proved to be totally insufficient to warrant the conclusion, which the adversaries of this doctrine deduce from them. Since it is a doctrine clearly taught in scripture, that all true saints shall infallibly persevere, it must be vain to hold up a few detached passages in opposition to this. The scriptures throughout must be consistent with themselves; so that if a few texts occur, which, to a superficial reader, may seem inconsistent with an established doctrine; there must be some principle of interpretation by which the apparent discrepancy can be reconciled. With respect to the doctrine under consideration, the passages seemingly opposed to it, are few in number, and to reconcile them with it, is easy; so that they can be of no weight whatever when laid in the balance, against that abundant mass of evidence, by which the doctrine has been established.

3. A third objection that has been advanced against the doctrine of the perseverance of the saints, is that it has a licentious tendency. But never was a more unjust insinuation thrown out against any doctrine. Let stubborn facts bear witness to the truth. Are those who deny this doctrine, more distinguished for devotedness of soul to God—greater watchfulness over the frame of their hearts, or more circumspection of external conduct than those who maintain it? Arminians themselves have never dared to say so. Was there ever a holier man, or a more zealous Christian than the apostle Paul, and yet do we anywhere read of an individual who had attained a stronger assurance than be of his interest in the love of God, and the certainty of his salvation?

In his mind, then, it is obvious this doctrine must have had the very reverse of a licentious tendency, and similar will be its effects upon all who view it in a proper light, and improve it in a scriptural manner. Ungodly men, indeed, as the apostle Jude speaks, may turn the grace of God into licentiousness, but it can be no valid objection against any doctrine that wicked men may pervert and abuse it. From the very nature of things, indeed, it were easy to show that the doctrine of the perseverance of the saints, has properly no licentious tendency. The certainty of succeeding in a secular undertaking never operates as a discouragement to engage in it with alacrity, and to prosecute it with diligence; but the reverse. Why then, may not the same thing hold with respect to religion? The Christian world, at the present day, is happily distinguished for great activity in disseminating the scriptures, and spreading the knowledge of the gospel among mankind; but will any maintain that the assurance of ultimate success, furnished to them by the light of prophecy, has a tendency to discourage Christians in this good work? Because the purpose and predictions of God have already made it a matter of certainty, that the Mediator's kingdom will be enlarged, and all nations converted to the Christian faith; do Christians think themselves warranted to stand by with folded arms, and to leave God to accomplish his prediction as he pleases? No, the idea is absurd, and the man would be in danger of being thought destitute of reason, who should seriously maintain it. But equally absurd is it to say, that believers are encouraged to become [remins] in holiness, from the consideration, that their salvation is already secured, and that God will never cast them off. The thought of this, so far from making them careless and negligent in running the ways of God's commandments, rather stirs them up to run with renewed alacrity. Never does the believer find his heart animated with a greater hatred of sin, and stronger resolutions to study universal holiness, than when he thinks of the unchangeable love of God, and the ample security furnished in the everlasting covenant for his preservation in grace and holiness, and perseverance to the end. God has promised never to cast off his people. This is the girdle with which the believer binds up his loins, to prosecute his spiritual journey; not the cloak in which he wraps himself to lie down and sleep by the way. God has promised to work in his people both to will and to do after his own good pleasure. This, so far from being an inducement to indolence, stirs them up to increased diligence, in working out their salvation with fear and trembling.

    A number of inferences might easily be deduced from the subject which we have been considering; but with two short remarks we must now conclude the discourse.

1. From this subject we may see the erroneous nature, and dangerous tendency of Arminian doctrine. It is only one of what are commonly called the five points of the Arminian controversy, that we have been at present considering; but from their sentiments on the single subject of perseverance, it is easy to see that the doctrines of the Arminian school are widely different from those of the gospel of Christ. Can any doctrine be more clearly taught in scripture, than that all true saints shall infallibly persevere? Yet Arminians altogether deny this; and maintain it to be quite possible for a real saint to perish forever. According to them, there is nothing unscriptural in supposing a man to be, today, in a state of justification and life, a child of God, and an heir of heaven; and, tomorrow, to be thrown back into a state of condemnation and death, and to become again a child of Satan, and an heir of hell. Nor is this doctrine only erroneous in its nature; it is also highly dangerous of in its tendency. It evidently tends to deprive the saints of God of much consolation—to discourage them in the exercise of committing the whole work of their salvation into the hands of their Redeemer, and limiting in him for confirming grace, to enable them to persevere. Nay, we may even go farther, and say, that it has a tendency to draw away their faith from the Saviour altogether, and to lead them to build their confidence on their own strength. For if Christians are taught that Christ keeps his people in the ways of truth and holiness, only as they choose to keep themselves, nothing can follow more naturally, than that their faith and expectations will be directed to that quarter whence their help is to come; and thus the Saviour will be dethroned altogether in their hearts, and that idol, self, on which

they are naturally too prone to trust, exalted in his room. Considering these, and many other things on which we cannot at present insist, it is not surprising that the friends of the truth as it is in Jesus, have always viewed Arminianism as a very dangerous system, and charged its abettors with corrupting and perverting the precious doctrines of the cross of Christ. At the present day, when Arminian doctrines are well known to have still an extensive prevalence, it is the imperious duty of all the friends of truth to oppose them to the utmost of their power, and to lay themselves out, by every prudent and laudable method, to counteract their influence, and disseminate the gospel in its purity. "A little leaven," says the apostle, "leaveneth the whole lump." A small departure from the truths of the Divine word will lead to dangerous consequences. Be it, then, our earnest study to be well established in the present truth, and to act the part of faithful witnesses for Christ, in lifting up a decided testimony against every error in doctrine, or corruption in worship and discipline, that may have crept into his church. Those who keep the word of his patience, he promises to keep from the hour of temptation, which shall come upon all the world, to try them that dwell upon the earth. "Be faithful to the death, and I will give thee a crown of life."

2. We may see from this subject, of what immense importance it is to be a real saint of God. The privileges connected with a justified state, are, in respect of intrinsic worth, of greater value that tongue can express or heart conceive; and they are confirmed to the believer by the promise and the oath of God, and the sure charter of the everlasting covenant, so that he can never be left to forfeit his interest in them, or to fall short of the heavenly inheritance. All the hearers of the gospel ought to think much on these things—those

who have as yet obtained no interest in the blessings of God's saving grace, that they may be impressed with a sense of their danger, and stirred up to flee from the wrath to come; and those who have, that they may thank God for his abundant goodness, and be quickened, by a grateful sense of his mercies, to greater diligence in his service. Since, too, believers are preserved from apostasy, and enabled to persevere, not by their own strength, but by the confirming grace of God, it should be their habitual exercise to commit the keeping of their souls into their Savior's hand, and to go forward in their spiritual journey in dependence upon his strength. To be diligent and persevering in the use of all the means of grace, and yet not to trust in our use of these means; to live denied to our own righteousness and strength, and to rely wholly upon our all sufficient Saviour for everything we need, seem to be exercises which constitute the very essence of that life of faith which true Christians live. In these exorcisms, then, be it our study to abound more and more, and thus to increase our diligence in working out our salvation with fear and trembling, trusting in God to work in us, both to will and to do of his good pleasure.

SERMON VII:
Grounds of Fear to Gospel Preachers

"I was with you in weakness, and in fear, and in much trembling."—1 Cor. ii. 3.

THESE words express the state of the apostle's mind, while he labored in word and doctrine among the Corinthians. Considering the natural intrepidity of the apostle's character, it may perhaps appear surprising to some that he should have been agitated with such feelings, while employed in such a work. From what is recorded of his history in scripture, it is easy to discover that he was not a man of a timorous disposition, or in much danger of being disturbed by groundless fears. In his unconverted state, his bold and intrepid spirit enlisted in the service of a blinded zeal, for what he considered the religion of his forefathers, discovered itself in the furious persecution which he carried on against the followers of Christ. Thinking it his duty to do everything in his power to extirpate the name of Jesus of Nazareth from the earth, he stealed his heart against the feelings of pity, and the calls of humanity, and barbarously made havoc of the church, in hauling multitudes of unoffending men and women, and committing them to prison. After his conversion, the same strength of zeal and intrepidity of character, that had distinguished him as a persecutor, characterized him as a preacher. Setting his face like a flint against the scorn of the world, and all the dangers of persecution, he began immediately to preach Christ in the synagogues, and continued ever afterwards a faithful and undaunted herald of the doctrine of the cross. In fulfilling the duties which devolved upon him, as an apostle of Christ, he was subjected to incessant fatigues and innumerable hardships; but all these he surmounted with fearless intrepidity. The dangers of persecution often stared him in the face, but his courage never deserted him. He was called before kings and councils for Christ's sake, but his undaunted spirit remained unshaken, and he spoke to them with dignity. Death itself seemed sometimes ready to swallow him up, but he trembled not at its approach. Respecting the greatest temporal hardships and dangers to which he was subjected, he resolutely declares, "None of these things move me, neither count I my life dear unto me, so that I might finish my course with joy, and the ministry which I have received of the Lord Jesus, to testify the gospel of the grace of God." Such, then, was the man whose heart was filled with fear and trembling while engaged in the work of preaching the gospel. But what, it will next be asked, was there in the nature of that work calculated to impress his mind with such feelings? To worldly men, unacquainted with the influence of religious motives, and who judge merely by natural principles, there will appear nothing in that work calculated to give rise to such fears. When the apostle stood and discoursed to his Corinthian audience on the doctrine of the gospel, what was there in his situation, so different from that of a Grecian orator haranguing a popular assembly, or a Roman counselor addressing the senate, that his feelings should have been so different? Why did not the consciousness of his talents support him against every fear, when his discourses fell with such a powerful effect upon the minds of his auditors? Why was not his heart filled with pride and self complacency, from the thought of the wonders which his eloquence had achieved? In this spirit, a man of unsanctified talents would, in all probability, have preached; but such was not the spirit of the apostle Paul. He thought on the infinite value of the immortal souls, with whose eternal welfare the truths which he delivered were so closely connected, and every feeling of vanity, every emotion of self complacency was banished from his mind. He reflected on the high responsibility of the watchman's office, and his heart trembled with fear. That spirit of undaunted intrepidity, which raised him above every fear in the presence of men, could not support him, in the same manner, when he stood in the presence of God. "1 was with you in weakness, and in fear, and in much trembling;" are the words in which he expresses the feelings which agitated his mind, when he stood up in the name of God, to deliver the messages of the gospel to fellow sinners.

In this text, the apostle uses three expressions, to describe the manner in which he felt and acted, when laboring in the work of the gospel among the Corinthians; he was with them "in weakness, and fear, and much trembling." As the first, of these words suggests a somewhat different idea from the two last, we mean to leave it in a great measure out of view, and to turn our attention, in this discourse, to some considerations which may be supposed to have given rise to that fear and trembling which the apostle felt when employed in preaching the gospel, and which ought to impress the mind of everyone who engages in that work with similar feeling. In selecting a subject of this kind for discussion, none, we think, will insinuate, that the speaker is studying merely the gratification of his own feelings in his present circumstances, to the neglect of the edification of his hearer. To those that hear the gospel, as well as those that preach it, it cannot but be an interesting inquiry, to endeavor to ascertain what it was that impressed the mind of the apostle with those deep anxieties of which he speaks in the text. Surely the messages of the gospel must be something of a very important and solemn nature, even to those who are its hearers, when such a man as the apostle Paul had his heart filled with fear and trembling, when employed in publishing these messages to his fellow-sinners. Besides, as this text is given to us as a part of the canon of scripture, a discussion of it is connected with the explanation of scripture, and cannot be thought uninteresting by any who view the whole word of God, as given them for their instruction and edification.

In our remarks on this subject, we propose to leave out of view the duties of the pastoral office, In the extensive sense of the expression, and to turn our attention to some circumstances connected with the work of merely preaching the gospel, or delivering its messages, calculated to impress the mind with fear. It is entirely of the preaching of the gospel, that the apostle is speaking in the context; "And I, brethren," he says, "came to you not with excellency of speech, or of wisdom, declaring the testimony of God. I determined not to know anything among you, save Jesus Christ, and him crucified: and my speech, and my preaching, was not with enticing words of man's wisdom, but in demonstration of the Spirit, and of power." All these expressions, obviously refer to preaching the gospel, or the simple delivery of its messages to sinners; so that, read in connection with the context, the words of the text convey the idea that, connected with the work of simply delivering the gospel messages, there are considerations which impressed the mind of the apostle with the deepest fear, and which ought, no doubt, to impress everyone who engages in that work in a similar manner. To mention, then, a few considerations, calculated to impress the mind of the gospel preacher with fear, and to conclude with some improvement, are all that is proposed in the present discourse.

1. The high responsibility connected with the work of preaching the gospel, is a consideration calculated to impress the mind of everyone who engages in that work, with the deepest fear. Every one that stands up to deliver the messages of the gospel, undertakes to warn his hearers from God; and if he does not faithfully deliver the messages with which he is put in trust, God will hold him responsible for the guilt of all the evils with which his unfaithfulness may be attended.

Responsibility to his great Creator and Lawgiver, for all that he does, is a view of the character of man, inseparably connected with his moral nature. Called into existence for the purpose of serving and glorifying his Creator, and endowed with rational and moral faculties, titling him for these duties; God justly holds him responsible for the use which he makes of these faculties, and the manner in which he lives to the great end of his being. Adam, in a state of innocence, was responsible to God for the improvement which he made of the exalted privileges which he enjoyed, and of the rational and moral powers with which he was endowed. His condemnation, on account of his rebellion and disobedience was not a matter of sovereignty with God, but an act of strict justice, founded on his moral nature, and necessary to maintain the glory of his perfections, and the honour of his righteous government. In their fallen state, sinners are unable to do anything in the way of glorifying God aright: still they are under obligation of his law, and amenable to his tribunal for all that they do. To deny this, were just to assert, that a creature may pass from being under the authority of God whenever it pleases, and deprives him of his right to punish it by the very act by which it renders itself deserving of punishment.

Man's responsibility to God, is frequently asserted in scripture; and the strong language that used on the subject, particularly with respect to the extent of his responsibility, is calculated to make a deep impression upon the mind of every one that seriously considers it, "God," it is expressly said, "will bring every work into judgment, with every secret thing, whether it be good, or whether it be evil." "God will judge," says the apostle, even "the secrets of men, by Jesus Christ, according to my gospel." "For every idle word that men speak," says our Redeemer himself, "shall they give an account in the day of judgment." Whatever, then, be the privileges or means of improvement which a man enjoys whatever be the duties in which he engages, the work which he performs, or the sins with which he is chargeable—for all these things God will bring him into judgment. This is the law which the unalterable appointment of his righteous Judge and Lawgiver has impressed upon his moral nature, he must give an account.

Accountable to God for every privilege that he enjoys, and amenable to his tribunal for everything that he does, man's responsibility increases in proportion to the extent of his privileges, and the importance of the duties which he is called to perform. Those who are born in a land of Christian light, and sit under the dispensation of the gospel, enjoy greater privileges, and are laid under a deeper responsibility, than those to whom the glad tidings of a God reconciled in Christ, were never communicated. Such as are called to publish the messages of the gospel to their fellow creatures, engage in a work of a peculiarly responsible nature; because consequences of inconceivable importance are connected with it, and it lays them under obligations to be accountable, to a certain extent, for others as well as for themselves. Standing up to speak to their fellow creatures, on subjects connected with their eternal welfare, they undertake to warn them from God; and if they do not faithfully deliver the messages with which they are entrusted, the guilt of all the evil which their unfaithfulness may produce, will be required at their hand. The description of the duties or the watchman, given in Ezek. xxxiii. seems to contain nothing but what is applicable to all who are called to preach the gospel; and the high responsibility which God himself there connects with that work, seems alone sufficient to impress the mind of everyone who engages in it, with fear and much trembling. "Son of man," says Jehovah to the prophet, "I have set thee a watchman unto the house of Israel; therefore thou shalt hear the word at my mouth, and warn them from me. When I say unto the wicked, O wicked man, thou shalt surely die; if thou dost not speak to warn the wicked from his way, that wicked man shall die in his iniquity; but his blood will I require at thine hand." The blood of a person is a common expression in scripture for the crime of murder, here, however, it is not the blood of the body, but the blood of the immortal soul, that is meant. What human heart is there that does not tremble at the thought! To have shed the blood of an innocent fellow creature, and to be called to account for this at the hands of men, is a situation in which any of us would shudder to be placed. The thought of the innocent blood which we had shed, crying for vengeance against us—the terrors of the earthly tribunal before which we were won to appear, and the ignominious punishment to which we must afterward be subjected, would rush upon our mind and almost drive us, with Job, to curse the day in which we were born. But far more awful still, than all this, is the thought of being called before the tribunal of God, to account for the blood of immortal souls, that had perished forever through our negligence and unfaithfulness. "It is a fearful thing," says the apostle, "to fall into the hands of the living God." To be called before hit tribunal to give an account for ourselves, is a thought which cannot but fill the serious mind with deep solemnity and awe; but to have our responsibility extended also unto others, is a consideration, under which, the man must be stout-hearted indeed, who can support himself without being impressed with the feelings which agitated the mind of the apostle, when laboring in the work of the gospel among the Corinthians, "I was with you in weakness, and in fear, and in much trembling."

2. The inconceivable value of the never-dying soul, is a second consideration strongly calculated to impress the mind of the gospel preacher with fear. The worth of an immortal spirit is a subject on which strong language has been used, but on which none too strong can ever be employed. "What is a man profited," says our Redeemer himself, "though he gain the whole world, and lose his own soul? or what shall a man give in exchange for his soul?" According to the common sentiments of mankind, the man who should gain the whole world, would obtain a prize of such extraordinary value, that he could scarcely purchase it at too high a price. A small part of the wealth of a single city, is thought sufficient to make a person rich. The man who possesses, as his property, a part of a single province of a single kingdom, is ranked among the great ones of the earth, to whose affluence and exalted station mankind are naturally disposed to look up as the summit of earthly felicity. But though all the wealth of all the cities of the world were collected into one heap—though its fertile provinces, and opulent kingdoms, were united into one property, and the whole offered to a man as the price of his soul, he could

not consent to the exchange without being an infinite loser. "What is a man profited though he gain the whole world, and lose his own soul?" Nay, the words of our Saviour warrant us to go farther than this: "What shall a man give in exchange for his soul?" Though the world were infinitely more valuable than it is—though its ponderous rocks, and massy mountains, were converted into silver, and its small stones into jewels, though its seas, and lakes, and rivers, were changed into precious oils, and the whole mass of earth into pure gold; nay, though, in addition to all this, the sun were changed into a diamond, the moon into pearl, and all the stars that bestud the azure firmament into the most costly gems, and the whole thrown into the balance against an immortal soul, one soul would outweigh them sill, and "call the astonishing magnificence of unintelligent creation poor!" There are two circumstances which contribute to raise the human soul to such an inconceivable value; it is immortal, and it must exist through all eternity either in a state of inconceivable happiness, or indescribable misery. Were its existence to terminate at death, or even at any period after it, however remote; or were its eternal duration a matter of little importance to itself, by being attended with no great degree, either of happiness or misery, its value would not be so inconceivably great. The truth, however is, that every human being possesses a soul, which shall not only outlast the moon and stars, and survive to eternity, but must exist in eternal duration either in a state of the most exalted and untangled felicity, or of the most consummate and indescribable misery: so that, of a soul that perishes, no language can paint the loss of a soul that is saved, no created mind can conceive the importance.

Now, if we consider that the work of the

preacher of the gospel is closely connected with the salvation of immortal souls, having this indeed for its very object, we must instantly perceive what abundant reason there is for his mind being impressed with deep solemnity and fear when engaged in his arduous duties, standing up to address immortal souls on subjects connected with their eternal welfare. What a trembling anxiety ought he to feel, lest by want of plainness in warning, of earnestness in expostulating, or by any kind of unfaithfulness in delivering the messages with which he is entrusted, he prove accessory to the eternal ruin of any of those whom he addresses! An immortal soul lost forever through his negligence or unfaithfulness, what an alarming thought! Were a man placed in such circumstances, that the preservation or destruction of a flourishing empire depended, under providence, on his single exertions and faithfulness to the duties of his trust, how would he feel the responsibility of his situation, and be constantly trembling with anxiety, lest by a moment's inattention, or any unguarded step he should contribute to bring about such a terrible disaster as the temporal destruction of a vast multitude of his fellow creatures? But the temporal destruction of the most populous and flourishing empire that ever existed, were but a trifling disaster, compared with the loss of an immortal soul. The aggregate of happiness destroyed in the one case, may be calculated and exhausted, that in the other, never can. A whole world, with all the animated beings, and gay inhabitants that it contains, swept away in a moment from existence, and made to become as if it never had been, were but a small calamity in the natural universe, compared with the spiritual calamity of an immortal soul shut out forever from the realms of bliss and felicity, and driven away with the devil and his angels into everlasting destruction. Even though God, then, had connected no responsibility at his own tribunal with the work of preaching the gospel, there is still enough in the very nature of the consequences depending upon it to impress the minds of all who engage in it with the deepest anxiety and fear. It is true, it is only the blessing of God which can make the most faithful preaching of the word effectual to the salvation of the hearers. This, however, ought by no means to diminish the gospel preacher's anxiety for the eternal welfare of those whom he addresses. The use of the means is what God requires at his hands, and it is only in the diligent and faithful use of the means that his blessing can be expected. While he looks habitually unto the Lord, then, for a blessing upon his labors, the gospel preacher ought to make it his constant, study, and earnest prayer, to be enabled to deliver faithfully the messages with which he is entrusted, and to fear and even tremble, lest by an unfaithful delivery of them he mar the success of his labors, and become accessory to the eternal ruin of immortal souls.

It is only in taking heed to himself and to his doctrine, and attending constantly to the duties incumbent upon him, that he has the promise of saving both himself and them that hear him.

3. A third consideration calculated to impress the mind with fear in delivering the messages of the gospel, is the solemnity of the very nature of the work. The gospel preacher stands in the presence of God, speaks in the name of God, and delivers messages as it were from his mouth; and ought, therefore, to have his mind impressed with all that fear and reverence which so solemn a work is fitted to inspire.

In all his religious exercises, fear and reverence highly become the Christian. The God whom he serves is a great God, and a terrible one. We are mere worms of the dust, yea, less than nothing in his sight, and ought never to come into his presence but with profound humility, and holy fear. As feeble unworthy creatures approaching our great Creator, fear and reverence highly become us—as sinners drawing near to the God whom we have offended, shame and confusion of face belong unto us. The seraphim before the throne cover their faces with their wings, when they cry, "Holy, Holy, Holy, is the Lord of hosts!" Much more ought we, polluted and sinful creatures, to be impressed with reverence and awe, when we engage in the worship, or come into the presence of a God so holy and glorious as Jehovah is. When Christians, then, come before God by assembling in the courts of his house, both speaker and hearers ought to view themselves as standing in the immediate presence of the great God of heaven and earth, and to be impressed with the humility and fear suited to such an occasion. "God," it is beautifully said, Psalm lxxxix. 7, "is greatly to be feared in the assembly of the saints, and to be had in reverence of all them that are about him." In his essential character, God is an object of terror unto sinners; and even now, under the gospel, were absolute purity and perfection required in our services, acceptance with him, in any duty, would be altogether unattainable. "We cannot," as Joshua said to the children of Israel, immediately before his death, "serve the Lord, for he is a holy God, he is a jealous God, he will not forgive our transgressions, nor our sins." Through the Mediator, however, Christians have their persons accepted in the sight of God, and even their imperfect, and polluted services, when presented in faith and sincerity of heart, come up with acceptance before his throne. But this, though it ought to free their mind from slavish dread in the exercises of religion, ought by no means to diminish their holy awe and filial reverence. It is to believers under the economy of grace, nay, to Christians under the last and better dispensation of the New Testament, a dispensation much more calculated to banish a servile spirit, and to inspire the mind with a holy confidence in the service of God, than the one which preceded it, that the apostle addresses the exhortation, "Let us have grace, whereby we may serve God acceptably, with reverence and godly fear, for our God," or as it is still more emphatically expressed in the original, "for even our God is a consuming fire." That there is a solemnity in the very nature of the preaching of the gospel, calculated to impress the minds of all who engage in it, with deep reverence and fear, is sufficiently obvious from its being an ordinance of Divine institution. In waiting upon this ordinance, we ought to be impressed with very different feelings from those with which we repair to a popular assembly, or engage in our worldly business. It is not a display of talents on the part of the speaker, nor a gratification of taste on that of the hearers, that is the object of our meeting together on the first day of the week, but it is that we may serve the Lord our God, and engage in a duty which he requires at our hand, when he commands us not to forsake the assembling of ourselves together. It is the appointment of God himself that men of like passions with others, who have been regularly called to the work, should publish to their fellow sinners the doctrines of salvation through a crucified Saviour; and this consideration invests their whole work with a sacredness of character, which belongs to nothing that is of merely human invention. When the gospel preacher stands up to speak to his hearers, on subjects connected with their eternal welfare, it is not to please men, but to serve God; it is not to speak in his own name, and to deliver messages on his own authority, but to speak in the name of God, and to deliver messages, which, through the medium of the holy scriptures, he has received from his mouth. "Thou shalt hear the word of my mouth," says the Lord to the prophet Ezekiel, "and warn them from me." And the thought, that in that work he is serving God, ought never to depart from his mind, nor to cease to impress him with a deep solemnity of spirit. But in addition to this, he ought to remember, that he is not only serving God, but serving him in his presence. God is not only his master, but his witness. He does not send him forth on his work, without taking notice how he executes it; but the eye of his omniscience constantly follows him, watching the secret motives by which he is actuated, and observing in what manner he discharges the important duties with which he is put in trust. This consideration is obviously calculated to impress the mind with deep solemnity and awe. That it had this effect on the mind of the apostle is evident, from the language which he uses on the subject: "We have renounced," he says, 2 Cor. iv. 2, "the hidden things of dishonesty, not walking in craftiness, nor handling the word of God deceitfully; but by manifestation of the truth, commending ourselves to every man's conscience in the sight of God." This last clause, in the sight of God, is subjoined in a manner that is very emphatic, and it plainly shows, that a regard to the presence of the Searcher of hearts dwelt constantly on the apostle's mind, and impressed him with fear and solemnity in his whole work. The same thing is obvious from his words in chap. v. 11, "Knowing therefore the terror of the Lord, we persuade men; but we are made manifest unto God; and I must also be made manifest in your consciences." And from what he says, in 1 Thes. ii. 4, 5, "As we were allowed of God to be put in trust with the gospel, even so we speak; not as pleasing men, but God, which trieth our hearts. For neither at any time used we flattering words, as ye know, nor a cloak of covetousness; God is witness." Whatever fears, then, the gospel preacher may have on account of his standing in the presence of men, he has a higher witness, the thought of whose presence ought still more deeply to impress him.

4. The adorable sovereignty which God exercises with respect to the effects of the gospel, making it the savor of life unto life only to some, perhaps only to a few, and leaving it to be the savor of death unto death unto others, is a consideration which ought to impress the mind of everyone who engages in the work of preaching it, with deep solemnity and fear. You are all aware, that it is not the faithfulness nor ability with which the word is preached, but the blessing of God alone, which makes it effectual to the salvation of those who hear it. A Paul may plant, and an Apollos water; but except God gives the increase, even Paul will plant, and Apollos water, in vain. Without the influences of the Holy Spirit, to bring home the word with power to the heart, the most persuasive reasonings, the most tender expostulations, the most impressive appeals to the conscience, the most alarming exhibition of the terrors of the law, and the most encouraging and constraining use of the alluring motives of the gospel, will all prove insufficient to awaken from the lethargy, or to overcome the obduracy of the unrenewed mind. Though the natural feelings should be excited, and a temporary impression produced, these impressions will soon die away, and become as if they had never been—as water is agitated for a little by a blow that is struck on its surface, but soon closes upon the impression which it had received, and returns to its former rest and stillness. Nor is it the mere absence of positively good effects that is to be remarked, where God does not accompany the

preaching of the word with his blessing; not proving the savor of life unto life, it becomes the savor of death unto death. When not made effectual for awakening, convincing, and converting its hearers, it generally hardens their hearts and stupefies their consciences more and more, and sinks them deeper and deeper in condemnation. Now, in these considerations, is there not something that may well impress the mind of everyone who engages in the work of preaching the gospel, with fear, and even trembling? When he stands up to deliver the messages of the gospel to his hearers, neither the word of God, nor the experience of the church in all past ages, gives him reason to expect anything else, than that many will reject the messages which he delivers, and aggravate their condemnation by so doing. While in the rich mercy and sovereign grace of God, he may be made the instrument of spiritual good unto some, he must also expect, in the depths of his adorable sovereignty, to become the occasion of increased guilt, and aggravated condemnation unto others. What is a worm of the dust, that he should be made an instrument of giving accomplishment to such high and mysterious purposes, as the rendering of men without excuse, as well as the saving of their souls? What is the feeble and unworthy preacher of the gospel, that consequences not only of a good and joyful, but of a most awful and affecting nature, should be connected with his labors?

That in mentioning the adorable sovereignty which God exercises with respect to the effects of the gospel, as a reason for solemn awe and fear to those that, preach it, we are making no undue intrusion into the secret counsels of God, nor perverting the doctrine of his sovereign purposes, by allowing it to have an effect on our minds, which he had no intention it should produce, may be satisfactorily proved from a passage, in which the apostle seems plainly to view the subject in this light: 2 Cor. ii. 15, 16, "We are unto God a sweet savor of Christ, in them that are saved, and in them that perish. To the one we are the savor of death unto death; and to the other the savor of life unto life: and who is sufficient for these things?" On this striking passage, to point out its application to our present purpose, two remarks may be made: 1st, The apostle plainly views his public labors, as attended with two different, and very opposite effects; and with the one of those he seems to lay his account, just as much as the other. To some he was the savor of death unto death; to others of life unto life. Nay, so far from separating these two things, he represents them as both united in the design of God—both glorifying to his name, and fulfilling his holy and adorable purposes. We are unto God a sweet savor of Christ in them that are saved, and not only this, but also in them that perish. When those that perish reject the gospel, through obstinacy and unbelief, the glory of God is displayed in the justice of their condemnation, as well as the riches of his grace are manifested, when those that are saved improve it by faith unto salvation. 2nd, While the apostle views his ministry as attended with these two so different effects, and acquiesces in the adorable sovereignty that has appointed it to be so, he is, at the same time, deeply affected with the thought. *Who is sufficient for these things!* is the exclamation to which a review of the solemn subject immediately leads him. This exclamation may refer to his insufficiency for the great and important duties of his office in general; at the same time, as it is plainly suggested by the preceding statement, and rises as it were out of it, it must be supposed to have a more particular reference to that view of his ministry of which he is speaking in the passage, than to any other. "To the one we are the savor of death unto death, and to the other the savor of life unto life; and who is sufficient for these things?" The mind of the apostle, then, it is evident, was impressed with deep solemnity and awe, when he thought of the adorable sovereignty which God exercised with respect to the effects of his preaching; and all who engage in the same work, ought, no doubt, to be impressed with similar feelings. It is true, we must beware of prying into the secret purposes of God, or acting as if these were the rule of our conduct. Whatever be the secret will of God, with respect to the success or effects of his labors, the preacher of the gospel must not murmur, nor be discouraged in pursuing what the revealed will of God declares to be the path of duty.

Even though he is called to fill a situation, then, in which he has reason to expect little else than to be the occasion of aggravated condemnation to not a few of his fellow creatures, in the will of God calling him to that situation, it becomes him to acquiesce; but while he acquiesces, it ought to be with "much trembling." When he contemplates the solemnity of the situation in which he stands, he may well adopt the language of the Psalmist, as peculiarly suited to his circumstances: "My flesh trembleth for fear of thee, and I am afraid of thy judgments."

5. The extensive and difficult duties connected with his work, is a consideration which may well impress the mind of the gospel preacher with deep anxiety, and fear. It is merely of the work of preaching the gospel that we are at present speaking; but how extensive and difficult are the duties connected with even this work? To declare unto men the whole will of God concerning the way of their salvation, to deliver faithfully the messages of the gospel, to give a luminous exhibition of its doctrines, to make a judicious use of the terrors of the law, in subserviency to it, to

encourage by its promises, to allure by its invitations, and to support with its consolations; all this is a work of so extensive and difficult a nature, that everyone who engages in it, may well tremble at the magnitude of his undertaking, and cry out with the apostle, "Who is sufficient for these things!" There is such a thing as an unfaithful delivery of the messages of the gospel; there is such a thing as an unskilful handling of the word of God; there is such a thing as placing a stumbling block in the way of the returning sinner; there is such a thing as marring the peace of the saints of God, and dealing untenderly with the doubting conscience. What anxiety, then, ought everyone who undertakes to preach the gospel to feel, lest he become chargeable with these things, and instead of proving a workman that needeth not to be ashamed, rightly dividing the word of life, prove an unfaithful and an unskillful steward of the mysteries of God!

The work of preaching the gospel may be regarded as consisting of two great branches, each of which involves duties of no ordinary importance and difficulty. The exhibition of the doctrines of salvation, in connection with the use of the terrors of the law, and the allurements of the gospel, for the conviction and conversion of sinners; and the elucidation of the higher mysteries of religion, for directing the exercises and promoting the edification of saints. To perceive the extent and difficulty of the first of these classes of duties, we need only contemplate for a moment the state in which sinners naturally are, and that into which, in order to their being savingly benefited by the gospel, they must be brought. They are naturally asleep in indifference and carnal security, and by what arousing motives shall they be awakened? They are naturally in ignorance and darkness; how shall they be enlightened? Their minds are filled with prejudices against the gospel scheme of salvation; how shall these be removed? A self-righteous disposition is predominant in their hearts, and interwoven with the whole texture of their thoughts and feelings; how shall this be rooted out, and their minds be brought to bury all their own pretensions to merit at the foot of the cross, and to rest exclusively on the righteousness of Christ, as the ground of their acceptance before God? They are naturally disposed to seek for happiness in the pleasures of sin and the enjoyments of the world; how shall they be convinced that these are but lying vanities, yea, worse than vanities, a deceitful reed that pierces the hand that lean on it, and be made to seek a felicity, suited to their rational and immortal souls, in the enjoyment of the favour of God, and a life of universal obedience to his law? These are only a few of the changes of views and feelings which the preaching of the gospel must effect on the minds of sinners, before it can be of any saving advantage to them, and may not then the preacher tremble at the greatness and difficulty of his work? It is true, no exertions of his can accomplish these changes, without Divine assistance; Still the utmost diligence and faithfulness that he can use are required of him as his duty, and he is to study, like the apostle, to be made all things to all men, that he may, by all means, save some.

The second class of his duties—the directing of the exercises, and the comforting and establishing of believers in faith and holiness, is not less extensive and difficult than the first. How diversified are the circumstances? How varied the experiences of the saints of God? Who is sufficient for the work of giving to every one of them his portion of meat in due season? What a holy skill, in dividing the word of life, is necessary, to apply it to the various cases of believers; to the comforting of those in darkness, the strengthening of the weak, the reclaiming of the wandering, the quickening of the slothful, the encouraging of the fearful, the directing of the tempted? What an arduous task to undertake, to be a guide to the people of God through the labyrinths of temptation, to fortify them against the assaults, and to warn them against the devices of Satan; and from the sacred storehouse of the Divine word, to furnish them with armor, for fighting the good fight of faith, and wrestling, yea, successfully wrestling with, and overcoming, principalities and powers? The danger of failing in such an undertaking cannot be small. How exclusively, then, ought those that engage in it, to trust in the all sufficient grace that is promised for their assistance; and how great ought to be their anxiety and fear, lest they prove unfaithful to the arduous and extensive trust that is committed to their hands!

6. His own weakness, and utter insufficiency for so great a work, is another consideration, fitted to impress the mind of the preacher of the gospel with deep humility and fear. Considering the extensive and difficult duties implied in the work of preaching the gospel, an angel's talents might be supposed to be indispensably necessary to the undertaking. Yet dying, feeble, and sinful men, men of like passions and infirmities with others, are called to engage in it. They are mortal men, creatures of a day with their breath in their nostrils, yet they are set up as guides to the land of immortality. They have a body of sin and death to struggle within their own souls, yet they are called to speak the words of eternal life to their fellow creatures; they are themselves children in the mysteries of God, yet they are made stewards of these mysteries, and called to exhibit them to others. Perhaps, on some occasions, they are called to this great and important work young in years, and in circumstances particularly

calculated to impress their minds with a sense of their utter insufficiency for such arduous duties. On such occasions, though they ought by no means to abandon their trust in God, or give way to despondency, as if they were sent a warfare on their own charges; it peculiarly becomes them to feel their own weakness, and to be impressed with their utter insufficiency for such a great undertaking as that to which they are putting their hand. Some of those holy men, whose lives are recorded in Scripture, were so impressed with their own weakness, that when God called them to public work in his church, their fears almost led them to resist the call of duty. When God appeared to Moses in the desert, proposing to send him to deliver his people from the hand of Egypt, Moses was so impressed with his unfitness and unworthiness, for so high a dignity, that he instantly replied, "Who am I, that I should go unto Pharaoh, and that I should bring forth the children of Israel out of Egypt?" After this, he went on to frame various excuses, and advance various objections; l all of which, God was graciously pleased to answer, but even when his objections were silenced, his fears and his reluctance were not at an end. "Send by the hand of him whom thou wilt send;" that is, *send by any person that thou wilt, provided it be not by me*, were the words that he still used, to evade the call of Jehovah, when he could find no better excuse to advance. The good Jeremiah also, when called to the work of a prophet, felt so deeply his unfitness for the duties of so high an office, that he replied to the call of God, by saying, "O Lord God! behold I cannot speak, for I am a child." The apostle Paul, too, felt so much of his own insufficiency for the high office to which he was called, that he declares he had no ability to discharge aright the least of its duties of himself:—" We are not sufficient," he says, "of ourselves, to think anything as of ourselves." In these words, the apostle is obviously speaking of his public duties, as an apostle of Christ; and the strong language that he uses deserves our attention: we are not sufficient, not merely to do or speak, but even to think, anything as of ourselves. But for a work of the Holy Spirit, assisting his natural faculties, and guiding the meditations of his mind, he would have been unable to devise a single idea, or to utter a single truth, calculated to be of any saving advantage to his hearers. His mind, instead of being directed into a useful and edifying train of thoughts, would have been barren in all those spiritual meditations and scriptural views of gospel truths, in the publication of which, the main part of his public work consisted. In these circumstances, the apostle must not only have approached the work of preaching the gospel with fear and trembling, but abandoned it in despair altogether, had he been called to discharge its arduous duties in his own strength. Here, however, lay his comfort, "We are not sufficient to think anything of ourselves; but our sufficiency is of God." All who are engaged in the same work with the apostle ought to learn to derive comfort from the same source. When they think of their own insufficiency for such great and important duties as those to which they are called, their hearts may well be filled with fear and trembling. But when they think of the grace that is promised to be sufficient for them, and the strength to be made perfect in their weakness; trust and confidence may mingle with their fear, and joy and comfort with their trembling.

7. The danger to which he is exposed of preaching solely to others, and himself losing an interest in the blessings of the gospel which he publishes, is another consideration that may contribute to impress the mind of the gospel preacher with the

feelings described in this text, "fear and much trembling." To any person, whatever be his circumstances, or his station in the church, or in society, no idea ought to be more alarming than the thought that he is a stranger to the power of true religion, and without a real personal interest in Christ as a Saviour. Without this, the greatest wealth, and the finest human accomplishments are empty trifles, yea, less than nothing in respect of real worth to their possessor. With this, the want of wealth and earthly comfort is no serious evil; nay, in all probability is a gracious appointment of Providence, designed for his spiritual good. Perhaps it may be thought that those that serve God in the work of the gospel possess peculiar advantages with respect to the working out of their salvation, and the cultivating of personal religion; and this opinion must be admitted in the main to be founded on truth. At the same time, their danger of misimproving these advantages, and being found at last wanting, with respect to personal religion, is not less than that of others. There is in them the same superlatively deceitful heart as in other men, a heart that is ever ready to trust in lying refuges, and to mistake excitements of natural affection, and other false evidences of the power of true religion for a saving work of the Spirit of God. Nay, that very work in which they are employed, and which, if properly improved, gives particular advantages, with respect to the cultivation of personal religion, is in no small danger of furnishing to the corrupt heart additional room for its deceitful character to manifest itself. Knowing that they are employed in an important and honorable work in the service of God, they are very ready to act as if their work alone would save them, and to merge the cultivation of personal religion in the duties and labors devolving upon them in their public character. Now, what an alarming consideration is this to the mind, when employed in delivering the messages of the gospel preaching the glad tidings of salvation to others, but never receiving these tidings for themselves; set up to point out to others the way to heaven, but themselves travelling directly to hell; receiving no personal advantage whatever from their official duties and public labors, but only abusing them to increase their guilt, and aggravate their condemnation. The apostle Paul himself, notwithstanding his high attainments in religion, and the strong assurance which he frequently expresses respecting his interest in the Saviour, and the certainty of his salvation, seems not to have been free from a holy fear and jealousy over himself, when he reflected on these alarming considerations. "I keep under my body," he says, "and bring it into subjection, lest that by any means, when I have preached to others, I myself should be a cast-away." This advice to his beloved Timothy, plainly discovers that he did not wish him to be free from anxiety on the same point. "Take heed unto thyself, and to the doctrine; continue in them: for in doing this, thou shall both save thyself, and those that hear thee." In both clauses of this passage, the attention and point which the apostle inculcates on Timothy, respecting himself, is not a little remarkable. "Take heed unto thyself and to the doctrine, thou shalt both save thyself and them that hear thee." Attention to their own vineyards, then, as well as those of others, is the imperious duty of those that serve God in the gospel of his Son. To prove negligent here, and to be found at last among the number of those who shall stand up, saying, "Lord open unto us, for we have prophesied in thy name, and in thy name done many wonderful works," but to whom the Lord will nevertheless declare, "Depart from me, I know you not whence ye are, ye workers of iniquity," is a consideration of so alarming a nature, that it may well contribute, at least, to cause every gospel preacher to engage in his public duties with similar feelings to those of the apostle, "I was with you in fear and much trembling."

8. The high ground on which he stands in respect of Christian profession, and the solemn and unreserved surrender, which he makes of his whole time and talents to the service of the Redeemer, and that, on some occasions, at least, in the circumstances of the church, he may have prospects before him of a peculiarly trying nature, are considerations calculated to impress the mind of the gospel preacher "with fear and much trembling." Every individual who offers himself to the work of serving God in the gospel of his Son, in answer to the question of Jehovah, "Whom shall we send? And who shall go for as?" professes to say, "Here am I, send me."' In a still higher sense than the disciples of Jesus in more private stations, he professes to deny himself, "to forsake all, to take up his cross and to follow Christ." Should Providence open up his way, and call him to continue his labors in the church, he professes his readiness to do so all the days of his life, and comes under obligations to know no other object, and to live to no other end, than that of serving God in the work of the gospel, and to allow no worldly hardships nor difficulties to turn Him away from his faithfulness, or to induce him to abandon the great work to which he has devoted himself. Putting his hand to the plough, he may not look back, else he is unfit for the kingdom of heaven. The ground on which he stands, then, in respect of Christian profession, is peculiarly high. The greatest holiness and circumspection of character are incumbent upon him. In the fall or unfaithfulness of one in his circumstances, the enemy will have particular cause of triumph, and a

reproach be brought on the ways of religion. Satan, who is well aware of these circumstances, will be incessantly plying his temptation, and using his influence, to move him away from his steadfastness. Could he succeed in this, he knows well how much the interests of his kingdom will he promoted. To be carried honorably through the great work which they have undertaken, then, ought to be the matter of earnest prayer and deep anxiety to all who devote themselves to the service of the Redeemer in the preaching of the gospel; and the danger which they are in of dishonoring God, and wounding the cause of religion, by proving deficient in this respect, ought at least to cooperate with other considerations, in making those men, like the apostle, who engage in their arduous duties, with fear and much trembling. The apostle's own mind was so deeply impressed with this consideration, that he felt far less anxiety from the greatest temporal dangers and hardships to which he was exposed, than from the thought of proving unfaithful to his trust, and failing to be carried honorably through the public work to which he had devoted himself. "None of these things," he says, "move me, neither count I my life dear unto me; so that I might finish my course with joy, and the ministry which I have received from the Lord Jesus to testify the gospel of the grace of God."

In connection with this remark we might also say a few things, on the idea, that there are sometimes certain circumstances of the church, and particular prospects before them, calculated to give rise to unusual anxiety in the minds of those who are devoting themselves to the work of publicly serving God in their generation. In seasons when the sword of persecution is unsheathed against the church, and the servants and people of Christ are called to maintain their testimony at the risk of their lives, and all that is most dear to them in the world, there are obviously greater temptations to unfaithfulness, and more grounds for fear and anxiety, with respect to being carried honorably through our generation work, than in seasons of outward peace and tranquility. There are some seasons, also, in which the affairs of the church come, as it were, to a kind of crisis. Errors may have been long abounding, and seem just ready to swallow up the cause of truth altogether, or perhaps the reign of error may have been for some time triumphant; but light is just beginning to rise, and there is now a prospect of bringing the dominion of error to an end. Those called to public work in the service of the church in seasons of this kind, are evidently placed in circumstances peculiarly trying, and unusually calculated to impress their minds with fear. We have read of the great reluctance and deep anxiety which was felt by our illustrious reformer, Knox, when he entered upon his public career in the service of the church; and can there be any doubt that at least a part of this arose from the critical state in which the cause of the Reformation at that time stood, and the peculiar danger that there was of the work of the gospel miscarrying in his hands at so extraordinary a period. On the situation of the Church at the present day, and the feelings with which those now entering, or already entered, upon public work in the service of Christ, ought to look forward to the prospects before them, I have no design to enlarge. Let it suffice to remark in a few words, that while our present prospects contain a good deal to animate and encourage, they also contain not a little to impress with anxiety and fear. Unprecedented exertions are making to propagate Christianity throughout the world. God, in his providence, is evidently making a way for diffusing the light of his gospel among all nations, and giving the kingdom of his Son an extent and a glory which has never yet been beheld. Here is something to animate and encourage. But along with this, is there not also a good devil to impress with anxiety and fear? Michael and his angels are plainly preparing, on the one hand, to fight against the dragon, and to bring his extensive dominions and usurped authority is to an end. But is not the dragon, on the other, also mustering his forces, and preparing to make a last and an obstinate struggle? The despots of the earth are confederating together to crush the rising spirit of civil liberty, and to plot "against the Lord, and against his Anointed." Ignorance has still an extensive dominion. Errors, and false systems of religion, retain a firm hold of the minds of a great part of mankind. Antichristian constitutions continue to be supported; and mighty concession must take place, before all these things can be thrown down. With respect to the final issue of such a contest, there is no ground for a single uneasy feeling. The Redeemer will unquestionably triumph. But with respect to the part which ourselves may be called to act in it, there is ground for not a little anxiety and fear. We, my friends, are this day preaching, and you are hearing, the gospel, in the communion of a church which has long counted it her duty to maintain her testimony in a separated capacity, and to stand aloof from the political and ecclesiastical associations around her. To faithfulness in the cause which she has undertaken to support, she is bound by the most weighty obligations. In addition to the moral obligation of the Divine law, there are the superadded bonds of solemn covenant engagements, and the blood of martyrs that has been shed to seal it. In undertaking to serve God in the gospel of his Son, and in connection with this, to support such a cause, so important in itself, and sanctioned by such solemn obligations, is there not much to impress with anxiety and fear? A high honour, we have every reason to think, awaits us, if we are faithful; but of our losing this honour there seems to be not a little danger. At all events, the present state of the Church and of the world is highly interesting. The generation now rising up have, in all probability, to pass through a season of a difficult and trying nature; and this; together with the high profession which we have long made, and the danger in which we are of proving unfaithful to the cause which we are under such solemn engagements to support, may, at least, have its influence in impressing the minds of those who are now entering upon public work in the Lord's vineyard, with similar feelings to those of the apostle, when he says, "I was with you in weakness, and fear, and much trembling."

With an inference or two, we shall now bring this discourse to a conclusion.

1. What a solemn and important work is the preaching of the gospel, and how seriously ought those who enter upon it to ponder well the paths of their feet, and to take good heed to the motives by which they are actuated! To all such it must be an impressive thought, that the mind of such a man as the apostle Paul was affected with fear and much trembling, when discharging those very duties in which they are engaged. Nothing, then, can be more unjustifiable, than to approach the duties of so solemn a work with levity and unconcern. The considerations connected with it, calculated to impress the mind with anxiety and fear, are great and important; and these ought to be seriously considered, and their influence felt and cherished. But while this work has its fears, blessed be God, it has also its encouragements; yea, encouragements amply sufficient to support the mind under all the fears which the thought of it is calculated

to inspire. This God whom we serve is not a hard master; he sends none a warfare on their own charges. To his people who put their trust in him, he has promised that his grace shall be sufficient for them, and his strength made perfect in their weakness. "As thy days, so shall thy strength be," is a promise calculated to convey comfort to the child of God in every situation in which he can be placed. While they are impressed with the ground of fear, connected with their work, on the one hand, and contemplate its ample encouragements on the other, those that serve God in the gospel of his Son, may unite trust and hope with their fear, and joy and confidence with their trembling. Our apostle, whom we find in one place exclaiming, "Who is sufficient for these things! I say with you in weakness, and fear, and much trembling," could also say, "our sufficiency is of God; I can do all things through Christ who strengthens me." even when fightings from without, and fears from within, assaulted him with the greatest violence; his faith in God remained unshaken. "We are troubled," he could say, "on every side, yet not distressed; we are perplexed, but not in despair; persecuted, but not forsaken; cast down, but not destroyed."

Those that serve God in the work of the gospel, are entitled to the Christian sympathy, and to an interest in the prayers, of those whom they address. To prove this remark, need I do more than remind Christians, what a great, and important, and responsible work it is, in which those that speak to them in the name of the Lord are employed, a work so arduous, that the apostle Paul himself engaged in it "with fear and much trembling." Nor is it for their own advantage and edification alone, but rather for that of others, that they are called to this work. So that Christians wishing to have their own spiritual interests promoted, will be careful to supplicate a blessing from God upon those that address them in his name, that a suitable message may be given to them, and that they may be enabled to speak a word in season to the weary soul. In the gospel, all the blessings of which we stand in need, are promised in answer to prayer: "Ask, and ye shall receive; seek, and ye shall find; knock, and it shall be opened to you." The necessity of earnest importunate prayer, for the blessing of God to accompany the preaching of the word, would be at once obvious and striking, did we only remember, that it is the blessing of God alone, that can make the gospel effectual to the salvation of those that hear it; and that his blessing, for that purpose, can only be expected, when it is devoutly and earnestly asked. The apostle Paul felt so deeply the necessity of the Divine presence to support him in his arduous duties, and to render his ministry a blessing to those that enjoyed it, that he scarcely writes a single epistle, in which he does not solicit an interest in the prayers of his Christian friends, "and who knows," it has been justly asked, "how much of the exemplary faithfulness and unwearied zeal, and distinguished success of that great apostle, were given to him in answer to the prayers that were presented throughout the churches in his behalf?" Let Christians, then, be impressed with the obligations under which they be, to remember those, at the throne of grace, that publish to them the messages of the gospel. The pastor whom God has set over them, has unquestionably the first claim to their remembrances in this respect; and ill, indeed, do they deserve the exalted privilege of a pastor to labor among them, and to dispense the bread of life unto their souls, who do not habitually pray for him, supplicating the blessing of God, to rest upon him both in his person and public labors. But whoever be the instrument that is called to deliver the messages of the gospel, he is entitled to the Christian sympathy, and to an interest in the prayers of his hearers. I hold that man to be guilty of a neglect of duty, who goes in a single instance to wait upon God in the preaching of the word, without first bowing his knees to God in prayer, supplicating the Divine presence to be with the speaker, and a blessing to accompany the truths which he delivers, that they may be made effectual for promoting the spiritual good of those that hear them.

3. The preaching of the gospel is something of a very solemn nature to those that wait upon it as hearers, as well as to those that are actively employed in it. There are many, I am afraid, in the world, who go to hear sermons, merely to have their taste gratified; the tedious hours of the Christian sabbath agreeably spent, and perhaps a religious character in the world supported; but who have no proper impressions of the high responsibility connected with the hearing of the word, or the solemn approach which they make into the presence of God, when they wait upon him in that ordinance. The whole responsibility connected With this work, they devolve upon the head of the speaker; and as for themselves, they may come and hear what he has to say, and go away as they came, without having anything more to do with what they have heard. Than such sentiments, none can be more false, none more dangerous. To hearers, as Well as speakers, there is a solemnity in the preaching of the gospel, which renders it most criminal and dangerous for them to wait upon it with levity or unconcern. To prove this, I need only remark, that the very same reasons which render the delivery of the messages of the gospel, a very solemn and important matter, prove the same thing With respect to the hearing of them. Is there a high responsibility connected with the preaching of the Word? So is there with the hearing of it. Those that

hear, will be called to give an account how they received and improved the messages of the gospel; as well as those that preach, how they delivered them. Is the inconceivable value of the immortal soul, a consideration calculated to impress the mind of the gospel preacher with fear and trembling? So is it to the gospel hearer. His own soul lost forever through his unbelief and rejection of the gospel? What an alarming thought! Is there a solemnity in the very nature of the preaching of the gospel, calculated to impress the mind with reverence and fear? This obviously applies alike to both preachers and hearers. God is equally the witness and the judge of both. His omniscient eye is observing the frame of mind with which the one hears, as Well as that with which the other preaches. Is the adorable sovereignty which God exercises with respect to the effects of the gospel, a solemn consideration calculated to impress the mind of the preacher with deep humility and awe? So is it to that of the hearer. The gospel is not made effectual to the salvation of all that hear it, but only gives occasion to some to harden themselves in guilt, and ripen themselves for destruction. What deep anxiety ought all to feel, that they may not rank among that unhappy number, but that they may be stirred up to flee from the wrath to come, and to improve the day of their merciful visitation while it lasts! In this way, it is easy to see, that the same remarks, which prove it to be a serious thing to preach the gospel, prove it also to be a serious thing to hear it. Be impressed, then, my friends, with the deep responsibility under which you place yourselves by coming to hear the gospel. The instrument that addresses you, may be feeble and unworthy; but the messages Which he is sent to deliver, are great and important. It is not on his authority, that their importance depends. If these truths, which he delivers, are founded on the Divine

Word, they possess a power to bind the conscience, which no human authority can either erect or set aside, a power which lays all who hear them under obligation to receive them, not as the word of man, but as they are in truth the word of God. The greatest danger, and the most aggravated guilt, are involved in a rejection of the gospel; but blessings of inconceivable value are connected with a believing reception of it. While the day of our merciful visitation then is continued, and the gospel is sounding its glad tidings in our ears; let us learn to know the things of our everlasting peace, while they are not yet hid forever from our eyes. While Jesus is exhibited to us as a Saviour able to save to the uttermost, let it be our exercise to receive him, and rest upon him alone for salvation as he is offered to us in the gospel. While he is tenderly inviting us, and saying, "Come unto me, all ye that labor and are heavy laden, and I will give you rest." Let it be our exercise to say in reply, "Lord, unto whom shall we go but unto thee, thou hast the words of eternal life." While he is exhibited in the gospel, like the brazen serpent upon a pole, from which healing virtue proceeds, to heal the wounds of all who look upon it; let it be our immediate exercise to direct to him an eye of faith, and to comply with his own invitation, "Look unto me, and be ye saved, all the ends of the earth; for I am God, and besides me, there is none else." Receiving in this manner the messages which the gospel brings, it will not prove our condemnation, but our unspeakable privilege, that light is come into the world, and that the glad tidings of salvation through the blood of the Lamb, have been sounded in our ears.

FINIS

POSTSCRIPT

Thomas Halliday is relatively little known by anyone in the Reformed community today, much less the Christian community. This is a tragedy. If you have come to this point in the work, you know his sermons are *outstanding*. As a matter of fact, his sermons are more than outstanding – they are a deep well where we may draw forth sweet things about Jesus Christ, God, salvation the work of the Holy Spirit and *more*. As my wife said about this work as she finished it, "Who preaches like this today? Relatively few. However, after they read this, they'll *want* preaching like it-if they are Christians. This work should be on a bestseller list." Unfortunately, this work will never make it to a bestseller list. It repels just about everything the world would like in a book. But for the Christian, it drips sweet drops of honey.

I have read many books over the past few years, and like most people, certain passages and certain chapters stand out more than others. There are certain parts that you retain because they affected you in a big way. In this work, I took this "affect" one step further. In the sermon on *The Atonement*, I italicized almost an entire paragraph (a lengthy one) because I believed it is one of the richest, most sublime paragraphs I have *ever* read. The italics were NOT in the original version of the work. I did that. I took the liberty to highlight that section, and I've reproduced it here – read it over slowly:

> When the sword of Divine justice was unsheathed against us, and our immediate destruction appeared to be inevitable, this illustrious personage, in the riches of his

unbounded love, graciously interposed, and warded off the stroke. Being both God and man in one person, he was every way qualified, as the Surety of an elect world, to endure that punishment, which the accumulated guilt of all their innumerable transgressions deserved. The infinite dignity of his person imparted to his mediatorial work an infinite value, and rendered his sufferings, though limited in respect of duration, infinitely efficacious as to merit. By the sufferings, both of body and mind, which he endured during the whole of his life, and particularly by those in the garden and on the cross, the justice of God has been satisfied, the honour of his holiness maintained, and a foundation laid for the salvation of guilty men, in a way perfectly consistent with the glory of all the Divine perfections.

This paragraph is worth the cost of the book. It is eminently constructed to hit almost every major doctrine in such a way as to press the reader towards being awed at the work of God. It is, no doubt, measured by the amount of information you may have stored in your mind and are able to unpack while reading Halliday's preached thoughts here. But even as a Christian who houses a cursory amount of information, this paragraph should cause joy to well up in you. *If it doesn't, something is dreadfully wrong with your understanding of the Gospel.*

Halliday would not be considered to be a minister in your church today if he lived during our time. Why? Too young. Too inexperienced. Sickly. Not fit for the ministry. *What a bunch of garbage.* But that does not make the fact that your church would not consider him as *your pastor.* We should take notice that this young, inexperienced, sickly, fervent, zealous, well-educated, thoughtful, precise, careful preacher of the Word of God had left his mark on the planet through his preaching; even to the point that someone like Andrew Symington would write a *memoir* about the young lad. If only we were as zealous to have the truth of God preached in such a way as to warrant THAT as the main requirement for preachers *today*!

Hopefully Halliday becomes more and more known through this work. If I come across any other manuscripts of this young preacher, or his sermons, I will immediately publish them. They are worth far more than their weight in gold and have specifically ministered to me. He is, like the young Puritan Christopher Love, one of my favorites. It is not often that I select a paragraph or two as being in the top 10 or 20 of best things I have ever read. Halliday is no doubt among them. I'm hoping he will be that for you as well. Through his preaching you will see Christ more clearly, which is what we want to see accomplished in every Christian.

In Christ's abounding Love and Grace,
C. Matthew McMahon, Ph.D.
September, 2011
A Puritan's Mind
www.apuritansmind.com

www.ingramcontent.com/pod-product-compliance
Lightning Source LLC
Chambersburg PA
CBHW020358100426
42812CB00001B/105